INFORMAL READING INVENTORY

INFORMAL READING INVENTORY

PREPRIMER to TWELFTH GRADE

BETTY D. ROE
Professor Emerita, Tennessee Technological University

PAUL C. BURNS
Late of University of Tennessee at Knoxville

Seventh Edition

HOUGHTON MIFFLIN COMPANY
Boston ◆ New York

Publisher: Patricia Coryell
Senior Sponsoring Editor: Sue Pulvermacher-Alt
Senior Development Editor: Lisa Mafrici
Editorial Assistant: Dayna Pell
Project Editor: Teresa Huang
Editorial Assistant: Katherine Leahey
Senior Art and Design Coordinator: Jill Haber Atkins
Composition Buyer: Chuck Dutton
Associate Manufacturing Buyer: Brian Pieragostini
Marketing Manager: Laura McGinn
Marketing Associate: Erin Lane

Cover image: Veer Incorporated

Printed in the U.S.A.

Library of Congress Control Number: 2005938726

Instructor's exam copy:
ISBN-13: 978-0-618-73231-9
ISBN-10: 0-618-73231-4

For orders, use student text ISBNs:
ISBN-13: 978-0-618-49598-6
ISBN-10: 0-618-49598-3

123456789-VGI-10 09 08 07 06

Contents

Appendix A

Appendix B

Preface

Audience and Purpose

The Roe/Burns *Informal Reading Inventory*, seventh edition, is designed for use by several different groups—pre-service college students who are learning about informal reading inventories in reading methods courses; special reading teachers who, as part of their training or their everyday work, need an easily administered assessment instrument for their students; and in-service classroom teachers in workshops dealing with reading methods or with informal assessment measures.

This test should prove to be a useful tool for college-level reading methods classes, elementary and secondary school classrooms, resource rooms, and reading clinics. Because it includes detailed instructions, a wide variety of school personnel should be able to use it with success. Teachers who have worked with similar assessment programs should be able to use the test even without practice sessions. Those who have not had prior experience with informal reading inventories should practice using the materials with a number of children, referring to the instructions in the text as necessary.

Features and Description

The first two sections of the inventory contain background information about different aspects of testing word recognition and comprehension and specific step-by-step directions on how to administer, score, and interpret an informal reading inventory. To illustrate the process of scoring and interpreting the inventory, case study information is presented for two situations: the administration of the oral passages to a fourth-grade boy and the administration of a complete inventory to a second-grade girl.

Through a numbered and clearly labeled format, samples of completed Worksheets and a Summary Form walk the student through an explanation of the scoring and interpretation of the test. The Summary Form allows for inclusion of all important data and highlights both quantitative and qualitative information. The two Worksheets facilitate calculation and recording of results.

The rest of the book consists mainly of word lists and graded passages from preprimer through twelfth grade with accompanying questions that can be used with a range of children, in order to determine appropriate levels of reading materials and each student's areas of strength and weakness. All passages have been chosen to fit the readability level for the grade, as measured by the Spache Readability Formula for preprimer level through grade 3 and the Fry Readability Graph for grades 4 through 12.

There are two equivalent sets of graded word lists and four equivalent forms of graded passages for each of the levels. The availability of so many forms enables the teacher to choose the material that is most appropriate for a particular assessment. Students can also be retested at intervals as such assessments are needed.

Appendix A, "Choosing Books to Develop and Support Children's Reading Proficiency," provides an extensive list of leveled trade books for preprimer through grade 12. These books can be used to develop and support children's reading proficiency through recreational reading or classroom instruction.

Appendix B describes the construction of this instrument for readers who are interested in the origins of the word lists and graded passages. Question construction is discussed in detail. Field testing of the inventory is also briefly discussed.

Field testing for this edition was coordinated by Sandra H. Smith, Assistant Professor of Curriculum and Instruction and Director of Teacher Education at Tennessee Technological University.

New to the Seventh Edition

Several key updates and improvements have been made to the Seventh Edition. These include:

- In response to user feedback, five reading passages have been replaced. (See Appendix B for details on the field-testing of new passages.)
- A new tabbing system has been designed to mark the various sections of passages and forms in an effort to increase the utility and navigation of this tool.
- A new rubric for retelling is offered in Section One to help guide the assessment of retellings by teachers.
- The appendix of leveled trade books has been expanded, thus providing a valuable resource for teachers planning instruction following administration of this tool.

Acknowledgments

The author is indebted to many people for their assistance during the preparation of this book. Although it is impossible to name them all, I would like to acknowledge the many teachers and students involved in the field testing of the material. I would also like to offer grateful recognition to the following reviewers whose constructive advice and criticism over several editions has helped me shape the revisions:

Rhea A. Ashmore, *University of Montana-Missoula*
Stacey L. Elsasser, *College of St. Rose*
Pamela W. Petty, *Western Kentucky University*
Evelyn J. Priddy, *Huntington College*
Ann Russell, *Southwestern Oklahoma State University*
Nancy Walker, *University of La Verne*
Marty B. Waring-Chafee, *Cabrini College*
Gail Yunk, *Loras College*

Appreciation is also expressed to those who have granted permission to use sample materials or quotations of their works. Credit for these contributions has been given in the footnotes.

Special recognition goes to Sandra H. Smith, the colleague who implemented the field testing for this edition. Without her assistance I would have been unable to field test materials within the needed time frame in multiple school settings. My appreciation for this mammoth task is great.

I also wish to acknowledge that some work of Paul C. Burns, a colleague and friend who was my co-author for the first edition, still remains in this edition. His death in the summer of 1983, before the second edition was begun, was a loss to all of us in the field of reading education.

Betty D. Roe

INFORMAL READING INVENTORY

SECTION ONE

Background Information

This section answers the following questions:

- What is an IRI?
- What can an IRI tell teachers?
- What are flexible ways to use an IRI?
- How do IRIs fit into literature-based programs?
- Who needs to take this informal reading inventory?
- When should the inventory be administered?
- How long does the inventory take to administer?
- Who can administer the inventory?

What Is an IRI?

An informal reading inventory (IRI) is a type of informal reading test designed to provide teachers with a variety of information. It can help a teacher discover the levels of reading material pupils can read both with and without teacher assistance, the reading levels at which pupils should not be asked to function, and the levels at which they can comprehend material that is read to them. It serves as a placement and monitoring tool for teachers. It measures students' performances against established criteria, not against the performances of other students. Invernizzi and colleagues (2005) point out that teachers often prefer to have the specific instructional information provided by such tests. Teachers know that numerical scores alone "usually don't provide a complete picture of what children know and can do" (Wilson, Martens, and Arya, 2005). The qualitative analyses of the IRI provide far more insight into their progress, and they can also help teachers diagnose some of the pupils' specific reading problems. As Johnson, Kress, and Pikulski (1987, p. 2) state: "The use of IRIs is aided by a series of guidelines for their construction, administration, scoring, and interpretation. However, use of these inventories is not bound by formal directions, defined time limits, or a restricted set of materials or procedures. Finally, the results of IRIs do not match an individual's performance against standardized or normed scores. Instead, the individual is evaluated against preestablished standards, which must be met if that individual is to become a successful, accomplished reader of the materials ultimately determined appropriate for use in classroom instruction. The emphasis is not upon comparing the performance of someone who is taking an IRI with others who have taken such inventories; instead, the emphasis is on learning about the skills, abilities, and needs of the individual in order to plan a program of reading instruction that will allow a maximum rate of progress." As Invernizzi and colleagues (2005, p. 611) point out, "teachers want assessments that are instructionally useful in the here and now." They need specific information about features of word recognition and comprehension that can guide them to appropriate instructional choices. IRIs can provide this information.

Although IRIs were originally teacher-made, they are time-consuming and difficult to construct. For this reason, published inventories, such as this one, have been developed. The goals for *this* inventory are the same as those for teacher-made IRIs. Directions for use, based on experience, research, and field testing, are offered, but teachers with experience are encouraged to use the materials flexibly to fit individual needs.

According to Barr, Blachowicz, and Wogman-Sadow (1995, p. 265), a commercial "informal reading inventory has many advantages over a diagnosis based on oral reading of a single passage. It allows for the comparison of silent and oral reading and for an assessment of fluency and word recognition proficiency at various levels of difficulty. These comparisons make it possible for you to determine more precisely the level of materials that a student should read under various conditions. Perhaps its greatest strength lies in the assessment of listening comprehension, which allows a more definitive conclusion to be drawn regarding the influence of word recognition on a student's comprehension."

Most commercial IRIs have graded word lists that function as placement tools to help the teacher decide where to start administering the graded passages that provide the bulk of the diagnostic information. In addition, an analysis of errors on the graded word lists can give the teacher information about phonics and structural analysis skills that need attention. Word recognition is a valid and reliable measure of overall reading ability because automatic word recognition frees the student to focus attention on comprehension (Invernizzi et al., 2005). The graded word lists and graded passages in this IRI are discussed below.

Graded Word Lists

Two lists of twenty words from each reading level (preprimer, primer, first reader, second grade, third grade, fourth grade, fifth grade, sixth grade, seventh grade, eighth grade, ninth grade, tenth grade, eleventh grade, and twelfth grade) are provided in this IRI.

The primary function of these lists is to provide the teacher with an indication of the level at which the administration of the graded passages should be started. The highest level at which the pupil knows all of the words on the list should be the starting point for administration of the passages (referred to in this text as the *placement level*). This estimate may have to be revised after the first passage has been administered, but it is a tentative indicator that may save the teacher some time by eliminating the tendency to begin the passages at too low a level.

Graded Passages

This IRI contains a series of carefully graded reading passages for all reading levels from preprimer through twelfth grade. Each selection has been checked for difficulty with a well-known readability formula and has been found to be at the designated level. The Spache Readability Formula was used for selections from preprimer through grade 3, and the Fry Readability Graph was used for selections from grades 4 through 12. Since formulas do not take into consideration many factors related to reading difficulty, during the field testing the passages were checked for increasing difficulty in word recognition and comprehension. They also were chosen primarily from graded materials in basal readers and literature books actually used in schools with students at that grade level. They include both fiction and nonfiction passages, since students are expected to read both types of passages in school. This choice of selections was made to ensure that the IRI presented the students with realistic reading tasks.

Following each selection is a group of questions designed to measure many types of comprehension strategies. Appropriate answers to the questions are provided for the convenience of the examiner.

Four selections (four forms) are provided at each reading level to facilitate pre- and post-testing. Most clinicians and some teachers like to use both an oral and a silent reading measure at each level and look at the combined results. This is the most desirable method, since it yields the most information for diagnostic purposes. In such a situation, two forms of the test are available for pre-testing and two forms for post-testing. In the interest of time, some teachers prefer to administer *only* an oral reading passage, or in some cases *only* a silent reading passage, at each level. In these instances the user of this IRI has available, in essence, four equivalent forms for use.

No pictures accompany the graded passages in this IRI because it was felt that the possible use of picture clues to obtain meaning from the paragraphs would lessen the accuracy of the test in determining the reader's ability to comprehend printed language. Students may be able to read more difficult material when picture clues are added to the context. Not all classroom reading tasks are accompanied by pictures, however. So testing performance without availability of picture clues seemed to be most helpful to teachers. If pictures are included in classroom material, many children will be able to handle material that is a grade level above the test result.

What Can an IRI Tell Teachers?

Two major types of information can be obtained from the use of this IRI: quantitative information expressed in grade equivalent scores to indicate the reader's independent reading level, instructional reading level, frustration level, and listening comprehension level; and qualitative information concerning the reader's word recognition and comprehension strengths and difficulties. These two categories of information are briefly explained as follows.

Quantitative Information

To analyze the results of an informal reading inventory in order to find a student's different reading levels, an examiner must use predetermined criteria. The criteria used are percentage of word recognition accuracy and percentage of correct answers to comprehension questions.

Various writers in the field suggest slightly differing percentages for independent, instructional, frustration, and capacity levels. The original criteria for establishing the levels were developed by Betts (1946). Powell (1970) and Powell and Dunkeld (1971) have suggested that the numerical standard used for determining the instructional level is too stringent, particularly at lower levels. At the same time, Ekwall (1974) presented evidence that the Betts criteria should be maintained, with repetitions counted as errors, in order to determine the frustration level accurately. That position also seems to agree with Johnston's idea that repetitions are "indicators of difficulty" (Johnston, 1997, p. 213). Taking these findings into account, we have utilized the criteria presented in Table 1–1. The set of criteria for the reading levels are basically those proposed by Johnson, Kress, and Pikulski (1987), with an adjustment suggested by Powell (1970) for word recognition for grades 1 and 2.

TABLE 1–1 **IRI Criteria**

Level	Word Recognition		Comprehension
Independent	99% or higher	and	90% or higher
Instructional	85% or higher (grades 1–2) 95% or higher (grades 3–12)	and	75% or higher
Frustration	below 85% (grades 1–2) below 90% (grades 3–12)	or	below 50%
Listening Comprehension			75% or higher

Independent Reading Level The independent reading level is the level at which a person can read with understanding and ease, without assistance. The reader has 99 percent or better word recognition (misses no more than one word in a hundred) and 90 percent or better comprehension (misses no more than one question in ten). At this level, reading is not accompanied by inappropriate habits (finger pointing, etc.) or signs of nervous tension (facial tics, frowning, etc.).

Material at a student's independent level is appropriate for homework assignments and recreational reading. The directions for classwork to be completed without teacher assistance should be written at this level.

Instructional Reading Level The instructional reading level is the level at which a person can read with understanding *with* the teacher's assistance. The reader has 85 percent or better word recognition (misses no more than fifteen words in a hundred) as a first or second grader or 95 percent or better word recognition (misses no more than five words in a hundred) as a third grader or above, and he or she has 75 percent or better comprehension (misses no more than two questions out of eight).

Material at a student's instructional level should be used for teaching reading strategies. It should be used during "reading class," where the teacher is available to support the students as they work with the written passages.

Frustration Level The frustration level is the level at which a person is unable to function adequately because the reading material is too difficult. The reader has *either* less than 85 percent word recognition (misses more than fifteen words in a hundred) as a first or second grader *or* less than 90 percent word recognition (misses more than ten words in a hundred) as a third grader or above, *or* has less than 50 percent comprehension (misses more than five of ten comprehension questions) as a student in any grade. At this level, attempts to read may be accompanied by finger pointing, frowning, squirming, facial tics, and other inappropriate habits and signs of nervous tension.

No student should be asked to read material written at his or her frustration level. Nothing can be learned from such material, and the experience can lead to negative attitudes toward both reading and school in general.

For a full explanation on what to do when a student's scores are not high enough for the instructional level, but not low enough to be frustration level, see FAQ #1 on page 32 of Section Two.

Listening Comprehension Level ■ The listening comprehension level (sometimes referred to as *capacity level* or *potential level*) is the level at which a person adequately comprehends material that is read by the teacher. The student has 75 percent comprehension of the material read.

This level is the one at which the student would probably be able to read if no limiting factors were present. Limiting factors could include physical or emotional disabilities, lack of motivation, or inadequate instruction. Comparing the student's capacity level with his or her instructional level can indicate potential for improvement. For example, a child who has an instructional reading level of 2.0, but a listening comprehension level of 6.0, has an excellent chance of improvement with a good program of instruction. In contrast, a child with an instructional level of 2.0 and a capacity level of 3.0 has less potential for advancement, but could improve some. It is generally possible to obtain a listening comprehension level by reading to the student passages from successively higher grade levels, after the frustration level has been found.

Some teachers use the word lists to make quick approximations of students' reading levels. However, because they involve only word recognition and not comprehension, word lists are not the best tool for determining levels. Still, comparison of the levels obtained from the word lists and the graded passages can provide some useful information. If students' levels are much higher on the word lists than on the passages, teachers can expect that instruction in comprehension and use of context clues is needed more than instruction in sight words, phonics, and structural analysis.

Qualitative Information

Word Recognition Miscue Analysis[1] ■ Both when the graded word lists are administered and when the informal reading inventory oral selections are administered, teachers should record word recognition miscues for use in determining reading skill strengths and weaknesses. The skill determinations can be used in setting up instructional groups or for individual instructional planning. The types of miscues made may provide the teacher with information about how the reader decodes words and about the reader's phonics and structural analysis skills.

Teachers should not overgeneralize from the results of an analysis of miscues on the word lists, however, for students' miscues on words in isolation often differ significantly from those on words in context. Readers tend to read words in context more accurately than words in isolation (Allington and McGill-Franzen, 1980). This finding should not be surprising, since more information is available to assist in decoding words when they are in context. In fact, comparison of the types of miscues made on words in isolation and words in context may alert teachers to needed instructional procedures. For example, if the two types of presentations result in identical miscues, the student is probably not making use of the semantic and syntactic information provided by the context. Such a student may be too bound to phonic and structural analysis techniques and may not be willing or able to use available context clues.

The word recognition miscues in the oral reading passages should be considered in terms of those that change meaning and those that do not. Even good adult readers often do not read the exact words when their minds are moving beyond the material that is being spoken. They often translate the material into different words that mean the same thing as the words in the text. For example, a reader may read "I will speak to him" as "I will talk to him," if *talk* is the word that seems more natural for the reader and if the reader's eyes are ahead of the voice, taking in different words that must be processed. Such a change obviously does not change the meaning and therefore is not a serious miscue. In contrast, if the reader reads "I will speed to him," the miscue disrupts the meaning, although not the syntax, and the miscue can go unnoticed, leaving the reader with a misleading impression. If the reader reads, "I will spinach to him," the miscue results in nonsense and as such is a serious impediment to the reader's comprehension. The fact that a word does not fit the syntax of a sentence should prevent such miscues, but if syntactic clues are ignored, serious miscues can result.

When analyzing miscues of different types, teachers should not worry about planning skill

[1]*Miscue* is a term that has grown out of the research of Kenneth Goodman and his associates. It is used to describe the unexpected responses students give when they misinterpret clues in the language that could help them decode words. Some people continue to use the term *errors,* but this term implies random response (Johnson, Kress, and Pikulski, 1987).

lessons for miscues that do not change the meaning of the passages; such miscues are likely due to the internal translation process of the reader and not to the reader's inability to decode the words in question. Miscues that change meaning should be examined more carefully. If students do not recognize the inappropriateness of miscues that produce nonsense, they should be given lessons that encourage the use of context clues.

When meaning is disrupted, a reader who is monitoring his or her comprehension may return to the point of confusion, reexamine the text, and correct the miscue. Such self-correction is a good sign, showing that the reader is demanding meaning from the text. Two important strategies for readers to acquire are self-monitoring and self-correction. Self-corrected miscues are not counted in miscue totals for determining reader levels, since they are considered positive evidence of reading skill. However, the repetitions of reading material that occur when the self-corrections are made *should* be counted in the miscue total for determining reader level. This decision is based on the results of a convincing study (Ekwall, 1974) indicating that repetitions should be counted as errors, if the criteria for levels that are used in this test are to be appropriate. The placement of students in materials is likely to be too high if repetitions are not counted as errors. Such artificially high placement could force children to try to read material that causes them discomfort and frustration.

The teacher can obtain a measure of the reader's sight vocabulary from the graded word lists when a more extensive testing procedure is not desired. Having two forms of the word lists facilitates retesting.

Comprehension Question Analysis ■ Following each reading selection is a set of comprehension questions. The following types of questions are used:

1. A *main idea* question asks for the central theme of the selection.
2. A *detail* question asks for bits of information directly stated in the material.
3. An *inference* question asks for information that is implied, but not directly stated, in the passage.
4. A *sequence* question requires knowledge of events in their order of occurrence.
5. A *cause-and-effect* question names a cause and asks for its effect or mentions an effect and asks for its cause.
6. A *vocabulary* question asks for the meaning of a word or phrase used in the selection.

The question types used in this inventory correspond to areas of comprehension addressed in instructional materials that are used in schools. Analysis of the types of questions most frequently missed can help teachers decide what specific lessons are needed to alleviate comprehension-skill deficiencies. Teachers should be careful to avoid drawing conclusions from extremely limited samples, however. If only four questions of a particular type have been asked and the student has missed two, deciding that this is a problem area may be inappropriate. Deciding that more assessment may be needed in this area is more reasonable. On the other hand, if a student has been asked ten questions of a particular type and missed nine, an instructional decision would be warranted.

Main Idea Questions. Main idea questions are asked primarily to determine whether the reader is able to obtain the central thought or topic of a passage. As Harris and Hodges (1981, p. 188) indicate, "[t]here is little agreement on what a main idea is." In beginning reading instruction students are often taught to recognize the topic of a passage, whereas at more advanced levels they are often asked to formulate a more complete statement of the central thought or message of the passage. Harris and Hodges (1995, p. 148) offer four definitions of main idea that range from "the chief topic" to the "central thought" of a passage.

A major problem in testing for knowledge of the main idea is that of phrasing the question in a way students can understand. Many young children are not familiar with the term *main idea* and therefore cannot simply be asked what the main idea of a passage is. The question "What is this story about?" often will elicit the main idea from such children; however, it may also elicit a summary of the entire story. The teacher may wish to follow a summary-type response with the question "Could you tell me what it is about in just one sentence?" or, for first graders who do not yet have a concept of sentence, "Could you tell me what it is about in a shorter way?" The way children respond to main idea questions will depend on their grasp of the terminology used in the questions and on what they have been taught about main ideas. A teacher giving this inventory will want to take both factors into account and adjust reactions to the questions accordingly.

Detail Questions. Detail questions, which are the kind of question most often asked by teachers, are important; they provide the building blocks from which answers to higher-order questions are constructed. However, they can easily be overemphasized. This inventory includes not only detail questions (which are easy to formulate and relatively easy to answer), but also higher-order questions that require manipulation of information and integration of ideas. Teachers should check the performance of students both on detail questions and on questions that require more advanced thought processes and then compare the results. Children in the United States tend to perform better on detail questions (on which they receive much more classroom practice) than on higher-order questions (which are sometimes neglected in the classroom).

Inference Questions. Inference questions are among the higher-order questions that require students to assemble clues from the reading material to determine information that is implied in the passage. To answer such a question, a reader must sometimes use information from his or her background of experience. For example, if the text says, "The sun was directly overhead," and the question is, "At what time of day did the event occur?" in order to answer the question correctly the reader must know that the sun is directly overhead at noon. Students who have broad backgrounds of experience therefore are likely to do better on inferential questions than are students with meager backgrounds of experience. However, on the basis of the answers to questions, teachers can often detect a lack in experiential background and can plan future instruction and choice of reading materials accordingly. Making inferences is essential to comprehending text (Valencia and Pearson, 1987). Applegate, Quinn, and Applegate (2002) point out that IRIs need to include assessment of thoughtful literacy. Use of inference questions at all inventory levels, as well as inclusion of main idea questions, is an attempt to meet such purposes of the IRI.

Sequence Questions. Recognition and understanding of sequences is important, both in following the plots of narrative materials and in comprehending expository material in areas such as social studies and science. In order to follow sequences, students must be able to respond to clues in the text such as the terms *first, second, third, next, then, finally, before,* and *after.* They must also use their knowledge of sequences of dates, months of the year, seasons, and times of day (morning, afternoon, evening, etc.). Sequence questions are designed to determine whether students are using this knowledge when they read.

Cause-and-Effect Questions. Causes and effects are important elements in the development of events in plots of narratives and in expository materials in areas such as science, health, and social studies. Causes and effects may be directly stated (i.e., be details) or may be implied (i.e., require inferences). Both types are found in materials that students are asked to read in school, and it is helpful for teachers to know how well students are able to identify causes and effects. Both types of cause-and-effect questions are found in this inventory. Sometimes causes and effects are signaled by words such as *because* and *since,* but often they are not. As with other types of inferences, students need to use their background knowledge to discern causes and effects that are implied rather than directly stated.

Vocabulary Questions. Understanding of the vocabulary in a reading selection is essential to comprehension of the selection. A vocabulary question in this inventory may ask for the meaning of a word that is important to comprehension of the selection, even if there are no clear-cut context clues to the meaning. Although these questions are by nature passage independent, they nevertheless illuminate the readers' comprehension of the passage. Other vocabulary questions may have context clues that will help students discern their meanings. An attempt was made to include in the vocabulary questions words that had multiple meanings that might cause misinterpretation.

What Are Flexible Ways to Use an IRI?

The previous sections explain traditional use of IRIs. However, since IRIs are *informal* tests, their use does not have to be limited to a restricted set of procedures. Teachers may vary their use of the materials in this IRI to fit their individual classroom needs. Following are some suggestions concerning flexible use of the IRI.

Retelling

Some educators feel that more complete data on comprehension can be gained from eliciting retellings of the selections than from merely asking comprehension questions. Johnston (1983, p. 54) sees retelling as "the most straightforward assessment . . . of the result of text-reader interaction."

The student retells the selection in his or her own words when a retelling, or free recall, technique is used to assess comprehension. The retelling may be written or oral. The teacher may have a list of the points that should be included in the retelling and may mark them off as they are mentioned by the student. After the student completes the retelling, the examiner may ask questions to probe for the information that is not provided by the student during the initial telling. The student can be given credit for each point recalled. This procedure takes more time than direct questioning, but may be chosen if the teacher wants to obtain an idea of the student's verbal facility.

There are possible problems with diagnostic use of the free recall process (Barr, Blachowicz, and Wogman-Sadow, 1995; Morrow, 1985; Morrow, 1988; Stein and Glenn, 1979; Bridge and Tierney, 1981; Brown and Cambourne, 1987). Students may have trouble with the process until they become familiar with it through repeated attempts. Morrow (1988, p. 128) points out that "[r]etelling is not an easy procedure for students, no matter what their ages and especially if they have no prior experience." Anthony and others (1991) caution that students must become familiar with what is expected from them in a retelling and must practice the procedure before it is used for assessment purposes.

Students also may not respond to directions as expected. For example, if the student knows that the examiner has read the selection, he or she may leave out important information on the assumption that the examiner knows it. This situation would be particularly likely if the passage was one that the student had just read orally to the teacher. For that reason, retelling may be more effective after silent reading of passages than after oral reading.

The quality of the free recall may be an indication of the verbal skills the student possesses as much as it is an indication of his or her comprehension. Written retellings may be affected by spelling and mechanical problems as much as, or more than, by comprehension difficulties. For that reason, oral retellings may be less demanding for certain students.

More information may be remembered in response to questions than can be remembered in free recall. Since poor readers have a greater tendency to provide additional information in response to questioning than good readers do, poor readers need questioning in order to demonstrate their comprehension more effectively.

Brown and Cambourne (1987) believe that a retelling procedure will not work effectively in classrooms that do not have a whole language/natural-learning climate. They see such classrooms as having friendly, supportive, nonthreatening social interactions and unpressured retelling opportunities, perceived as relevant to the students' needs. Brown and Cambourne used retelling as a learning procedure rather than as a testing procedure, and therefore allowed student discussion of retellings, rather than just having teacher evaluation.

Different methods have been devised to guide the assessment of retellings by teachers. A number of the systems of analysis of retellings are complicated and unmanageable for many classroom teachers. One of the less complicated systems is shown in Figure 1–1. Another one is found in Figure 1–2.

Nevertheless, retellings can offer teachers insights both into students' ability to organize the material read in a coherent manner and into students' recall of passage content. Moss (2004) suggests having a student predict what the material will be about based on the title, before reading takes place. In the passages for this IRI, a user who wants to incorporate this feature of testing could include a title for each passage derived from the answers suggested for the main idea questions to provide an opportunity for prediction. Personal response questions can also be added after the retelling is done to discover how much the student is making connections between the selection and his or her own life experiences, attitudes, interests, and needs.

When retelling is to be used, the students should be informed before they start reading a selection that they will be asked to retell it. The teacher should encourage each student to retell as much of each selection as he or she can. The teacher may say something similar to "Retell this selection for someone who has not read it, so that the person would understand it as well as you do." As the student retells the selection, the teacher may offer encouragement to continue when the student pauses by saying, "Can you tell anything else that it said?" After the student finishes retelling, the teacher can probe further by asking the comprehension questions that were not answered in the retelling. (There is, of course, no need to ask those questions that were clearly answered in the retelling.) Teachers can figure the comprehension based on the percentage of questions answered under either condition. In making the qualitative analysis, they can also consider the students' grasp of the organization of the material as indicated by the order of retelling. Much judgment goes into the final analysis of the students' reading, and the data from the retelling can be useful in forming that final judgment.

Tapings of retellings can make analysis of them easier for the teacher, who can listen again to any

FIGURE 1–1 **Free Recall Processing Checklist**

Answer each of these questions according to the following scale:

- **5** Yes, very well
- **4** Yes, more than adequately
- **3** Yes, adequately
- **2** No, not too well
- **1** No, poorly
- **NA** Not applicable or can't tell

1._____ Did the student recall a sufficient number of ideas?

2._____ Did the student recall the ideas accurately?

3._____ Did the student select the most important details to recall?

4._____ Did the student understand explicit pronouns and connectives?

5._____ Did the student infer important implicitly stated information?

6._____ Did the student include the explicitly stated main points?

7._____ Did the student create any new summarizing statements?

8._____ Did the student use the organizational pattern used by the author?

9._____ Did the student elaborate appropriately?

10._____ Did the student know how to adjust strategies to the purpose given?

What effective comprehension processes were evident in the student's recall?

What comprehension processes were not evident, or seemed to be causing problems?

To what extent was the student's performance as just described affected by each of the following?

1. Limited prior knowledge or vocabulary.
2. Limited motivation or interest.
3. Cultural differences.
4. Decoding problems.
5. Difficulties in the text.
6. Social context.
7. Discomfort with the task.
8. Other environmental influences.

Source: From Judith Westphal Irwin, *Teaching Reading Comprehension Processes*, 2d ed., p. 202. Copyright © 1991. Published by Allyn and Bacon, Boston, MA. Copyright © 1991 by Pearson Education. Reprinted by permission of the publisher.

FIGURE 1–2 **Rubric for Oral or Written Retelling of a Narrative**

3	2	1
Characterization		
Accurately recalls both primary and secondary characters	Accurately recalls only primary or secondary characters, not both	Incorrectly identifies the characters
Uses vivid, appropriate descriptive words when discussing the characters	Provides limited, correct descriptions of the characters	Provides no descriptions or inaccurate descriptions of the characters
Setting		
Recalls the setting: both place and time	Recalls only the time or the place, not both	Provides minimal information or inaccurately describes the setting
Plot		
Recalls the action or plot in correct sequence as it happens in the story	Describes some of the events as they occur in the story sequence	Inaccurately describes events as they happen in the story sequence or describes events out of sequence
Conflict/Resolution		
Accurately discusses both the conflict and the resolution	Discusses only the conflict or the resolution, not both	Discusses fragmented sections of the story with little mention of a conflict or problem with a resulting resolution

Name of student: ______________________________

Story: ______________________________

Circle type of response: Written Oral

Source: From Betty D. Roe, Sandy H. Smith, and Paul C. Burns, *Teaching Reading in Today's Elementary Schools*, 9th ed., p. 470. Copyright © 2005 by Houghton Mifflin Company. Reprinted with permission.

parts that are confusing or that were presented very quickly by the student. Overreliance on taping slows down the assessment, so taping may simply serve as a backup to be used in special cases, rather than as a regularly analyzed aspect of each session.

Teachers who wish to use a retelling component for assessment may want to consult some writings on this topic for help in implementing a personally effective procedure (Clark, 1982; Irwin and Mitchell, 1983; Kalmbach, 1986a; Kalmbach, 1986b; Barr, Blachowicz, and Wogman-Sadow, 1995; Morrow, 1985; Morrow, 1988; Stein and Glenn, 1979; Bridge and Tierney, 1981; Brown and Cambourne, 1987). Given the current lack of generally accepted criteria for evaluating retelling, most teachers will probably be more comfortable with the standard questioning procedure.

Assessing Use of Context Clues

The use of context clues is an aspect of comprehension that can sometimes be more easily ascertained by examination of word recognition miscues made while reading the passages than by examination of question responses or retellings. Students who make miscues that fit the context and do not distort meaning are using context clues to good advantage; in contrast, students who make miscues that distort meaning or result in nonsense and who fail to correct these miscues need help with using context clues.

Reading Rate

The measurement of reading rate is not essential to obtaining accurate results from the inventory, but information about rate can be beneficial to teachers in a number of ways. First, rate is an important part of fluency, because slow, laborious reading lacks proper phrasing and intonation. Second, the slow rate overtaxes memory and thereby reduces comprehension. Third, too fast a rate may also impede comprehension because it often results in careless reading that may result in misconceptions.

Partial Assessments

This instrument can also be used to obtain more limited information than administration of the complete inventory would provide, such as silent reading independent level only or oral reading instructional level only, by using just the portions of the material that are needed. Teachers may do this to find out if a written work that they plan to use for homework or in the class (and for which they have a grade level designation) is likely to be at an independent, instructional, or frustration level for the students who will be asked to read it.

Many secondary teachers feel that only a silent reading assessment is appropriate for students in grades 7 through 12, and many primary grade teachers feel that an oral assessment will give them the best picture of performance if they have limited time available. Not every assessment needs to be a complete assessment. Indeed, classroom teachers would be hard-pressed to administer complete assessments to all of their students without some additional assistance, such as a paraprofessional to oversee other activities while the assessments are being done. As Barr, Blachowicz, and Wogman-Sadow (1995) have indicated, teachers need to be familiar with the procedures for a complete assessment, but they also need to know when following only a portion of these procedures is appropriate.

Users whose purpose is to analyze the word recognition miscues carefully to decide what strategies are being used may administer the word lists and oral passages only and compare the word recognition strategies used in isolation with those used in context, but some teachers may not use the word lists, because students are not generally asked to read words out of context in authentic literacy activities.

Instead of doing a standard complete inventory, some teachers may administer two different forms to compare the results of having the students read orally at sight and having them read orally after they have read silently. This oral reading after silent preparation may be used primarily to assess oral reading fluency.

Cautions About Partial Assessments One caution is that administration of a single passage will not give a definitive level for instructional purposes. Students must have a chance to read progressively difficult passages to determine the highest level at which the criteria for a specific level are met.

Another caution is that any one passage may give a misleading level because background of experiences and interests strongly influence comprehension. Some passages will test abnormally high because of extensive background on the topic. Similarly, a passage may test abnormally low because of lack of background about the topic or lack of interest in the topic.

How Do IRIs Fit into Literature-Based Programs?

Norton (1992, p. 107) points out that IRIs "are especially valuable for assessing the reading ability of students in literature-based programs because the IRIs can be constructed from passages and questions that are similar to those in the materials read by the students." Literature-based programs generally focus on having students interact with larger chunks of language than the single, isolated sounds, words, and sentences often used for assessment in traditional standardized tests. Informal reading inventories provide students with more connected text to read, and facility with individual skills can be determined from the analysis of the students' performance when reading connected text.

The format of the reading passages in an informal reading inventory is more like the text found in books that the children read than is the format of traditional, multiple-choice-type standardized tests. In fact, the passages in this inventory come primarily from actual materials that students are asked to read in school. They are not passages just designed to highlight particular skills. Anthony and others (1991, pp. 68–69) point out that "the teacher needs to know how well children can cope with real texts."

Informal reading inventories are not timed tests that put unnatural time constraints upon decoding and understanding text. The untimed nature of these tests allows students the freedom to use strategies, such as rereading to utilize context clues, that are often not encouraged by timed tests.

Open-ended questions, as opposed to multiple-choice items, require more than random choices for answers. This inventory includes not only open-ended questions, but also a mixture of literal and higher-order questions, in order to get a more complete picture of the students' comprehension.

Emphasis is on what levels of material are best for individual students and what instructional needs the students have, instead of on comparisons with other students. The IRI provides specific information about each individual student's reading strategies that can provide a base for developing instructional activities and assigning independent reading of literature from trade books.

Winograd, Paris, and Bridge (1991, p. 110) encourage teachers to "[c]larify the purpose of an assessment and then select the tools most appropriate for that purpose." An informal reading inventory meets the requirements for assessments that are designed to diagnose instructional needs of students and to place the students in materials that are on appropriate levels. Other tests may be more appropriate for meeting other assessment goals.

Strategic readers "are able to handle a variety of authentic texts for a variety of different purposes, . . . and they are adept at planning their approach to reading depending upon their purpose, their familiarity with the topic, the type of text, and so forth." (Winograd, Paris, and Bridge, 1991, p. 112). This inventory provides varying topics and types of text, both fiction and nonfiction, that are typical of ones the students might encounter in classroom instruction to facilitate decisions about students' ability to handle them.

Who Needs to Take This Informal Reading Inventory?

Ideally, every student would be given the informal reading inventory so that the teacher could place him or her at the correct level in the reading program, supply appropriate content-area reading material, and recommend recreational reading. Because an all-inclusive assessment is not likely to be possible for classroom teachers, at least pupils known to have reading problems and pupils for whom reading skills information is not available should be assessed. Students who score low on standardized reading achievement tests are appropriate candidates for assessment, as are students who arrive from other schools without accompanying records. The administration of an informal reading inventory provides a unique opportunity for close pupil–teacher contact. This may increase the teacher's chances of providing effective remedial assistance.

Teachers will also find inventory results for gifted students to be helpful in planning instruction. They can determine the level of advanced material that can be used to challenge these students and keep them interested in school assignments.

When Should the Inventory Be Administered?

Probably the best time for administering a reading assessment is at the beginning of the school year. However, there are other times when it can be equally useful, such as when a child is having difficulty with classroom reading material, after a student's prolonged absence from school, or when a new student transfers into the classroom.

For students with notable reading difficulties, two or more forms of the inventory may be administered at various times during the year. Thus it is possible to measure the progress made in eliminating problems discovered during the first assessment.

How Long Does the Inventory Take to Administer?

Administration of this reading inventory will take a bit longer the first few times than after the administrator has gained some experience. Administration of an abridged form of the inventory (for example, a word list plus only oral selections) usually takes only twenty to thirty minutes. For the complete form, including administration of both oral and silent passages and a measure of listening comprehension, an experienced inventory user often needs forty to fifty minutes. The time required will vary from student to student.

Some ideal times for an assessment session are during supervised study periods or during regularly scheduled reading classes, if another capable person is available either to administer the inventory or to teach the class. It is not necessary to administer the inventory in one sitting.

Who Can Administer the Inventory?

The person who will be working most closely with the student in reading instruction, content areas, and recreational reading is the best one to administer the inventory, since much may be observable that is not readily recordable—and, of course, first-hand observation is likely to be more revealing than a study of the record alone. Normally, the administrator is the classroom teacher; however, if the teacher cannot administer the inventory, he or she should still be able to accumulate sufficient data about the student by studying the record and discussing it with the administrator. Thus, the assessment could be administered by a reading teacher or other person who has the necessary skill; it need not always be done by the classroom teacher.

Prospective teachers are frequently taught to administer informal reading inventories in methods courses that deal with developmental reading and/or focus on diagnosing and correcting classroom reading problems. Although this is valuable preparation, much additional practice in administering and scoring an inventory is needed before a valid administration can be ensured. Practice in scoring tapes of students reading aloud is helpful. After the scoring, these tapes can be replayed so that the markings can be checked for accuracy.

SELECTED REFERENCES

Allington, Richard L., and McGill-Franzen, Anne. "Word Identification Errors in Isolation and in Context: Apples vs. Oranges." *The Reading Teacher* 33 (April 1980): 795–800.

Anthony, Robert J., Johnson, Terry D., Mickelson, Norma I., and Preece, Alison. *Evaluating Literacy: A Perspective for Change.* Portsmouth, N.H.: Heinemann, 1991.

Applegate, Mary DeKonty, Quinn, Kathleen Benson, and Applegate, Anthony J. "Levels of Thinking Required by Comprehension Questions in Informal Reading Inventories." *The Reading Teacher* 56 (October 2002): 174–80.

Barr, Rebecca, Blachowicz, Camille L. Z., and Wogman-Sadow, Marilyn. *Reading Diagnosis for Teachers: An Instructional Approach.* White Plains, N.Y.: Longman, 1995.

Bear, Donald R., and Barone, Diane. *Developing Literacy: An Integrated Approach to Assessment and Instruction.* Boston: Houghton Mifflin, 1998.

Betts, Emmett A. *Foundations of Reading Instruction.* New York: American Book Co., 1946.

Bridge, C. A., and Tierney, R. J. "The Inferential Operations of Children Across Text with Narrative and Expository Tendencies." *Journal of Reading Behavior* 13 (1981): 201–14.

Brown, Hazel, and Cambourne, Brian. *Read and Retell.* Portsmouth, N.H.: Heinemann, 1987.

Cagney, Margaret A. "Measuring Comprehension: Alternative Diagnostic Approaches." In *Reexamining Reading Diagnosis: New Trends and Procedures,* edited by Susan Mandel Glazer, Lyndon W. Searfoss, and Lance M. Gentile, pp. 81–93. Newark, Del.: International Reading Association, 1988.

Christie, James F. "The Qualitative Analysis System: Updating the IRI." *Reading World* 18 (May 1979): 393–99.

Clark, Charles H. "Assessing Free Recall." *The Reading Teacher* 35 (January 1982): 434–39.

Ekwall, Eldon E. "Informal Reading Inventories: The Instructional Level." *The Reading Teacher* 29 (April 1976): 662–65.

Ekwall, Eldon E. "Should Repetitions Be Counted as Errors?" *The Reading Teacher* 27 (January 1974): 365–67.

Forell, Elizabeth. "The Case for Conservative Reader Placement." *The Reading Teacher* 38 (May 1985): 857–62.

Glazer, Susan Mandel, Searfoss, Lyndon W., and Gentile, Lance M., eds. *Reexamining Reading Diagnosis: New Trends and Procedures.* Newark, Del.: International Reading Association, 1988.

Goodman, Yetta M. "Reading Diagnosis—Qualitative or Quantitative?" *The Reading Teacher* 50 (April 1997): 534–38.

Harris, Theodore L., and Hodges, Richard E., eds. *A Dictionary of Reading and Related Terms.* Newark, Del.: International Reading Association, 1981.

Harris, Theodore L., and Hodges, Richard E., eds. *The Literacy Dictionary: The Vocabulary of Reading and Writing.* Newark, Del.: International Reading Association, 1995.

Hunt, Lyman C., Jr. "The Effect of Self-Selection, Interest and Motivation Upon Independent, Instructional, and Frustration Levels." *The Reading Teacher* 50 (December 1996/January 1997): 278–82.

Invernizzi, Marcia A., Landrum, Timothy J., Howell, Jennifer L., and Warley, Heather P. "Toward the Peaceful Coexistence of Test Developers, Policymakers, and Teachers in an Era of Accountability." *The Reading Teacher* 58 (April 2005): 610–18.

Irwin, Judith Westphal. *Teaching Reading Comprehension Processes.* Englewood Cliffs, N.J.: Prentice-Hall, 1991.

Irwin, Pi A., and Mitchell, Judy Nichols. "A Procedure for Assessing the Richness of Retellings." *Journal of Reading* 26 (February 1983): 391–96.

Johnson, Marjorie Seddon, Kress, Roy A., and Pikulski, John H. *Informal Reading Inventories,* 2nd ed. Newark, Del.: International Reading Association, 1987.

Johnston, Peter H. *Knowing Literacy: Constructive Literacy Assessment.* York, Maine: Stenhouse Publishers, 1997.

Johnston, Peter H. *Reading Comprehension Assessment: A Cognitive Basis.* Newark, Del.: International Reading Association, 1983.

Kalmbach, James R. "Evaluating Informal Methods for the Assessment of Retellings." *Journal of Reading* 30 (November 1986a): 119–27.

Kalmbach, James R. "Getting at the Point of Retellings." *Journal of Reading* 29 (January 1986b): 326–33.

Morrow, Lesley Mandel. "Retelling Stories: A Strategy for Improving Young Children's Comprehension, Concept of Story Structure, and Oral Language Complexity." *Elementary School Journal* 75 (1985): 647–61.

Morrow, Lesley Mandel. "Retelling Stories as a Diagnostic Tool." In *Reexamining Reading Diagnosis: New Trends and Procedures,* edited by Susan Mandel Glazer, Lyndon W. Searfoss, and Lance M. Gentile, pp. 128–49. Newark, Del.: International Reading Association, 1988.

Morrow, Lesley Mandel. "Using Story Retelling to Develop Comprehension." In *Children's Comprehension of Text: Research into Practice,* edited by K. Denise Muth, pp. 37–58. Newark, Del.: International Reading Association, 1989.

Moss, Barbara. "Teaching Expository Text Structures Through Information Trade Book Retellings." *The Reading Teacher* 57 (May 2004): 710–18.

Norton, Donna E. *The Impact of Literature-Based Reading.* New York: Merrill, 1992.

Pikulski, John J. "Informal Reading Inventories." *The Reading Teacher* 43 (March 1990): 514–16.

Powell, W. R. "Reappraising the Criteria for Interpreting Informal Reading Inventories." In *Reading Diagnosis and Education,* edited by J. DeBoer. Newark, Del.: International Reading Association, 1970.

Powell, William R., and Dunkeld, C. G. "Validity of the IRI Reading Levels." *Elementary English* 48 (October 1971): 637–42.

Roe, Betty D., Smith, Sandy H., and Burns, Paul C. *Teaching Reading in Today's Elementary Schools,* 9th ed. Boston: Houghton Mifflin, 2005.

Rubin, Dorothy. *Diagnosis and Correction in Reading Instruction.* Needham Heights, Mass.: Allyn and Bacon, 1996.

Smith, G. G., and Keister, D. "Learning about Literacy Through Retelling." In *Literacy Assessment for Today's Schools,* edited by M. D. Collins and B. G. Moss, pp. 16–31. Pittsburg, Kans.: College Reading Association, 1996.

Spiegel, Dixie Lee. "Meaning-Seeking Strategies for the Beginning Reader." *The Reading Teacher* 31 (April 1987): 772–76.

Stein, N. L., and Glenn, C. G. "An Analysis of Story Comprehension in Elementary School Children." In *Advances in Discourse Processes, Vol. 2: New Directions in Discourse Processing,* edited by R. O. Freedle. Norwood, N.J.: Ablex, 1979.

Valencia, Sheila W., and Pearson, P. David. "Reading Assessment: Time for a Change." *The Reading Teacher* 40 (April 1987): 726–32.

Wilson, Pat, Martens, Prisca, and Arya, Poonam. "Accountability for Reading and Readers. What the Numbers Don't Tell." *The Reading Teacher* 58 (April 2005): 622–31.

Winograd, Peter, Paris, Scott, and Bridge, Connie. "Improving the Assessment of Literacy," *The Reading Teacher* 45 (October 1991): 108–16.

SECTION TWO

Instructions for Use

This section answers such questions as:

- How is the inventory administered?
- How is the inventory scored and interpreted?
- What are some frequently asked questions about the IRI?

This section also provides two case studies in scoring and interpretation: one interwoven into the explanation of the administration, scoring, and interpretation of the inventory and one in a separate part of the section.

How Is the Inventory Administered?

Overview of Basic Procedures

Figure 2–1 provides an overview of the procedures that are followed when a complete inventory is administered.

As this figure shows, the administrator of the assessment must first set the stage for the testing, including choosing an appropriate location and establishing rapport; then decide upon a starting level for administration of the inventory, using the Graded Word Lists or another method; administer the Graded Passages, alternating oral and silent passages (or the reverse), asking comprehension questions about each passage administered until independent reading, instructional reading, and frustration levels have been located; read higher-level passages to the student and ask accompanying comprehension questions until the listening comprehension level has been located; analyze the findings; and interpret the results qualitatively and quantitatively to help make instructional decisions. If the administrator has prior knowledge of a level at which the student is

FIGURE 2–1 **Basic Procedures**

Set the stage for the testing
(choose appropriate location, establish rapport, inform the student about procedures).

↓

Administer Graded Word Lists for placement
(or choose starting passage in some other manner).

↓

Administer Graded Passages
(alternating oral and silent passages, starting with either oral or silent, depending upon the student), including comprehension questions for each passage to discover independent, instructional, and frustration levels.

↓

Administer listening passages to determine listening comprehension level.

↓

Analyze the findings.

↓

Interpret the results
(qualitatively and quantitatively).

likely to meet with success, which is likely if the administrator is the classroom teacher, he or she may dispense with administration of the word lists unless a measure of word knowledge in isolation is desired. If any administrator feels that there is insufficient time available to administer both the word lists and the graded passages, he or she may simply start administration of the passages at the level two grades below the student's grade placement. This placement procedure has not consistently proven to be as accurate as use of the word lists, in the author's personal experience, but both procedures are only approximations. Therefore, if the administrator is willing to adjust the passage administration downward if the initial passage is too difficult, starting two grade levels below the grade placement is a feasible procedure, and it sometimes does save a significant amount of time.

Setting the Stage

The place used for testing should be quiet and free from distractions. A child who can see other children running around on the playground while he or she is being tested is unlikely to give the examiner undivided attention.

In each testing situation, time should be provided for establishing rapport before the assessment starts, if the administrator has not already established rapport with the student. Students respond best if they are at ease.

The student should be informed that the administrator will be taking notes; even so, all note-taking should be done unobtrusively. Some administrators have found it effective to tape students' test performances, replaying them later to note the word recognition miscues and comprehension errors. If the session is taped, there will be less need for the administrator to write while the student is reading. Furthermore, replaying the tape as needed when the analysis of errors is done will increase the accuracy of recording and interpretation.

If the session is to be taped, the administrator should spend some time desensitizing the student to the presence of the recorder. For example, the teacher might tape the student reading a paragraph or two unrelated to the test and have him or her listen to the playback. The student also should be told the purpose of the taping and should indicate a willingness to be taped. Taping can make some students nervous enough to affect the test results.

It is a good idea to laminate both the student versions of the word lists and passages (so that they can be used a great many times) and the teacher passages (to facilitate note-taking, cleaning, and reusing). The lists and passages may be reproduced for classroom or clinic use, but they may not be reproduced in any form for any other purpose without written permission from the copyright owner.

Graded Word Lists

The general procedure for administering the word lists is shown in Figure 2–2. For students who have had little reading experience, individual words printed on index cards may be used instead of the complete twenty-word lists as they appear in this book. The words should be printed in good manuscript handwriting in black ink, and the cards should be numbered and arranged in the same order as the words on the test sheet. The examiner will have a copy of the test sheet on which to keep a record of words missed. When the test sheet is used, the student should have a cardboard marker to place under each word as he or she proceeds down the page. Both the pupil and the examiner should have copies of the test sheet. (The teacher's copies may be duplicated for this purpose.)

FIGURE 2–2 **Administration of Graded Word Lists for Placement**

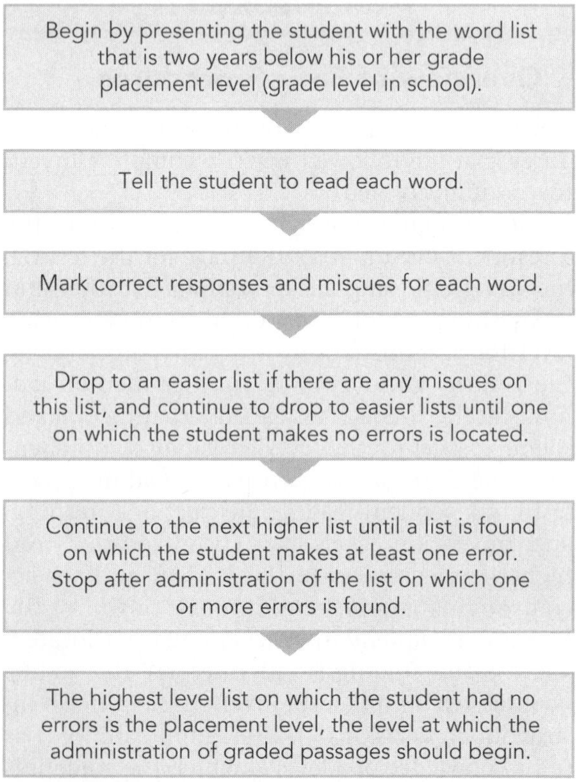

Begin by presenting the student with the word list that is two years below his or her grade placement level (grade level in school).

↓

Tell the student to read each word.

↓

Mark correct responses and miscues for each word.

↓

Drop to an easier list if there are any miscues on this list, and continue to drop to easier lists until one on which the student makes no errors is located.

↓

Continue to the next higher list until a list is found on which the student makes at least one error. Stop after administration of the list on which one or more errors is found.

↓

The highest level list on which the student had no errors is the placement level, the level at which the administration of graded passages should begin.

When administering the word list portion of the test, the examiner should follow these steps:

1. Tell the student to read each word, even if it is a difficult one. If the correct response is given, the examiner should draw a line through the word on his or her test sheet (or place a checkmark on the line beside the word, if that seems easier).
2. If the student mispronounces a word and does not correct the pronunciation, the examiner should record the child's miscue on the test sheet and should not give credit.
3. If the pupil mispronounces a word but then corrects it before going on, the examiner should record the miscue on the test sheet and write a *C* in front of the word to indicate that the miscue was corrected. Credit is given for this word.
4. If the student mispronounces a word and gives more than one mistaken word before getting the correct pronunciation, no credit should be given. The examiner should record all erroneous responses for later analysis.
5. If the student makes no effort on a word for ten seconds, the examiner should point to or present the next word. "Don't know" should be written on the test sheet, and no credit should be given.
6. The student's score is the number of words lined through (or checkmarked) or marked with a *C*.

The teacher should start administering the test with a list that is at least two years below the student's grade placement level. If the student mispronounces and does not correct any words on the initial list, the teacher should drop to easier lists until no errors are made. The highest level list on which the student makes no errors is the level at which the teacher should start administering graded passages. These lists are included with the inventory mainly to provide a tool for placement in the graded passages, allowing teachers to bypass the administration of passages that are much too easy for the students. The word lists are not infallible guides to placement, however, since they contain no measure of comprehension. Therefore, if it becomes clear that administration of the passages has been started too high on the basis of the word list administration, it is important for the administrator to drop back to a lower level.

The use of word lists is an unreliable means of determining independent, instructional, and frustration levels when compared with the use of graded passages, in part because word list scores may be inflated for children who have good phonics and structural analysis skills and less developed comprehension skills. Nevertheless, word lists are used by some teachers to get extremely rough estimates of independent, instructional, and frustration levels. When using the lists for this purpose, the teacher should have the student read from increasingly difficult lists until at least five words are missed. The level at which the student misses no more than two out of twenty words is probably his or her independent reading level; three or four errors on a list indicate the probable instructional reading level; and five or more errors identify the level at which reading material is likely to be too difficult.

The marking of a graded word list is illustrated in Figure 2–3. This sample list was administered to a fourth-grade student named Jason. Jason was a boy who changed schools when he went to live

FIGURE 2–3 Sample Marking of a Word List

LEVEL 4

1. ~~amused~~ ________
2. ancient ānk' ənt
3. ~~award~~ ________
4. cemetery kĕm' ē·ter' ĭ
5. ~~echo~~ ________
6. ~~elastic~~ ________
7. ~~flock~~ ________
8. ~~government~~ ________
9. ~~invade~~ ________
10. ~~jealous~~ ________
11. ~~lizard~~ ________
12. mechanic mə·chă' nĭk (as in church)
13. ~~mysterious~~ ________
14. ~~portion~~ ________
15. ~~savage~~ ________
16. ~~scarlet~~ ________
17. signal sĭg' năl
18. ~~statue~~ ________
19. ~~stout~~ ________
20. vicious vĭk' us

with a relative in a different town. His previous school records were slow in arriving at his new school, and he did not appear comfortable with the fourth-grade reading material that his new teacher first gave him, so the teacher administered the oral portion of the informal reading inventory to give her some guidance in placing him in an appropriate reading group for instruction and in assigning him homework reading. The teacher administered the word lists to determine the correct level on which to start the reading passages and to get an idea of Jason's word recognition skills for words in isolation. The placement level (level at which the reading passages should be started) indicated for Jason by the word lists was second grade, because he had no errors on that list, but three errors on the third-grade list. The list shown in the example is the fourth-grade list.

Graded Passages

The general procedure for administering the graded passages is shown in Figure 2–4. To obtain maximum information, it is suggested that both an oral and a silent reading passage be administered at each level. Nevertheless, some teachers may prefer to use only one or the other. Although traditionally the oral passages have been administered first, there is often good reason for administering the silent passages first. The decision should be made by the teacher who is administering the test, based on his or her knowledge of the student being tested.

Oral Reading ■ The oral reading sequence should begin on the highest level at which the student achieved a perfect score on the graded word list section of the inventory. The student should be told what is expected during the assessment process. For example, the teacher might say, "I want you to read some stories for me. Some of them will be easy for you; others will be hard. You are not expected to read everything perfectly. Just do your best. If you don't know a word, try to figure it out instead of just skipping it. After you finish each story, I'm going to ask you some questions about it." Then the teacher may read aloud the introductory statement preceding the passage.

As the student reads, the examiner should not indicate correctness or incorrectness. If the child hesitates or looks to the examiner for reassurance, a response such as "Go on" should be used. If the pupil hesitates for more than five seconds, the teacher should supply the problem word and mark *TP* on the passage (for "teacher pronounced").

As the child reads, the examiner should mark all unexpected responses or miscues. Although some of the items marked, such as omitted punctuation, will not count in the quantitative count of miscues that is used to determine levels, they may nevertheless be helpful to the teacher in a qualitative analysis for use in planning future instruction. Some of the miscues that are marked may be counted for determination of levels, but may prove not to be significant in the qualitative analysis. It is wise not to make decisions during the administration about what to mark; instead, the examiner should mark everything that differs from the text and then, after the recording is complete, decide how to interpret the markings.

The examiner should mark any reading miscues according to the sample system illustrated in Table 2–1. A passage so marked might look like the one illustrated in Figure 2–5, which is the frustration level passage for Jason, the fourth grader whose word list for this level was examined.

Any standard system for marking miscues may be used; the important thing is that it be consistent and reproducible. A teacher who does not know a standard system should not use self-designed markings, the meanings of which may not be interpretable later. Such a teacher should learn a standard marking system thoroughly before beginning the test administration. The reading will seem to go incredibly fast for an inexperienced examiner in any event, and, if practice with the system has not taken place, it will be easy for the student to outdistance the examiner's marking skills. An examiner who makes up marking symbols as the reading takes place is likely to use more than one way to mark similar miscues and be confused by this during the analysis stage.

After the oral reading, the selection should be removed from the student's view, and the teacher should ask questions about its content. The student's answers may simply be marked correct (+) or incorrect (0), or they may be marked (+) or (0) and simultaneously recorded exactly as given for further analysis later. Although teachers must record tentative correctness or incorrectness as the test is proceeding in order to have an immediate idea of the comprehension level, it is generally wise also to record exact responses, because snap judgments made about the correctness of answers during the testing may prove to be inadequate when there is time to consider the responses more fully. In addition, qualitative analysis of comprehension skills is facilitated by having the student's exact answers. With such information, the teacher can decide, for example, if the child is trying to answer strictly from past experience and is

FIGURE 2–4 Administration of the Graded Passages

Locate a passage at the student's placement level.
Decide whether you are going to administer the oral or the silent reading passages first.
(In this example the oral passages are listed first only because it is the traditional system. Many students may be more comfortable with doing the silent reading first, and the teacher should use this order with them.)

↓

Tell the student what will be expected during the assessment process.

↓

Present the student's copy of the first passage to the student, and read the introductory statement to him or her.

↓

Ask the student to read the passage orally. Mark all miscues on the teacher's copy as the student reads.

↓

Remove the passage from the student's view, and ask the accompanying comprehension questions
(or, if you prefer, have the student retell the passage and then follow up the retelling by asking any comprehension questions that were not covered in the retelling).
Record incorrect responses for later analysis.

↓

Present the student with a passage from a different form of the inventory at the same grade level and read the introductory statement to him or her.

↓

Ask the student to read the passage silently and look up at you when he or she is finished.

↓

After the student is finished reading the passage, remove it from his or her view and ask the accompanying comprehension questions
(or have him or her retell the passage with the questions that are left unanswered used as follow-up probes).
Record all incorrect responses.

↓

If the student met both the criteria (word recognition and comprehension) for the independent level at this level, move on to the next higher level and administer oral and silent passages from the same two forms in the same manner as before.
If he or she did not meet the criteria for the independent level, drop back to the next lower grade level passage and administer both forms at that level. Continue to drop back until the independent level is located. Then, if the initial passage presented was not at the frustration level, go to the next level above that passage and continue to administer passages until the frustration level is met.

↓

When the student reaches frustration level on the oral passage, discontinue having him or her read to you, and read aloud the passage at the next higher level to him or her.

↓

Ask the student the accompanying comprehension questions
(or have him or her retell the passage, following up with any unanswered questions).

↓

Continue to read progressively higher passages until the student falls below 75 percent comprehension on a passage.
The last passage on which the student had 75 percent comprehension will be the listening comprehension level. (It may be necessary to read a passage from another form at the same level as the frustration level. It may even be necessary to drop back and read one at the same level as the instructional level in order to locate the listening comprehension level if the student is reading about as well as he or she is capable and is not in need of any corrective procedures, just good developmental reading instruction at the correct level.)

TABLE 2–1 Word-Recognition Miscue-Marking System

Miscue	Marking	Comment
Mispronunciation	~~went~~ (wert written above)	The student attempts to pronounce the word but produces a nonsense word, rather than a real one.
Substitution	~~went~~ (want written above)	The student substitutes a real word that is incorrect.
Refusal to pronounce	went (TP written above)	The student neither pronounces the word nor attempts to do so. The teacher pronounces the word so that testing can continue.
Insertion	sent ^ to (on written above caret)	The student inserts a word or a series of words that does not appear in the text.
Omission	to (the) school (the circled)	The student omits a word or a continuous sequence of words in the text but continues to read.
Repetition	in the little house (the little underlined with wavy line)	The student repeats one or more words that have been read. Groups of adjacent words that are repeated count as one repetition.
Reversal	that he saw (he and saw marked for reversal)	The student reverses the order of words or letters.

Note: If the student makes a miscue and then corrects it without prompting from the teacher, the teacher should place a check (✓) beside the miscue to indicate a spontaneous correction and should not include the miscue in the error count.

ignoring the passage content. Once again, as the student answers the comprehension questions, the teacher should not communicate feedback about correctness or incorrectness. If two responses are needed and the youngster gives only one, it is acceptable to ask, "Anything else?", but prompting with specific clues is *not* acceptable. If the pupil seems to have understood but has not adequately expressed himself or herself, the teacher may ask, "Could you tell me more?"

Although the most likely answers have been provided to assist the teacher, there will be some correct answers that have not been listed, especially on main idea and vocabulary questions. If the teacher *knows* that an answer is correct, he or she should not feel restricted by the fact that it is not included in the suggested responses, but should count it as correct. When a main idea question asks what the story is about, some children will respond with a single word, such as "Buddy," or a short phrase. It is acceptable to ask, "What about Buddy?" If the child is unable to elaborate, however, he or she should not be prompted further. If the child gives an entire summary of the story, the teacher should ask for a shorter way of saying what it is about or for one sentence that tells what it is about, assuming that the student understands the concept of sentence. Once again, the student should not be prompted further if the additional question does not elicit a correct response.

The answers to sequence questions may have several steps. Credit must not be given for these steps if they are given in incorrect order, but partial credit may be given for correct steps given in order, even if some step has been omitted. Similarly, if there are two-part detail questions, half credit can be given for getting one of the two parts.

Some questions are accompanied by notes to help the examiner decide about the scoring of a particular answer. The examiner should look for any explanatory notes as the testing progresses. Figure 2–6 shows the marked set of comprehension questions for Jason's frustration level passage (shown in Figure 2–5).

Silent Reading ■ Next the examiner presents the student with a passage at the same level for silent reading. The examiner reads the introductory statement to the student and then asks the student to read the passage silently. There is no time limit for the reading of the selection, but some examiners time the reading for additional diagnostic information. The examiner does not offer help with unknown words or answer student questions. If the student asks for assistance, the examiner should simply say, "Do the best you can. I want to find out how well you can read it without help." When the student finishes reading the passage, the selection should be removed from view, and the examiner should ask comprehension questions about the selection.

Monitoring the Administration ■ When a student falls below 90 percent in word recognition on the oral passage (or 85 percent for students in first

FIGURE 2–5 **Sample Marking of an Oral Reading Passage**

On the corner, one block away from the closed library, Matthew saw the long green bookmobile. He walked up to the truck, climbed the three little steps, and walked inside. A girl who looked a little like Claudia took his book from him. The woman from the library was standing next to her, stamping books for people to take home. She smiled when she saw Matthew. "Look at the titles," she said. "I'll come over as soon as I can and help you find a book you'll like."

Matthew smiled back and walked around the bookmobile, looking for the children's section. There were other people walking around, too. They were all close together because there wasn't a lot of room. The books were lined up against the wall on shelves. When you walked around them, you couldn't find a place to be by yourself. Matthew saw that he couldn't stay at the bookmobile the way he could at a real library. So when he came to the children's section, he looked through the shelves and tried to find a book as fast as he could. He looked at the titles and all the bright book covers. His eyes fell on a book with a picture of a boy on it. The boy had brown skin just like Matthew's, and he looked about the same age. Matthew thought it would be nice to read a book about a boy who looked so much like himself. He picked it up and took it to the librarian. She said, "You picked out a really good book." Then she took his card and stamped the book.

Source: "A Quiet Place," by Rose Blue, in Leo Fay and others, *Star Show* (Chicago: The Riverside Publishing Company, 1989), pp. 212–213.

[*Note*: Do not count as miscues mispronunciation of the names Matthew and Claudia. You may pronounce these names for the student if needed.]

1. **Miscues (scored or counted):**

Substitutions (8):

away for *around*
a for *the*
child's for *children's*
Where for *There*
then for *when*
title for *titles*
Matthew for *Matthew's*
(The proper noun is not the problem in this case; the *'s* ending is.)
When for *Then*

Insertion (1):

the

Omission (1):

stamping books for people to take home. She smiled when

Repetitions (8):

his
and
you'll
at the
the
all the bright
fell
up

2. **Other items (marked on teacher's passage, but not scored):**

Spontaneous corrections (2):

bookmobile
really

Refusal to pronounce a proper noun (1):

Claudia

FIGURE 2–6 **Sample Marking of Comprehension Questions**

COMPREHENSION QUESTIONS

Score	Type	Question
o	main idea	1. What is this story about? (Matthew visits the bookmobile because the library is closed; Matthew makes his first visit to the bookmobile.)
o	detail	2. Where did Matthew see the bookmobile? ~~(on the corner; one block away from the library)~~ *(at the library)*
o	vocabulary	3. What is a bookmobile? (a library in a truck or bus or van)
+	cause and effect/ inference	4. Why did Matthew go to the bookmobile? ~~(He had a book to turn in and~~ wanted another ~~one~~ *book* and the library was closed.)
o	inference	5. Was the librarian friendly? (yes) What did the story say that made you think that? ~~(She smiled at Matthew and offered to help him.)~~ *They have to be.*
o	sequence	6. What was the first thing Matthew looked for after he returned his book? ~~(the children's section)~~ *(a book)*
o	inference	7. Was the bookmobile crowded? (yes) What did the story say that made you think that? ~~(People were close together; there wasn't a lot of room; there was no place to be by yourself.)~~ *Don't know. It doesn't say.*
+	detail	8. What two things did Matthew look at to help him pick out a book? (the titles and the book covers)
+	vocabulary	9. What does the phrase "his eyes fell on a book" mean? (He saw a book.)
o	inference	10. What did Matthew look like? (He had brown skin.) *Don't know*

and second grades), achieves below 50 percent in comprehension on either the oral or silent passage (answers less than half of the questions correctly), or exhibits signs of extreme frustration (such as facial tics, body tension, excessive squirming, and other signs of frustration), he or she should not be asked to read at a higher level. The examiner should be careful not to confuse signs of fatigue with frustration. If a student indicates that he or she is tired or shows indications of tiredness, rather than tension and upset, a rest period is in order.

Options for Administration ■ Optionally, the material read silently may be reread orally and scores compared with earlier oral reading. In this way it is possible to discover if a student's oral reading with prior preparation is markedly superior to his or her oral reading at sight. Oral reading with prior preparation more closely approximates classroom oral reading than does oral reading at sight, but does not readily reveal a student's word recognition strategies. Upper-grade teachers who feel confident of the word recognition skills of their students may wish to use only silent passages for determining levels. They may use oral rereading of the same passages if they wish to check fluency of oral reading rather than word recognition procedures.

If the silent reading is being timed to give some indication of the student's reading rate in words per minute (WPM), the student should be told to wait for a signal to begin reading and to look up as soon as he or she has finished reading. A clock with a second hand or a stopwatch may be used for timing the reading. The time of reading in seconds is needed for figuring the reading rate. The number of words read is multiplied by sixty, and this number is divided by the time spent reading the passage.

Listening Comprehension ■ When a student reaches frustration level, it is appropriate to begin listening comprehension testing. The examiner should read aloud one selection from each successive level (beginning with the next level in the form currently being used or with an alternate form of the level at which frustration was reached) and ask the student the accompanying comprehension questions. Progressively higher levels should be administered until the student is unable to answer at least 75 percent of the questions asked. The highest level at which the student still gives correct answers to at least 75 percent of the comprehension questions is the listening comprehension level.

Other Considerations ■ If at any point during the administration of the test the student becomes fatigued or the passages become difficult enough to cause some tension, pausing briefly between passages for a "stretch break" can help. The examiner should be alert for signs of both fatigue and tension, since either can adversely affect the test results.

How Is the Inventory Scored and Interpreted?

To score the inventory, the examiner must use predetermined criteria for word recognition and comprehension accuracy to ascertain the reading levels. The criteria to be used for this inventory were presented in Table 1–1 in Section 1.

As the testing proceeds, it is necessary for the examiner to have some idea of the word recognition and comprehension percentages the student is attaining, so that he or she will know when to stop asking the student to read passages and when to begin reading to the student. A scoring aid for this IRI is provided in the teacher section for each passage. (See Figure 2–7 for an example.) It is located on the page with the passage and the comprehension questions, where it is easy to find quickly. The scoring aid for word recognition shows the percentages resulting from various numbers of miscues made in the oral reading of the passage. The number of words in the passage on which the word recognition percentages are based is also given in each scoring aid. This number is the total number of words minus the difficult proper nouns and special words that are not counted as errors but that can be supplied for the student. The total number of words in the passage is also given to show the basis for the rate calculations provided in the scoring aid. The scoring aid for comprehension shows percentages based on the number of errors made in answering the comprehension questions. In addition to being useful for quick tallying during administration of the test, these scoring aids are helpful for filling out the Summary Form, which aids in interpretation of data gathered during the testing.

FIGURE 2–7 **Scoring Aid for a Reading Passage**

SCORING AID

Word Recognition

%–Miscues

99–3

95–13

90–25

85–36

Comprehension

%–Errors

100–0

90–1

80–2

70–3

60–4

50–5

40–6

30–7

20–8

10–9

0–10

237 Words
(for Word Recognition)

244 Words
(for Rate)

WPM
14640

■ Completing the Worksheets

Two worksheets that teachers may wish to use to help them organize and analyze the information collected through the administration of the informal reading inventory are presented in Figures 2–8 and 2–9. These worksheets are not a required part of completing the inventory, but filling them out generally facilitates completing the Summary Forms for Quantitative and Qualitative Analysis.

Figure 2–8 shows the Worksheet for Word Recognition Miscue Tally Chart. This chart is designed to help the examiner consolidate counts of types of word recognition miscues from the various passages that were read orally. This allows the examiner to total errors of each type across a number of passages and see more clearly which types of errors predominate for a particular student. The examiner looks at each passage that the student read orally and counts the total number of uncorrected mispronunciations, substitutions, insertions, omissions, reversals, repetitions, and

FIGURE 2–8 Worksheet for Word Recognition Miscue Tally Chart

Miscue		PP	P	1	2	3	4	5	6	7	8	9	10	11	12	Totals	
Mispronunciation	A					3										A	3
	MC					3										MC	3
	SC						1									SC	1
Substitution	A				1	3	8									A	12
	MC					2	4									MC	6
	SC				1	1	1									SC	3
Insertion	A						1									A	1
	MC						1									MC	1
	SC															SC	
Omission	A						1									A	1
	MC						1									MC	1
	SC															SC	
Reversal	A															A	
	MC															MC	
	SC															SC	
Repetition	A						8									A	8
Refusal to pronounce	A															A	
Totals	A				1	6	18									A	25
	MC					5	6									MC	11
	SC				1	1	2									SC	4

A = All miscues of that type (excluding ones that were self-corrected)
MC = Miscues that resulted in a meaning change
SC = Self-corrected miscues

Miscue Analysis of Phonic and Structural Analysis Skills

(Tally total miscues on appropriate lines.)

Miscue	For Words in Isolation	For Words in Context
Single consonants	|||	||||
Consonant blends		|
Single vowels	~~||||~~	||||
Vowel digraphs		
Consonant digraphs	||	||
Diphthongs		|
Prefixes		
Suffixes		
Special combinations	||	
Word beginnings	|	||||
Word middles	~~||||~~ |	~~||||~~
Word endings	|||	||||
Compound words		|
Inflectional endings		|||
Syllabication		
Accent		

(*Note:* In order to fill out the analysis for words in context, it is helpful to make a list of expected reader responses and unexpected responses for easy comparison as to graphic similarity, syntactic acceptability, and semantic acceptability. See page 108 for a good way to record this information.)

FIGURE 2-9 **Worksheet for Qualitative Analysis of Uncorrected Miscues in Context**

(Include mispronunciations, substitutions, insertions, omissions, and reversals.)

Passage	Type of Miscue	Expected Response	Unexpected Response	Graphic Similarity	Syntactic Acceptability	Semantic Acceptability
2	*substitution*	*grandfather*	*father*	*yes*	*yes*	*yes*
3	*mispronunciation*	*fife*	*fĕf*	*yes*	*yes*	*no*
3	*mispronunciation*	*fife*	*fĕf*	*yes*	*yes*	*no*
3	*mispronunciation*	*fife*	*fĕf*	*yes*	*yes*	*no*
3	*substitution*	*setting*	*selling*	*yes*	*yes*	*no*
3	*substitution*	*fiddling*	*feeling*	*yes*	*yes*	*no*
3	*substitution*	*pockets*	*pocket*	*yes*	*yes*	*yes*
4	*omission*	*stamping . . . when*	—	—	*no*	*no*
4	*substitution*	*around*	*away*	*no*	*no*	*no*
4	*substitution*	*the*	*a*	*no*	*yes*	*yes*
4	*substitution*	*children's*	*child's*	*yes*	*yes*	*yes*
4	*substitution*	*There*	*Where*	*yes*	*no*	*no*
4	*substitution*	*when*	*then*	*yes*	*no*	*no*
4	*substitution*	*titles*	*title*	*yes*	*yes*	*yes*
4	*substitution*	*Matthew's*	*Matthew*	*yes*	*yes*	*yes*
4	*substitution*	*Then*	*When*	*yes*	*no*	*no*
4	*insertion*	—	*the*	—	*no*	*no*

refusals to pronounce, inserting each total under the correct grade level beside the letter *A* (all miscues of the type except ones that were self-corrected). Next, these miscues are examined to determine whether or not they resulted in a meaning change. The number that resulted in a meaning change is recorded under the appropriate grade level for each miscue type beside the letters *MC* (miscues that resulted in a meaning change). Then self-corrected miscues of each different type are counted and recorded under the appropriate grade level for the appropriate type beside the letters *SC* (self-corrected miscues). Rows and columns can be totaled, giving a quick look at miscues grade-by-grade and type-by-type. The results make a portion of the Summary of Quantitative Analysis (shown in Figure 2–10) easy to fill out. This worksheet also has a place to tally types of miscues made on words in isolation and on words in context, allowing a visual comparison. Figure 2–8 shows the Worksheet for Word Recognition Miscue Tally Chart filled out for Jason, the fourth grader whose results have been shared in earlier figures.

Figure 2–9 shows the Worksheet for Qualitative Analysis of Uncorrected Miscues in Context. It helps the examiner decide whether the student is paying attention to, or ignoring, graphic clues, syntactic clues, and semantic clues in the context of the passages. To fill out the sheet, the teacher looks at each passage that the student has read orally and writes down, for each mispronunciation, substitution, insertion, omission, and reversal, the passage number, the type of miscue, the expected response (none will be appropriate for insertions), the unexpected response (what the student actually said), whether the unexpected response was graphically similar to the expected response (*yes* or *no* for most words, *identical* if the wrong pronunciation of a homograph was given), whether the unexpected response was syntactically acceptable in the sentence (*yes* or *no*), and whether the unexpected response was semantically acceptable in the sentence (*yes* or *no*). Examination of this completed worksheet may help the examiner fill out the Summary of Qualitative Analysis found in Figure 2–10. The completed Worksheet for Qualitative Analysis of Uncorrected Miscues in Context shown in Figure 2–9 summarizes information gathered from the same inventory from which the worksheet in Figure 2–8 was taken.

Summary Forms

Two summary forms for the teacher/administrator—a Summary of Quantitative Analysis and a Summary of Qualitative Analysis—appear after each set of passages. These forms, which should be copied and used to record the data accumulated during the testing, are shown in Figure 2–10, summarizing the data on Jason, the fourth grader whose results have been shown in previous examples. Figure 2–10 includes circled numbers as guides to the following discussion of use of the form. The user should refer to each numbered section of the form as that part of the form is discussed. The actual form does not have these circled numbers.

Teacher Summary Form for Quantitative Analysis

(1) *Identifying Information.* Identifying information includes the student's name and grade placement, the date of administration, the name of the administrator of the test, and the form or forms used for various parts of the test.

(2) *Performance Levels Based on Graded Word Lists.* The main use for the graded word lists for most examiners will be as a placement tool for deciding where to begin administering the graded reading passages of the inventory. For these users, only the section indicating the placement level needs to be completed. In this space the user should insert the highest level at which the student had no errors. If the examiner wishes to compare the performance levels as indicated by the graded word lists with the performance levels based on reading passages, he or she will fill in the spaces on the chart for independent, instructional, and frustration levels, based upon these criteria:

1. Independent reading level—the highest level at which there were no more than two errors
2. Instructional reading level—the highest level at which there were no more than four errors
3. Frustration level—the lowest level at which there were five or more errors

(3) *Types of Miscues in Context.* In the appropriate boxes in this chart the examiner should place the totals for the following types of miscues from all levels of graded passages that were given orally: mispronunciation, substitution, insertion, omission, reversal, repetition, and refusal to pronounce. Self-corrected miscues are not counted in the totals entered on the top row of this chart, but they are entered in the bottom row of the chart under the appropriate category. Of the uncorrected miscues, those that resulted in meaning changes are entered under the appropriate category in the middle row. The Worksheet for Word

FIGURE 2–10 Completed Sample Summary Forms

SUMMARY OF QUANTITATIVE ANALYSIS

(1) **Student's Name** *Jason Brooks* **Grade** *4* (1) **Date** *2/24/92* (1) **Administrator** *Mrs. Bingham*

(1) **Forms Used:** Word Lists, Form *1* Oral Passages, Form *A* Silent Passages, Form ___ Listening Comprehension, Form *B*

(6) **Performance Levels Based on Full Inventory (Oral & Silent):** Independent ___ Instructional ___ Frustration ___ Listening Comprehension ___

(6A) **Performance Levels Based on Oral Passages:** Independent *2* Instructional *3* Frustration *4* Listening Comprehension *4*

(6B) **Performance Levels Based on Silent Passages:** Independent ___ Instructional ___ Frustration ___ Listening Comprehension ___

(6C) **Optional Comparison Levels:** Independent ___ Instructional ___ Frustration ___ (7) **Rate of Reading:** High ___ Average ___ Low ___

(2) **Performance Levels Based on Graded Word Lists:** Placement *2* Independent *2* Instructional *3* Frustration *4*

(3) Types of Miscues in Context

	Mispronunciation	Substitution	Insertion	Omission	Reversal	Repetition	Refusal to Pronounce	Row Totals
Total	3	2	1	1		8		15
Meaning changed	3	6	1	1		0		11
Self-corrected	1	3	0	0		0		4

(4) Comprehension Skill Analysis Chart

Skill	Number of Questions	Number of Errors	Percent of Errors
Main idea	5	1	20%
Detail	12	4½	37.5%
Sequence	5	3	60%
Cause and effect	9	0	0%
Inference	10	4	40%
Vocabulary	7	4	57%

(5) Summary Table of Percentages

Level	Word Recognition	Oral Comprehension	Silent Comprehension	Average Comprehension	Listening Comprehension
PP					
P					
1					
2	99	100			
3	96	85			
4	92	30			80
5					60
6					
7					
8					
9					
10					
11					
12					

FIGURE 2–10 *(continued)*

SUMMARY OF QUALITATIVE ANALYSIS

(8) Summary of Strengths and Weaknesses in Word Recognition

(Include all of the important data that have been collected on word recognition skills.)

When Jason was reading words orally in context, by far the most frequent type of miscue (almost half of the total) was substitutions, and half of these resulted in a meaning change. Jason expects to make real words from the collections of letters and rarely settles for a nonsense word. In fact, all three of the nonsense productions were an attempt at the word "fife." About a third of his miscues were rather random repetitions in the fourth grade passage, on which he had reached frustration level. Jason appears to pay less attention to the middles of words presented in isolation, but he is careless with all parts of words in context. This appears to be due to his desire to read rapidly. He needs to be encouraged to slow down and think about the meanings of sentences and paragraphs, not about just producing real words for unfamiliar groups of letters. He sometimes leaves off s and 's inflectional endings. This may also be due to haste and carelessness. He frequently confuses th and wh word beginnings. This was consistent with his teacher's other observations of his reading practices. His insertion was made without consideration of syntax or semantics. He did little self-correction of errors.

(9) Summary of Strengths and Weaknesses in Comprehension

(Include all of the important data that have been collected about comprehension.)

He had the most trouble with sequence and vocabulary questions, missing 60 percent and 57 percent of those questions, respectively. He also showed possible weaknesses in making inferences and recalling details. These areas need to be monitored carefully during classroom reading activities, since there was a small number of questions involved in the test, particularly for sequence. On the other hand, Jason didn't miss any of the 9 cause-and-effect questions. His listening comprehension level is two grade levels above his instructional reading level, indicating that he has the potential for improvement with instruction.

(10) Checklist of Reading Behaviors

(Place a [+] by areas that are strong and a [–] by areas that are weak.)

1. Reads in phrases __–__ *(except 2nd grade passage)*
2. Reads with expression __–__ *(except 2nd grade passage)*
3. Attends to punctuation __+__
4. Pronounces words correctly __–__
5. Sounds out unfamiliar words __–__ *(not effectively)*
6. Uses structure clues, when available, to recognize unfamiliar words __–__
7. Uses context clues __–__ *(not well or consistently)*
8. Makes strategic attempts to recognize unfamiliar words (applies word recognition skills flexibly) __–__
9. Keeps place in material being read *(Not always)*
10. Shows few signs of tension when reading __+__
11. Holds book at appropriate distance from face when reading __+__
12. Self-corrects errors without prompting *not always*

Recognition Miscue Tally Chart in Figure 2–8 can be helpful in preparation for filling out this portion of the Summary Form. It allows the total, meaning change, and self-corrected miscues to be tallied by level and then added to provide the figures needed for the summary.

If the single sample marked passage in Figure 2–5 were to be entered on the Summary Form, there would be no need to tally it first on the Worksheet for Word Recognition Miscue Tally Chart, since no other passage results would be added to it. The results of the sample passage would be entered on the form as follows: an 8 in the box for total substitutions (*away, a, child's, Where, then, title, Matthew, When*), a 1 in the box for total insertions (*the*), a 1 in the box for total omissions (*stamping books for people to take home. She smiled when*), and an 8 in the box for total repetitions (*his, and, you'll, at the, the, all the bright, fell, up*).

The miscue on the name *Claudia* is not counted. The examiner is instructed to tell the student this name if necessary, as is the case with all proper names (except ones that are also common words, like *Brown* and *Pat*).

Only 1 is put in the box for omissions, even though several words were omitted, because the words were omitted as a part of a continuous sequence. The appearance here is that the reader lost his place and accidentally switched lines. Such carelessness is a part of this reader's general profile. Only one repetition is counted for *at the* and only one for *all the bright* because in each of these cases the words were part of a continuous phrase.

A 4 should be placed in the box for substitutions that caused a meaning change, because the substitutions of *away, Where, then,* and *When* all resulted in a loss of meaning. A 1 should also be placed in the box for insertions that caused a meaning change and another 1 placed in the box for omissions that caused a meaning change, since both of these miscues distorted meaning.

A 1 should be placed in the box for self-corrected mispronunciations (*bookmobile*) and in the box for self-corrected substitutions (*really*). Self-corrections are good signs because they signal use of metacognitive skills by the student.

The Summary of Quantitative Analysis in Figure 2–10 combines the information from this selection with information from two other passages that Jason read orally. Therefore, the types of miscues in context on that form include some miscues not pointed out previously. (See the worksheet in Figure 2–9 for more detail.)

Meaning changes and self-corrections will be discussed further in relation to the next part of the form, which includes qualitative factors to be considered in a skills analysis.

(4) *Comprehension Skill Analysis Chart.* A record of the student's performance is placed on the Comprehension Skill Analysis Chart in Figure 2–10. For each question type, the teacher records the number of questions asked and the number of errors the student made on that type of question. Cause-and-effect questions are labeled both as "cause and effect" and as either "detail," if the cause or effect is directly stated in the passage, or "inference," if the cause or effect is implied. The examiner may choose whether to tally *all* cause-and-effect questions under the category "cause and effect" or to tally the cause-and-effect/inference questions under the "inference" category and the cause-and-effect/detail questions under the "detail" category. After recording the numbers of questions and errors for each question type, the examiner calculates the percentage of errors for each one. This percentage is figured by dividing the number of errors by the number of questions and multiplying the result by 100. (Example: The student was asked twenty detail questions. He missed five of them: 5 ÷ 20 = .25; .25 × 100 = 25%. His rate of error for detail questions was 25 percent. This would indicate a moderate need for help with this type of question.)

In the example in Figure 2–10, Jason missed three of five sequence questions, for a 60 percent error rate, and four of seven vocabulary questions, for a 57 percent error rate. Both of these percentages are high enough to indicate possible problems in these areas. However, a word of caution is in order at this point. Generalizations about skill deficiencies based on extremely limited samples are not advisable. Since only five sequence questions and seven vocabulary questions were asked, the conclusions that can be drawn from these small samples are much less certain than the finding in the example above in which twenty questions were involved. Recognizing that both the word recognition and comprehension analyses are limited measures of specific skills, the teacher can best use the results of this assessment to determine which skill areas need additional observation.

(5) *Summary Table of Percentages.* The Summary Table of Percentages is used to record the percentages of accuracy for word recognition and comprehension for each of the passages that is administered as a part of the test. The first diagram on page 28 illustrates percentage calculation for word recognition scores.

When both the oral and the silent selections have been administered, the comprehension percentages for each may be obtained separately. A combined score can then be obtained for average comprehension. The calculation procedure for comprehension, which is the same for all three calculations, is shown in the second diagram.

1. *Word recognition*: oral passages only

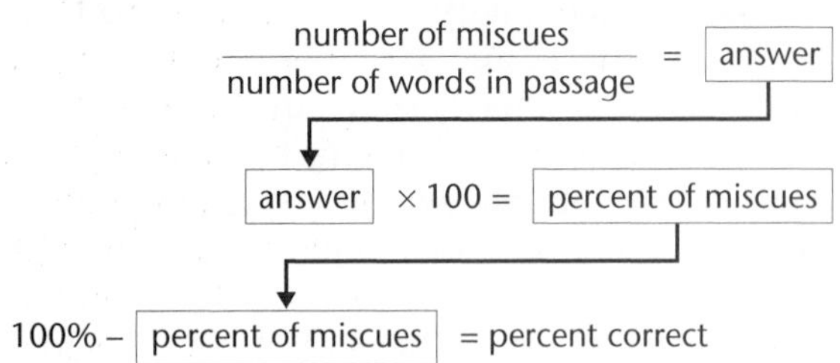

2. *Comprehension*: oral and silent passages

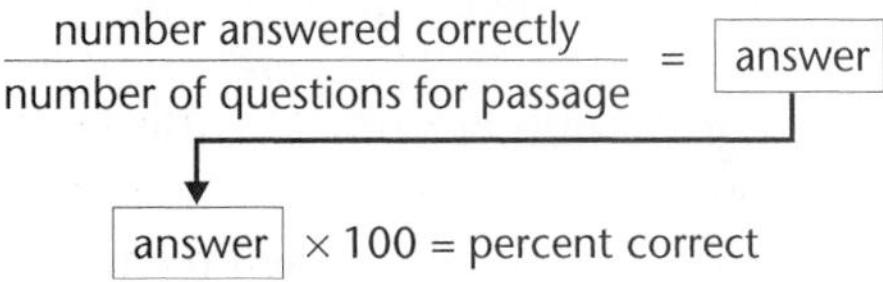

Assume, for example, that both a silent and an oral passage are administered at each level and that there are ten questions for each passage. If the student misses two questions on the oral passage and one question on the silent passage, that student would have 8/10 = .8 × 100 = 80 percent correct for the oral passage and 9/10 = .9 × 100 = 90 percent correct for the silent passage. The student's average comprehension would be 17/20 = .85 × 100 = 85 percent. Obviously, if only one passage has been given at each level, as in Jason's case, no average comprehension is found.

The examiner reads passages to the student after the frustration level has been reached and then asks comprehension questions based on these passages. The percentages for these passages are included in the table under listening comprehension.

(6) *Performance Levels Based on Reading Passages.* In order to determine a student's independent, instructional, frustration, and listening comprehension levels, the teacher compares the percentages in the Summary Table of Percentages with the criteria in Table 1–1. Here is an example of how this is done:

If the student's word recognition score on the oral passage for a level was 96 percent and his or her comprehension score was 85 percent, the passage would be considered to be at an instructional reading level for the student. Performance levels based on the full inventory consider both silent and oral passages. The administrator must remember that both criteria (word recognition and comprehension) must be met to establish the independent and instructional reading levels; in contrast, only one of the criteria needs to be met to establish the frustration level.

(6A) or (6B) *Performance Levels Based on Oral Passages* or *Performance Levels Based on Silent Passages.* If only oral passages or only silent passages are administered, the results should be recorded on either line 6A or 6B. If a complete inventory is given, both of these lines should also be completed, for they will indicate whether silent or oral reading is stronger than the other. If silent reading comprehension appears to be better than oral reading comprehension, pronunciation of words may be taking too much of the student's attention, so that it is difficult for him or her to focus on meaning. On the other hand, if the oral reading comprehension appears to be better, the student may still be translating the print symbols to sound in order to understand them, as beginning readers tend to do, instead of moving directly from print to meaning.

(6C) *Optional Comparison Levels.* The examiner may also want to compare the levels that are obtained by reading the material at sight and answering comprehension questions with the levels obtained when the student is allowed to read passages silently first and then reread them orally before being questioned. The reading of passages with prior preparation more closely approximates classroom oral reading than does oral reading at sight, but oral reading at sight reveals more about a student's word recognition strategies. In that case, he or she may record the results of the silent reading with oral rereading on the line labeled OPTIONAL COMPARISON LEVELS. These results may then be compared with the line PERFORMANCE BASED ON ORAL PASSAGES.

(7) *Rate of Reading.* Testing of reading rate is optional when administering this inventory. Timing of the passages is not necessary for setting levels.

To obtain a reading rate, the examiner takes the product of the number of words in the selection times 60 and divides this product by the number of seconds it takes for the pupil to read; the result is a words-per-minute rate.

The scoring aid for each passage includes two word counts. The word count on which word recognition is based excludes difficult proper nouns in the passages. The word count on which the rate is based includes all words, since all must be dealt with to the extent of being looked at, even if they are not counted in the decoding analysis. For example, if there are 100 words in the passage and 4 of them are difficult proper names, the word count on which the word recognition percentage is based would be 96, whereas the word count on which the rate is based would be 100. The scoring aid uses the calculation

$$\frac{\text{Words in passage} \times 60}{\text{Reading time in seconds}}$$

to compute the pupil's reading rate in words per minute (WPM). The words-in-passage-×-60 portion of the calculation has already been computed and is printed in the scoring aid, ready for the examiner to divide by the number of seconds the pupil took to read the selection. Continuing our example of a 100-word passage, the scoring aid would show a value of 6,000 under the division sign (100 words multiplied by 60 seconds = 6,000). If the pupil read the passage in 50 seconds, the examiner would divide the 50 seconds into the 6,000 shown in the aid, yielding a rate of 120 words per minute.

Table 2–2 shows the median silent reading rates that Albert J. Harris and Edward R. Sipay (1990) found on several tests of reading rate for grades 2 through 9 and grade 12. According to their findings, a fourth-grade student who reads a passage at 73 words per minute is clearly reading below the median rate for that grade level as determined by standardized tests. Similarly, a fourth-grader who can read the passage at 240 words per minute is obviously reading above the median rate. Although a teacher may be interested in such information, it should be interpreted with caution. Reading rate is influenced by purpose for reading, interest in the material, and passage difficulty, among other factors. These variables should be taken into account when a rate score is interpreted.

If a student is checked for rate on more than one instructional-level passage—that is, if the student meets the criteria for instructional level at several levels that are timed—the range of rates on these passages should be considered because of the range of variables just mentioned that affect rate. For example, a student may read more slowly in material in which he or she is not interested. For a student in the second grade who reads instructional-level passages at from 82 to 88 words a minute, the examiner would compare the student's rate with the Harris and Sipay chart, see that these scores are nearest to the median for grade 2, and check "Average" on the form. Rates from frustration-level passages should not be considered; they are not a fair representation of rate, since the student should not be asked to function at that level in a school setting.

Teacher Summary Form for Qualitative Analysis ■ (Note: The Worksheet for Qualitative Analysis of Uncorrected Miscues in Context is particularly important because it supplies the basis for the information needed to fill in three crucial sections of the Summary Form: the Miscue Analysis of Phonic and Structural Analysis Skills, the Summary of Strengths and Weaknesses in Word Recognition, and the Summary of Strengths and Weaknesses in Comprehension. The arrangement of the Worksheet page facilitates comparisons of miscues.)

(8) *Summary of Strengths and Weaknesses in Word Recognition.* This is a very important section for bringing together all of the data that have been collected on word recognition skills and for interpreting the meaning of the data in terms of the

TABLE 2–2 Median Rates of Reading for Different Grades as Determined by Several Standardized Reading Tests

	Grade								
	2	3	4	5	6	7	8	9	12
Highest test	118	138	170	195	230	246	267	260	295
Median test	86	116	155	177	206	215	237	252	251
Lowest test	35	75	120	145	171	176	188	199	216

Note: The number of tests included in the table is 7 for grades 2, 3; 8 for grades 4, 5, 6, 7; 6 for grades 8, 9; and 3 for grade 12.

Source: *How to Increase Reading Ability: A Guide to Developmental and Remedial Methods*, 9th ed., by Albert J. Harris and Edward R. Sipay. Published by Allyn and Bacon, Boston, MA. Copyright © 1990 by Pearson Education. Reprinted by permission of the publisher.

student's abilities and needs. The chart showing types of miscues in context on the quantitative analysis part of the Summary Form, the chart related to miscue analysis of phonic and structural analysis skills on the worksheet in Figure 2–8, and the worksheet in Figure 2–9—which brings in the recording of the graphic similarity of miscues, syntactic acceptability, and semantic acceptability—all provide data from which a narrative about the student's strengths and weaknesses in word recognition can be formed. Some considerations for judging miscues include the following:

1. Does the miscue change the meaning? If the meaning is not changed, the student is comprehending to some degree. If the meaning is changed, the miscue is a significant one.
2. Is the reader using syntactic cues? If a pupil says "walk" for *chase* (the same type of word), she shows some use of syntactic cues, but if she says "boy" for *beautiful* (different types of words), she is probably not following the syntactic pattern.
3. Is the student using graphic cues? Comparing the sounds and spellings of miscues and expected words in substitutions will reveal how a reader is using graphic cues. Examples of miscues in which some graphic cues are being used include "house" for *horse*, "running" for *run*, and "dogs" for *dog*.

When analyzing a student's miscues, the teacher should distinguish between trivial and significant errors. For example, if a student has read the word *the* correctly seven or eight times and then substitutes *a* or *an* once in the passage, it is probably safe to assume that the child is familiar with the word. Meaning was not substantially affected, and the substitution may have been due to nervousness or haste. Similarly, if a word has been correctly called several times in a selection and is later omitted, carelessness is likely to be the cause of the omission. As Goodman (1997, p. 534) said, "The number of miscues a reader makes is much less significant than the meaning of the language that results when a miscue has occurred."

Noting if students are using semantic (meaning), syntactic (grammatical), and graphic (symbol) clues when reading will help teachers determine which strategies need to receive instructional attention. For example, failure to use syntactic information may stem from the fact that a student's spoken dialect is unlike the "standard English" presented in the passage. Additional exposure to spoken standard English may be valuable for such a student. Disregard of semantic clues might signal a need for vocabulary and concept development and use of context clues, whereas inability to employ graphic clues could indicate a need for phonics and structural analysis instruction.

All errors are recorded and counted in the process of determining performance levels; however, when the miscues are analyzed for semantic and syntactic acceptability, those that do not violate either criterion are not considered significant enough to necessitate instructional attention.

The worksheet in Figure 2–8 provides a place to tally miscues of various types that were recorded during the administration of the graded word lists and the graded reading passages. The miscues for the graded word lists are recorded beside the appropriate miscue type in the column for words in isolation. The miscues for the graded reading passages are recorded beside the appropriate miscue type in the column for words in context. These miscues are indicated in separate columns because miscues in isolation often differ in type from miscues in context. Few miscues in context and many in isolation indicate that the student is using clues in the passage beyond graphic clues to help in word recognition—a good sign. The frequencies of different types of miscues can be used as a guide to help the teacher focus instruction on appropriate phonic and structural analysis skills.

To facilitate the tally for words in context, it is helpful to make a list showing the expected and unexpected reader responses for each error. The worksheet in Figure 2–9 is useful for recording this information. This worksheet also provides a place to record information needed in the next section of this Summary Form. Expected and unexpected responses will already be recorded side by side in the graded word list section for those who use this portion of the test. Not all examiners will give the graded word lists for miscue analysis purposes, since they may be primarily concerned with miscues in context and feel that time is best spent concentrating on that portion of the test.

(9) *Summary of Strengths and Weaknesses in Comprehension.* This section is important for incorporating all information that has been collected about comprehension abilities and weaknesses and for interpreting the meaning for instructional purposes. The analysis can be done on the basis of the information recorded in the Summary Table of Percentages, the Comprehension Skill Analysis Chart, and the chart called Types of Miscues in Context (all on the Summary Forms)

and in the worksheet in Figure 2–9, in which miscues in context are analyzed for semantic and syntactic acceptability.

Examination of the Summary Table of Percentages can help the examiner determine whether the student performs better in comprehension when reading orally or silently. If these two scores differ drastically in the same direction for all passages given, it may be wise not to use average comprehension for that student. Some students perform similarly in comprehension when reading silently and orally, but for a variety of reasons, some do much better at one type of reading or the other. Some students, especially young ones, need to hear words in order to absorb their meanings. In contrast, for others both the pressure of pronunciation in oral reading and the need to try to use expression distract from concentration on the meaning of the passage. As students become more proficient in reading, their silent reading abilities often outdistance their oral reading abilities.

Question types that had high error rates should be considered areas in which instruction may be needed. However, conclusions drawn on the basis of exceedingly small samples are not as valid as ones drawn from larger samples are. For example, the conclusion that a child needs instruction on main ideas because she missed two of four main idea questions (50-percent error) is not warranted, because the sample is too small. An advantage of giving both silent and oral passages as a part of the inventory is that decisions are based upon a larger question base. Even small samples can provide tentative indications that may be followed up by further investigation, however. Incorrect answers on all four main idea questions asked, for example, would give a stronger indication that help might be needed in this area, and the teacher could do further analysis in this area with classroom materials. Areas in which the error rate is very small are indications of comprehension strengths.

Study of the Types of Miscues in Context chart and the syntactic acceptability and semantic acceptability columns on the worksheet in Figure 2–9 will give the examiner insight into whether the student is using context clues and reading for sense or is producing nonsense as he or she struggles with the passage. The number of self-corrections made is a sign of whether or not the reader is monitoring the sense of what he or she is reading. Self-correction of responses that do not make sense is a good sign.

The examiner may also consider if the student read orally with expression, read in phrases, and used punctuation appropriately. All of these may be indicators of comprehension of material.

Comprehension of material that is read is a complex process. Interest in the topic and background of experience with the topic both play large roles in the comprehension of any given passage. When a student is given this inventory, or any other reading comprehension test, these factors come into play. For this reason, a student will sometimes have a very high comprehension score on a passage or a very low comprehension score on a passage that does not fit the pattern of increasingly difficult material that is expected, given the careful grading of these passages according to readability formulas. An unexpectedly high score may result from extremely high interest or rich background knowledge. An unexpectedly low score may result from extremely low interest or meager background knowledge. Interest and background knowledge related to various subjects differ greatly from student to student in the same classroom. The effects of these variables cannot be eradicated from the test because every passage has content that may be affected by interest and background knowledge. Teacher judgment is needed to place the passages in perspective.

For example, a first grader read the preprimer, primer, and first reader selections of Form C with the following comprehension percentages: 100, 87.5, 75. The student was following a typical pattern at this point. Then she read the second reader selection with a comprehension score of 100 percent. She said, "My grandfather has a greenhouse. He grows plants like that." The link with her background experiences and knowledge and the interest this link created evidently caused her to read the last passage with much more understanding than might have been expected. This idea was confirmed when she dropped to 50-percent comprehension on the third reader passage. For her silent reading performance on preprimer, primer, first reader, second reader, and third reader passages on Form D, her comprehension percentages were 100, 100, 87.5, 75, and 62.5, respectively. She did slightly better at silent reading on all passages except the second reader level, which reinforced the deduction that her interest and background had given a spuriously high reading.

In this section the examiner should include anything that would contribute to an understanding of the student's comprehension levels and strategies. Observations of the child when reading and the child's informal comments during the testing may provide insights into the effects of background, interest, and other factors on comprehension performance.

(10) *Checklist of Reading Behaviors.* This section is used to record aspects of oral reading skill, word recognition strategies, and general reading behaviors.

Aspects of oral reading skill, such as reading in phrases, using expression when reading, attending to punctuation, and pronouncing words correctly, are important for reading to audiences, for they enhance communication with listeners. Often, presence of these skills indicates fairly good comprehension, but this is not always the case. Some children sound good when reading orally but do poorly on comprehension checks. This may be due to excessive attention to pronunciation of words and lack of concentration on meaning. The teacher should be alert for such a circumstance and record it. Emphasizing attention to meaning in oral reading, rather than just pronunciation, will be especially important for these children. Observations of students as they read orally at sight can help a teacher discover which strategies are being applied, if they are being applied rigidly or flexibly, and what general reading behaviors are displayed when reading.

What Are Some Frequently Asked Questions About the IRI?

1 *What do I do when the student's scores are not high enough for the instructional level, but not low enough to be a definite frustration level?*

An area that often causes confusion is the gray area in which students' scores are not quite high enough to be considered a firm instructional level, but higher than the frustration level percentages. For example: What level should be assigned if a student makes a word recognition score of 90 to 95 percent and/or scores between 50 and 75 percent on comprehension? To answer this question that covers a fairly common occurrence, the teacher should study all the data gathered through the informal inventory. The appropriate decision is sometimes that it is a "questionable instructional level" and sometimes that it is a "questionable frustration level." A few examples will illustrate how the examiner must use personal judgment in deciding the level at which a student should be ranked.

Student A:
Word recognition—94%
Comprehension—100%

Since the word recognition score is so close to the instructional level criterion, and since comprehension is perfect, this could be accepted as a probable indicator of instructional level.

Student B:
Word recognition—92%
Comprehension—45%

Though the word recognition score is slightly above the frustration level criterion, the comprehension score reflects inadequate responses to more than half the questions. Thus, this student may be considered to have reached frustration level when reading this material.

Student C:
Word recognition—93%
Comprehension—70%

This mixture of scores indicates a need to analyze the types of errors made. Based only on the data provided, the best conclusion might be that at this point the pupil is at either the instructional or the frustration level; instructional level is more likely if signs of tension and frustration are absent.

2 *Which passages should be administered first—oral or silent?*

The explanation earlier in this text concerning administration of the informal reading inventory describes the oral reading section as being given first because that has been traditional; however, there is no well-established reason that this must always be the case, and there is often far more reason to do the reverse. For a child who is especially sensitive about reading orally or who is known to have better silent reading skills than oral reading skills, the silent passage may be given first to relax the child before the oral reading begins. Many older students seem to respond better to this order. This recommendation is based strictly on observation of different sequences of administration of passages over a period of years; it is not based on controlled research.

3 *What can I do if I don't have time to give the entire inventory?*

Some users will, of course, wish to administer the entire inventory in order to gain a picture of both silent and oral reading abilities; word recognition strategies; areas of strengths and weaknesses in comprehension; and independent reading, instructional reading, frustration, and listening comprehension levels, but much information can be gained by administering less than the complete inventory. Your purpose for administration may dictate how much you decide to give. Some users elect to administer only a silent inventory or only an oral inventory in the interest of time or because they wish to analyze only one specific area of reading expertise. Some may administer only a passage at the grade level of the material that they intend to use with the students in their class, in order to see whether the material is appropriate for homework or class instruction. Still others may administer two different forms to compare the results of having the students read orally at sight and having them read orally after they have read silently, a common classroom strategy. Some users may analyze the word recognition miscues carefully to decide what strategies are being used or may analyze the comprehension question results to see what types of comprehension appear to need attention, whereas others may look only for the levels that they can derive from miscue counts.

4 *Are my results valid if I give only a portion of this inventory?*

Yes, they can be. They will be if giving a portion of the inventory provides the specific information you need, such as what level of material can the student read silently with adequate comprehension without the assistance of the teacher. In this case, you could administer enough of the inventory to determine an independent reading level and cease administration. The purpose for testing will have been met.

5 *What if I want to test comprehension in a way other than questioning?*

Although most test administrators use the comprehension questions included in the inventory because they have been chosen to represent a variety of areas of comprehension and have been field-tested, others use a retelling procedure to assess comprehension. That is perfectly acceptable for users who have skill in evaluating retellings.

6 *Why can't I just use the word lists to establish independent, instructional, and frustration levels and save the time needed for administering the passages?*

Use of the word lists alone to determine reading levels is unreliable because these lists involve only word recognition without a comprehension measure. This type of assessment should never be considered to provide more than temporary approximations of levels until a more complete assessment can take place. Comparison of levels obtained with the word lists and with passages may tell a teacher something about the student's ability to make effective use of context in reading at different reading levels. Some users skip the word lists altogether, feeling that reading of words out of context is not indicative of typical reading situations in the classroom.

7 *What value might word list administration have, other than for placement purposes?*

Some users may administer the word lists in order to compare the word recognition strategies used in isolation with those used in context, and such comparisons are often valuable. They can help determine the relative need for instruction in use of context clues and instruction in phonics and structural analysis.

8 *How can I decide if a particular error pattern is significant?*

You should remember that generalizations about skill or strategy deficiencies should be based upon large samples of behavior, rather than extremely limited ones. If only two sequence questions have been asked of a student, a 50-percent error rate does not provide you with clear-cut information about the student's ability to detect sequence in reading materials in general. On the other hand, if the student has been asked twenty-six questions of a particular type and missed thirteen, there is greater cause for concern. Similarly, if a student mispronounces the short *a* sound in two words, there are many possible reasons for this occurrence, and it is not possible to indicate with certainty that there is a problem in this area. On the other hand, if he or she mispronounces every short *a* sound in a series of selections in which the short *a* occurs frequently, concern would be in order.

9 *What causes students to suddenly drop down or increase in scores abruptly during the administration of the reading passages? What should I do when this happens?*

All students come to a testing situation with background knowledge, interests, and attitudes that can affect their comprehension of passages. If a student suddenly scores extremely low on a passage, when he or she has done *much* better on the previous passage, it may signal low background knowledge about the topic, disinterest in the topic, or a negative attitude toward the topic. You may wish to administer the same level passage from another form of the inventory to determine if this is the case. You also may wish to continue with the next passage in the form you have been using. You may find that the student will do better on it than on the previous one, and that the succeeding passages give expected gradations of performance. In that case, you may disregard the passage that produced abnormal results. Questioning of the student about interest in, attitude toward, and knowledge of the topic may offer confirmation of inferences about the passage performance. In like manner, if a student suddenly does *much* better on a passage than he or she has done on one or more lower level passages, his or her background knowledge about, or interest in, the topic may be extremely high. In such a case, administration of the next higher passage is likely to produce scores in line with the earlier passages, but *much* lower than the abnormal passage response. Once again, the passage affected by experience and interest may be disregarded. Another passage at that level from another form of the inventory may be administered, if more information on that level is needed. For example, if grade 3 had been instructional, grade 4 had been independent, and grade 5 had been frustration level, you might want to give grade 4 from a different form to discover if that passage is still at instructional level or is already at frustration level.

Hunt (1996/1997) pointed out that highly motivated readers can understand, at least partially, material that is considerably difficult for them. He also indicated that silent reading allows the reading to be a search for ideas, not a struggle with pronunciation, so that there may be much better performance on silent reading than there is on oral reading for these students.

10 *Is the inventory useful for advanced/gifted readers, as well as average and below-average readers?*

Yes, the inventory results can help a teacher choose appropriate recreational and instructional materials for gifted readers—who are often capable of reading and studying written works that are rarely accessible to the others in their grade placements. These readers can be placed in useful and challenging materials that are not beyond their ability levels with the help of the inventory results.

These readers also may have word recognition and comprehension skill needs that should be addressed—often manifested at higher grade levels than for most of their classmates—but real needs for them, nevertheless. Because the inventory has material through twelfth-grade level, it often makes possible the detection and analysis of these needs.

11 *Is it ever appropriate to give partial credit for an answer?*

Yes. If the question is a two-part detail question, half credit can be given for correctly providing one of the parts, and if a sequence question has several parts, partial credit may be given for correct steps given in the appropriate order, even if some step has been omitted. If any step is given out of order, however, no credit is given for the question.

12 *Are proper names that are mispronounced or have to be prompted by the teacher counted as miscues?*

They are only counted as miscues if they are also common words such as *green* or *art*. Any words not intended to be counted as miscues are pointed out in bracketed notes located below the passages on the teacher's copy.

Further Comments and Clarifications

The informal reading inventory must be viewed as a sampling procedure designed to give the teacher some guidance in choosing instructional strategies. Perfect precision is rarely available from a single administration of a single assessment inventory of any sort. The teacher must continue to evaluate the student's performance during instructional periods and alter instructional strategies accordingly.

This inventory can yield many types of information, depending upon the way that the individual administrator uses it. It is not intended to be used in a single, unvarying way, as is the case with standardized instruments.

A Case Study in Scoring and Interpretation

This section shows a sample set of graded word lists and graded oral and silent passages administered to one second-grade child (Figure 2–11). The data are interpreted and sample records are illustrated following the marked test sheets.

FIGURE 2–11 **Melissa Gordon's IRI Materials**

LISTS — LIST 1 — TEACHER

PRIMER □		FIRST READER ◇		SECOND READER ○○		THIRD READER □□	
1. all		1. after		1. also		1. air	aid
2. am		2. again		2. always		2. cold	
3. any		3. book		3. around		3. dear	C did
4. came		4. boy		4. best		4. drink	
5. day		5. come		5. box		5. every	even
6. find		6. hand		6. color		6. food	
7. had		7. how		7. fall	C fit	7. bold	
8. into		8. keep		8. five		8. learn	laugh
9. now		9. long		9. grow		9. move	
10. out		10. many		10. head	hid	10. number	none
11. put		11. never		11. light		11. often	over
12. ran		12. next		12. made		12. several	don't know
13. say		13. once		13. part		13. start	stay
14. soon		14. open		14. people	don't know	14. such	
15. there		15. room		15. read	ride	15. table	take
16. two		16. school		16. same		16. today	
17. well		17. them	when	17. small		17. try	
18. what		18. think		18. town		18. wash	
19. with		19. up		19. turn	torn	19. wrong	write
20. yes		20. where	there	20. wish		20. yellow	

Independent level: 0–2 errors **Instructional level:** 3–4 errors **Frustration level:** 5+ errors

TEACHER 1 ◇

INTRODUCTORY STATEMENT: Read this story to find out why no one wanted to play with Harriet. (READ ORALLY.)

Harriet ran home.
"Mom, Mom!" she said. "School is out!
No more books. No more work to do.
I can play all day."

"Oh?" said Harriet's mom. "No work?
You'll help me with the housework.
Won't you?"

"Yes, Mom," said Harriet.
"I'll help you.
But I'll have time to play, too."

TP
So vacation time was here.
Harriet played and played.
She played with Pat.
She played with Jack and David.
She did many things.

But one day no one wanted to play.
Harriet went to see Pat.
"Come on, Pat," she said. "Let's play."

"No," said Pat. "I don't want to play.
I want to read.
I've had too many days of play.
Now I'm all played out."

SCORING AID

Word Recognition

%–Miscues

99–1
95–5
90–12
85–18

Comprehension

%–Errors

100–0
87.5–1
75–2
62.5–3
50–4
37.5–5
25–6
12.5–7
0–8

111 Words
(for Word Recognition)

118 Words
(for Rate)

WPM
7080

Source: Leo Fay, Ramon R. Ross, and Margaret LaPray. Rand McNally Reading Program, "All Played Out," in *Red Rock Ranch*, Level 6 (Chicago: The Riverside Publishing Company, 1978), pp. 7–9.

[*Note*: Do not count as miscues mispronunciation of the names Harriet, Jack, and David. You may pronounce these words for the student if needed.]

COMPREHENSION QUESTIONS

_+_ main idea	1. What happens to people when they get to play as much as they want? (They get all played out.)
_+_ detail	2. What did Harriet want to do when school was out? (play)
_+_ sequence	3. What did Mother say to Harriet after Harriet said, "No more work to do. I can play all day."? (You'll help me with the housework.)
_+_ inference	4. What time of the year was it? (summer)
_+_ inference	5. How did Harriet feel about summer vacation? (excited)
_+_ detail	6. Who wanted to read? (Pat)
_+_ cause and effect/ detail	7. Why didn't Pat want to play? (He was all played out.)
_+_ vocabulary	8. What is the meaning of "all played out"? (tired of playing)

◇ 1 PASSAGE

FIGURE 2–11 *(continued)*

TEACHER 1 ◇

INTRODUCTORY STATEMENT: Harriet has just left her friend Pat as this story begins. Read to find out what Harriet thinks is a good vacation. (READ SILENTLY.)

Then Harriet went to see Jack and David.
David was eating, and Jack was reading a book.

"This is no time for reading," said Harriet.
"You can do that in school.
This is vacation time. It's time to play.
Come on, Jack. Let's go!"

"Not now," said Jack. "I want to read.
Why don't you get a good book?
Then you can read too."

"Read? When I can play?" said Harriet.
"No! I'll find someone to play with.
Someone will want to have a good vacation."

Away went Harriet.
She looked up all of her friends.
But no one wanted to play.

Source: Leo Fay, Ramon R. Ross, and Margaret LaPray. Rand McNally Reading Program, "All Played Out," in *Red Rock Ranch*, Level 6 (Chicago: Rand McNally, 1978), pp. 9–11.

[*Note*: Do not count as miscues mispronunciation of the names Harriet, Jack, and David. You may pronounce these words for the student if needed.]

SCORING AID

Word Recognition

%–Miscues
99–1
95–5
90–9
85–15

Comprehension

%–Errors
100–0
87.5–1
75–2
62.5–3
50–4
37.5–5
25–6
12.5–7
0–8

92 Words (for Word Recognition)

102 Words (for Rate)

WPM
6120

COMPREHENSION QUESTIONS

+ main idea	1. What did Harriet think was a good vacation? (all play)
+ sequence	2. Who did Harriet go to see after Pat? (Jack and David)
+ detail	3. What was Jack doing when Harriet visited him? (reading a book)
+ detail	4. What was David doing? (eating)
+ inference	5. Did Jack like to read? (yes) What does he do that makes you answer this way? (He wants to read instead of play. He tells Harriet to read.)
+ cause and effect/ inference	6. Why did Harriet leave Jack? (He wouldn't play with her, and she didn't want to read.)
+ vocabulary	7. What is the meaning of "vacation time"? (time away from usual activities)
+ detail	8. What did Harriet do after she left Jack? (looked up other friends)

◇ 1 PASSAGE

INTRODUCTORY STATEMENT: Read the story to find out about Dan's problem. (READ ORALLY.)

The ball came fast. Dan ran to catch it. He jumped for it. ~~Swish!~~ *Swat* The ball flew past (him). The game was over. Dan's team (had) lost.

Poor Dan. He wanted so much to play well. His baseball team was a *very* good one. But they couldn't win games if Dan always missed the ball—and he had missed it again.

As Dan walked ~~slowly~~ *went storly* ✓ home, he saw something on the ground. It was a baseball mitt. Dan picked it up and put it on. He walked along thinking. Why couldn't he catch the ball? He always tried so hard. Lost in thought, he threw a ball into the air and caught it. He threw the ball again, and again he caught it.

Source: Leo Fay, Ramon R. Ross, and Margaret LaPray. Rand McNally Reading Program, "Dan and the Magic Mitt," in *Boxcars and Bottle Caps*, Level 7 (Chicago: The Riverside Publishing Company, 1978), pp. 54–55.

SCORING AID

Word Recognition

%–Miscues

99–1
95–6
90–12
85–18

Comprehension

%–Errors

100–0
87.5–1
75–2
62.5–3
50–4
37.5–5
25–6
12.5–7
0–8

123 Words
(for Word Recognition)

123 Words
(for Rate)

WPM
7380

COMPREHENSION QUESTIONS

+ main idea	1.	What was Dan's problem? (He couldn't catch the ball.)
+ sequence	2.	What was the first thing that Dan did in the story? (He ran to try to catch a ball and missed it.)
+ detail	3.	What kind of a team did Dan play on? (good, baseball)
+ cause and effect/ detail	4.	Why didn't Dan's team win games? (Dan missed the ball.)
o inference	5.	How did Dan feel about losing the game? (sad, unhappy, disappointed) What in the story makes you believe that? (He walked slowly and worried about why he couldn't catch the ball.) ***(I don't know.)***
+ detail	6.	What did Dan find? (baseball mitt)
+ detail	7.	What was Dan thinking about after he found the mitt? (why he couldn't catch the ball)
+ vocabulary	8.	What does "lost in thought" mean? (thinking so hard that he didn't notice what was happening around him)

FIGURE 2–11 *(continued)*

TEACHER 2

INTRODUCTORY STATEMENT: Read the story to find out why Dan thought he was becoming a better ball player. (READ SILENTLY.)

Suddenly Dan thought about what he had been doing. He threw the ball as high as he could throw it. The ball landed right in his mitt. He threw the ball again and again. Each time it landed in his mitt.

"The mitt!" he cried. "The mitt must be magic!"

The rest of the day he threw the ball into the air so that he could catch it with his magic mitt. He caught the ball just about every time.

The next day Dan got up early and worked out with the magic mitt. He couldn't wait until the game!

At last it was time to go to the ball park. A few boys were warming up when Dan got there. Dan worked out with them.

Source: Leo Fay, Ramon R. Ross, and Margaret LaPray. Rand McNally Reading Program, "Dan and the Magic Mitt," in *Boxcars and Bottle Caps*, Level 7 (Chicago: The Riverside Publishing Company, 1978), pp. 55–56.

SCORING AID

Word Recognition
%–Miscues
99–1
95–6
90–12
85–19

Comprehension
%–Errors
100–0
87.5–1
75–2
62.5–3
50–4
37.5–5
25–6
12.5–7
0–8

125 Words
(for Word Recognition)

125 Words
(for Rate)

68 WPM
110 ⟌ 7500

COMPREHENSION QUESTIONS

+ main idea	1. What did Dan think was the reason he was able to catch the ball? (He thought the mitt was magic.)
+ detail	2. What did Dan do the rest of the day and the next morning? (He practiced catching.)
+ inference	3. Did Dan believe in his own ability to catch the ball? (no) Why did you answer that way? (He thought the mitt was helping him.)
+ vocabulary	4. What does "worked out" mean? (practiced)
o cause and effect/ inference	5. What caused Dan to be eager for the game to be played? (He was catching the ball so well that he wanted the others to see.) *(He liked to play ball.)*
+ detail	6. Who was at the ball park when Dan got there? (a few boys)
+ vocabulary	7. What does "warming up"' mean? (gradually building up to full-speed activity)
+ sequence	8. What was the last thing Dan did in the story? (He worked out with some boys.)

PASSAGE 2

TEACHER 3

INTRODUCTORY STATEMENT: Read the story to find out about a Pilgrim girl who lived many years ago. (READ ORALLY.)

"Hurry, Elizabeth," called her mother. Your cornmeal mush will be cold."

Elizabeth jumped out of bed and quickly put on her warm clothes. She shivered in the cold morning air. She must hurry, for today there was work for everyone to do in the little colony of Plymouth. Tomorrow was the day of the big Thanksgiving feast.

Elizabeth ate her mush. As she did, she wished again that she didn't have to eat the same thing for breakfast every day. But she knew that she really should be thankful for each bite.

There had been hard years in the past. But now Elizabeth's family had plenty of food for the cold winter which lay ahead. Friendly Indians had shown the group of Pilgrims how to plant corn. And they had taught them the best ways to hunt for animals.

"At least I won't eat mush tomorrow," Elizabeth said.

"No, not tomorrow," said her mother.

Handwritten miscue marks: meat (mush); will circled; the (inserted before bed); coat (clothes); hurry, circled; TP (colony); TP (Tomorrow); mush (mush); wanted (wished); TP (breakfast); really should be underlined with wavy line; ✓ think (thankful); party (plenty); of circled; The friend (Friendly); TP (Pilgrims); last (least); TP (tomorrow)

SCORING AID

Word Recognition

%–Miscues

99–1
95–8
90–15
85–23

Comprehension

%–Errors

100–0
90–1
80–2
70–3
60–4
50–5
40–6
30–7
20–8
10–9
0–10

147 Words
(for Word Recognition)

154 Words
(for Rate)

WPM
9240

Source: From *Jack and Jill* magazine, copyright © 1961 by Curtis Publishing Company. Reprinted by permission of the publisher, Children's Better Health Institute, Ben Franklin Literary and Medical Society, Indianapolis, Indiana.

[*Note:* Do not count as miscues mispronunciation of the nouns Elizabeth, Plymouth, and Pilgrims. You may pronounce these for the student if needed.]

COMPREHENSION QUESTIONS

+ main idea — 1. What important event were the Pilgrims preparing for? (Thanksgiving feast)

+ sequence — 2. Name, in order, the three things Elizabeth did in this story. (She jumped out of bed, put on her clothes, and ate breakfast.)

o vocabulary — 3. What does "shivered" mean? (shook from cold) ***(A piece of wood.)***

o cause and effect/detail — 4. What caused Elizabeth to shiver? (the cold morning air) ***(She didn't like her food.)***

+ cause and effect/detail — 5. What caused Elizabeth to hurry? (There was work for everyone to do.)

o detail — 6. Where did Elizabeth live? (Plymouth Colony) ***(In the country.)***

o detail — 7. What did Elizabeth have for breakfast? (cornmeal mush) ***(I don't know.)***

o inference — 8. What season was it? (fall) ***(Winter)*** Why do you say that? (Thanksgiving feast, cold winter ahead.) ***(It was cold.)***

+ detail — 9. Who taught the Pilgrims how to plant corn? (Indians)

o inference — 10. Did the Pilgrims have meat to eat? (yes) What in the story caused you to say that? (The Indians taught them to hunt animals.) ***(I don't know.)***

PASSAGE 3

FIGURE 2–11 *(continued)*

TEACHER 3

INTRODUCTORY STATEMENT: Read the story to find out what Elizabeth did to get ready for the special day. (READ SILENTLY.)

"Tomorrow is a special day. The men have been hunting and fishing. They have brought in wild turkey, duck, deer, fish, oysters, and clams. Tomorrow is going to be a big day of celebrating and feasting and prayer."

Elizabeth thought of the good baking odors that had filled the kitchen for days. Her mother and the other Pilgrim women had spent many hours baking and cooking. Elizabeth, too, wanted to help, but she wasn't old enough to do any of the baking. So far she had only been able to help with little jobs. If there were only something big she could do for the Thanksgiving celebration.

"I'm going to need a lot of help this morning," said her mother. "There is still much to be done. Why don't you begin by sweeping the floor?"

Elizabeth slowly picked up the twig broom and began to sweep. Her mother went to the woodshed for firewood. In a few moments she returned with a straw basket in her hands.

SCORING AID

Word Recognition

%–Miscues

99–2
95–8
90–16
85–24

Comprehension

%–Errors

100–0
90–1
80–2
70–3
60–4
50–5
40–6
30–7
20–8
10–9
0–10

163 Words
(for Word Recognition)

167 Words
(for Rate)

WPM
10020

Source: From *Jack and Jill* magazine, copyright © 1961 by Curtis Publishing Company. Reprinted by permission of the publisher, Children's Better Health Institute, Ben Franklin Literary and Medical Society, Indianapolis, Indiana.

[*Note*: Do not count as miscues mispronunciation of the nouns Elizabeth and Pilgrim. You may pronounce these for the student if needed.]

COMPREHENSION QUESTIONS

__+__ main idea — 1. What is the main idea of this story? (Everybody helped with the Thanksgiving feast.)

__+__ detail — 2. What were four animals the men had caught for the feast? (wild turkey, duck, deer, fish, oysters, clams)

__+__ detail — 3. What had the Pilgrim women been doing for days? (cooking and baking)

__+__ vocabulary — 4. What is meant by "feasting"? (eating a large meal)

__o__ cause and effect/detail — 5. Why couldn't Elizabeth help with the baking? (She wasn't old enough.) *(She was a bad cook.)*

__o__ inference — 6. Was Elizabeth content with the jobs she had been given? (no) What in the story makes you say this? (She wanted to do something big for the celebration.) *(I don't know.)*

__+__ detail — 7. What was the first job Mother gave Elizabeth? (sweeping the floors)

__o__ detail — 8. For what did Mother go to the woodshed? (firewood) *(For a basket.)*

__o__ inference — 9. Was Mother at the woodshed long? (no) What did the story say that made you answer that way? (She returned in a few moments.) *(I don't know.)*

__o__ sequence — 10. What did Mother do after she went to the woodshed? (She came back with a straw basket.) *(I don't know.)*

3 PASSAGE

Melissa was a second-grade student who changed schools at the beginning of the school year. The teacher used an informal reading inventory to assess her performance levels and skills for quick placement in reading instructional activities. Some of the marked materials are included here to indicate her performance. In addition to completing the material shown here, Melissa read an oral and a silent passage at the primer level with no word recognition miscues and no comprehension errors. Passages at the third- through sixth-reader levels were read to her as a means of determining listening comprehension. She missed one cause-and-effect question at the third-reader level, one inference question at the fourth-reader level, one cause-and-effect question and one inference question at the fifth-reader level, and one cause-and-effect question and two inference questions at the sixth-reader level.

Information to aid in data analysis is found on the two completed worksheets (Figures 2–12 and 2–13). A summary of Melissa's performance is provided on the completed Summary Forms (Figure 2–14).

Analysis

On the basis of this example, the following observations may be made about Melissa's reading skills.

Graded Word Lists The child achieved a perfect score on the primer word list. This was the level at which she should begin to read the graded passages of the test. On the first reader level, two words were miscalled, both of them frequently confused basic sight words. This result indicates a first reader independent reading level. On the second reader word list, Melissa mispronounced three words and said "don't know" for one word. She made substitutions by incorrectly pronouncing medial vowel sounds. According to the criteria, these results indicate that Melissa's instructional reading level is at the second reader level. The nine errors made on the third reader list confirm that a higher level can be considered frustrating for this youngster. The errors on miscalled words tended to involve word middles and endings. The child seemed to be looking only at the beginnings of words and then guessing the rest.

Graded Passages The completed summary forms show Melissa's scores on the oral and silent passages and discuss her strengths and weaknesses in word recognition and comprehension. The various levels may be designated as follows:

Independent reading level—first reader
Instructional reading level—second reader
Frustration level—third reader

After the pupil's level of frustration had been reached, the examiner read aloud passages beginning with the third reader level and becoming progressively more difficult. (These are not included as samples.) Melissa correctly answered 90 percent of the comprehension questions about the third- and fourth-grade reading material and 80 percent of the fifth-grade questions. At the sixth-grade level, Melissa was able to answer only 70 percent of the questions. Thus, the fifth-grade reading level can be considered the child's present level of listening comprehension.

This student appeared to have much room for improvement in reading skills, even though she was currently reading at her grade placement level. She could comprehend material that was read to her at higher levels than material she could read for herself with understanding. She showed a need to be encouraged to use graphic clues in the middles and at the ends of words, since she appeared to look primarily at word beginnings and then guess. When the words were in context, the guesses were often semantically and syntactically acceptable, showing that she did make some use of context as she read. She did tolerate some disruption of understanding without attempts at self-correction, however. The teacher should have encouraged Melissa to consider whether or not what she read made sense and to try to correct a problem when one was recognized.

The teacher should have considered classroom instruction in making inferences and recognizing causes and effects to help Melissa build her comprehension abilities. The teacher might also have wanted to work with Melissa to improve her oral reading skills, using primer level materials as a beginning point, since she did not read in phrases or with expression.

FIGURE 2–12 **Completed Sample Worksheet for Word Recognition Miscue Tally Chart**

Miscue		PP	P	1	2	3	4	5	6	7	8	9	10	11	12	Totals
Mispronunciation	A				I	I										A 2
	MC				I	I										MC 2
	SC															SC
Substitution	A				I	𝍸I										A 7
	MC					III										MC 3
	SC				I	I										SC 2
Insertion	A				I	I										A 2
	MC															MC
	SC															SC
Omission	A				II	II										A 4
	MC					I										MC 1
	SC															SC
Reversal	A															A
	MC															MC
	SC															SC
Repetition	A				I	I										A 2
Refusal to pronounce	A			I		𝍸										A 6
Totals	A			1	6	16										A 23
	MC				1	5										MC 6
	SC				1	1										SC 2

A = All miscues of that type (excluding ones that were self-corrected)
MC = Miscues that resulted in a meaning change
SC = Self-corrected miscues

Miscue Analysis of Phonic and Structural Analysis Skills

(Tally total miscues on appropriate lines.)

Miscue	**For Words in Isolation**	**For Words in Context**
Single consonants	IIII	I
Consonant blends	II	II
Single vowels	III	𝍸I
Vowel digraphs	II	I
Consonant digraphs	II	III
Diphthongs		
Prefixes		
Suffixes		I
Special combinations		
Word beginnings	I	
Word middles	𝍸II	𝍸II
Word endings	𝍸II	III
Compound words		
Inflectional endings		
Syllabication		
Accent		

(*Note*: In order to fill out the analysis for words in context, it is helpful to make a list of expected reader responses and unexpected responses for easy comparison as to graphic similarity, syntactic acceptability, and semantic acceptability. See page 108 for a good way to record this information.)

FIGURE 2–13 **Completed Sample Worksheet for Qualitative Analysis of Uncorrected Miscues in Context**

(Include mispronunciations, substitutions, insertions, omissions, and reversals.)

Passage	Type of Miscue	Expected Response	Unexpected Response	Graphic Similarity	Syntactic Acceptability	Semantic Acceptability
2	*Substitution*	*Swish*	*Swat*	Yes	Yes	Yes
2	*Omission*	*him*	—	—	Yes	Yes
2	*Omission*	*had*	—	—	Yes	Yes
2	*Insertion*	—	*very*	—	Yes	Yes
2	*Mispronunciation*	*slowly*	*storly*	Yes	Yes	No
3	*Substitution*	*mush*	*meat*	Yes	Yes	Yes
3	*Omission*	*will*	—	—	No	No
3	*Insertion*	—	*the*	—	Yes	Yes
3	*Substitution*	*clothes*	*coat*	No (except 1st letter)	Yes	Yes
3	*Mispronunciation*	*mush*	*mūsh*	Yes	Yes	No
3	*Substitution*	*wished*	*wanted*	Yes	No	No
3	*Substitution*	*plenty*	*party*	Yes	No	No
3	*Omission*	*of*	—	—	Yes	Yes
3	*Insertion*	—	*The*	—	Yes	Yes
3	*Substitution*	*Friendly*	*Friend*	Yes	No	No
3	*Substitution*	*least*	*last*	Yes	Yes	Yes

FIGURE 2–14 Completed Sample Summary Forms

SUMMARY OF QUANTITATIVE ANALYSIS

Student's Name *Melissa Gordon* **Grade** *2* **Date** *9/14/88* **Administrator** *Mr. Wilson*

Forms Used: Word Lists, Form *1* Oral Passages, Form *X* Silent Passages, Form *Y* Listening Comprehension, Form *Z*

Performance Levels Based on Full Inventory (Oral & Silent): Independent *1* Instructional *2* Frustration *3* Listening Comprehension *5*

Performance Levels Based on Oral Passages: Independent *1* Instructional *2* Frustration *3* Listening Comprehension *5*
probably (Administration stopped at 3 because of 50% comprehension and tension signs)

Performance Levels Based on Silent Passages: Independent *1* Instructional *2* Frustration *3* Listening Comprehension ______

Optional Comparison Levels: Independent ______ Instructional ______ Frustration ______ **Rate of Reading:** High ______ Average *✓ (68 WPM)* Low ______

Performance Levels Based on Graded Word Lists: Placement *P* Independent *1* Instructional *2* Frustration *3*

Types of Miscues in Context

	Mispronunciation	Substitution	Insertion	Omission	Reversal	Repetition	Refusal to Pronounce	Row Totals
Total	2	7	2	4		2	6	23
Meaning changed	2	3		1				6
Self-corrected		2						2

Comprehension Skill Analysis Chart

Skill	Number of Questions	Number of Errors	Percent of Errors
Main idea	11	0	0
Detail	31	3	9.8
Sequence	11	1	.09
Cause and effect	14	6	42.8
Inference	12	8	66.7
Vocabulary	12	1	8.3

Summary Table of Percentages

Level	Word Recognition	Oral Comprehension	Silent Comprehension	Average Comprehension	Listening Comprehension
PP					
P	100	100	100	100	
1	99	100	100	100	
2	95	87.5	87.5	87.5	
3	88	40	50	45	90
4					90
5					80
6					70
7					
8					
9					
10					
11					
12					

FIGURE 2–14 *(continued)*

SUMMARY OF QUALITATIVE ANALYSIS

Summary of Strengths and Weaknesses in Word Recognition

(Include all of the important data that have been collected on word recognition skills.)

In reading oral passages, the most frequent miscues were substitutions and refusals to pronounce. The refusals to pronounce show a reluctance to take risks in word recognition. On isolated word lists and in reading oral passages, she showed attention to word beginnings, but not word middles or (frequently) endings. Although she had several problems with single vowels, there was no one vowel for which there was a pattern of a problem. It seems that she looks at the beginning of a word and, in context, sometimes at the ending and guesses a word that is graphically similar, often syntactically acceptable, and often semantically acceptable. She had no reversals of letters or words. None of her miscues appeared to be related to dialect. She did very little self-correction of miscues.

Checklist of Reading Behaviors

(Place a [+] by areas that are strong and a [–] by areas that are weak.)

1. Reads in phrases __–__
2. Reads with expression __–__
3. Attends to punctuation __+__
4. Pronounces words correctly __–__
5. Sounds out unfamiliar words __–__
6. Uses structure clues, when available, to recognize unfamiliar words __–__
7. Uses context clues *(some use—not strong)*
8. Makes strategic attempts to recognize unfamiliar words (applies word recognition skills flexibly) __–__
9. Keeps place in material being read __+__ *(Never seemed fully at ease.)*
10. Shows few signs of tension when reading __–__
11. Holds book at appropriate distance from face when reading __+__
12. Self-corrects errors without prompting __–__

Summary of Strengths and Weaknesses in Comprehension

(Include all of the important data that have been collected about comprehension.)

She had the most trouble on comprehension with inference and cause-and-effect questions. Instruction in these areas may be in order. She missed no main idea questions and only one sequence question. She missed few detail and vocabulary questions, indicating probable strengths in these areas. She appears to have the ability to understand material at levels above the one at which she can read for herself with understanding. This shows the potential for improvement with instruction.

She needs help with self-monitoring of her reading for meaning, since she had some miscues that did not make sense in context and that she did not correct.

Her reading lacked the expression that generally comes with good comprehension, and her reading was mainly word-by-word beyond the primer level. She did attend to punctuation most of the time.

Key to Symbols on Passages

Special symbols are used on student passages to help the administrator of the inventory identify the grade level of the passage without identifying it to the student. For example, a filled-in circle designates a sixth-grade passage. These symbols *and* the grade levels are included on the teacher passages to allow the teacher easy classification of each passage by referring to these symbols. The complete set of symbols is as follows:

Key to Symbols

Preprimer	○	Level 6	●
Primer	□	Level 7	■
Level 1	◇	Level 8	◆
Level 2	○○	Level 9	●●
Level 3	□□	Level 10	■■
Level 4	◇◇	Level 11	◆◆
Level 5	☆	Level 12	★

SELECTED REFERENCES

Allington, Richard L., and McGill-Franzen, Anne. "Word Identification Errors in Isolation and in Context: Apples vs. Oranges." *The Reading Teacher* 33 (April 1980): 795–800.

Anthony, Robert J., Johnson, Terry D., Mickelson, Norma I., and Preece, Alison. *Evaluating Literacy: A Perspective for Change*. Portsmouth, N.H.: Heinemann, 1991.

Barr, Rebecca, Blachowicz, Camille L. Z., and Wogman-Sadow, Marilyn. *Reading Diagnosis for Teachers: An Instructional Approach.* White Plains, N.Y.: Longman, 1995.

Brecht, Richard D. "Testing Format and Instructional Level with the Informal Reading Inventory." *The Reading Teacher* 31 (October 1977): 57–59.

Brown, Hazel, and Cambourne, Brian. *Read and Retell.* Portsmouth, N.H.: Heinemann, 1987.

Cagney, Margaret A. "Measuring Comprehension: Alternative Diagnostic Approaches." In *Reexamining Reading Diagnosis: New Trends and Procedures*, edited by Susan Mandel Glazer, Lyndon W. Searfoss, and Lance M. Gentile, pp. 81–93. Newark, Del.: International Reading Association, 1988.

Caldwell, JoAnne. "A New Look at the Old Informal Reading Inventory." *The Reading Teacher* 39 (November 1985): 168–73.

Cunningham, Patricia. "Match Informal Evaluation to Your Teaching Practices." *The Reading Teacher* 31 (October 1977): 51–56.

D'Angelo, Karen, and Wilson, Robert M. "How Helpful Is Insertion and Omission Miscue Analysis?" *The Reading Teacher* 32 (February 1979): 519–20.

Ekwall, Eldon E. "Informal Reading Inventories: The Instructional Level." *The Reading Teacher* 29 (April 1976): 662–65.

Ekwall, Eldon E. "Should Repetitions Be Counted as Errors?" *The Reading Teacher* 27 (January 1974): 365–67.

Farr, Roger, and Carey, Robert F. *Reading: What Can Be Measured?* Newark, Del.: International Reading Association, 1986.

Forell, Elizabeth. "The Case for Conservative Reader Placement." *The Reading Teacher* 38 (May 1985): 857–62.

Glazer, Susan Mandel, Searfoss, Lyndon W., and Gentile, Lance M., eds. *Reexamining Reading Diagnosis: New Trends and Procedures*. Newark, Del.: International Reading Association, 1988.

Gonzales, Philip C., and Elijah, David V., Jr. "Rereading: Effect on Error Patterns and Performance Levels on the IRI." *The Reading Teacher* 28 (April 1975): 647–52.

Goodman, Yetta M. "Reading Diagnosis—Qualitative or Quantitative." *The Reading Teacher* 50 (April 1997): 534–38.

Goodman, Yetta. "Using Children's Reading Miscues for New Teaching Strategies." *The Reading Teacher* 23 (February 1970): 455–59.

Harris, Albert J., and Sipay, Edward R. *How to Increase Reading Ability*, 9th ed. New York: Longman, 1990.

Hollander, Sheila K. "Why's a Busy Teacher Like You Giving an IRI?" *Elementary English* 51 (September 1974): 905–7.

Hunt, Lyman C., Jr. "The Effect of Self-Selection, Interest and Motivation Upon Independent, Instructional, and Frustration Levels." *The Reading Teacher* 50 (December 1996/January 1997): 278–82.

Irwin, Judith Westphal. *Teaching Reading Comprehension Processes*. Englewood Cliffs, N.J.: Prentice-Hall, 1991.

Johnson, Marjorie Seddon, Kress, Roy A., and Pikulski, John J. *Informal Reading Inventories*, 2nd ed. Newark, Del.: International Reading Association, 1987.

Johnston, Peter H. *Constructive Evaluation of Literate Activity.* New York: Longman, 1992.

Johnston, Peter H. *Knowing Literacy: Constructive Literacy Assessment.* York, Maine: Stenhouse Publishers, 1997.

Johnston, Peter H. *Reading Comprehension Assessment: A Cognitive Basis.* Newark, Del.: International Reading Association, 1983.

Kibby, Michael W. "Passage Readability Affects the Oral Reading Strategies of Disabled Readers." *The Reading Teacher* 32 (January 1979): 390–96.

Livingston, Howard F. "Measuring and Teaching Meaning with an Informal Reading Inventory." *Elementary English* 51 (September 1974): 878–89.

Marzano, Robert J., et al. "The Graded Word List Is Not a Shortcut to an IRI." *The Reading Teacher* 31 (March 1978): 647–51.

Morrow, Lesley Mandel. "Retelling Stories as a Diagnostic Tool." In *Reexamining Reading Diagnosis: New Trends and Procedures*, edited by Susan Mandel Glazer, Lyndon W. Searfoss, and Lance M. Gentile, pp. 128–49. Newark, Del.: International Reading Association, 1988.

Morrow, Lesley Mandel. "Using Story Retelling to Develop Comprehension." In *Children's Comprehension of Text: Research into Practice*, edited by K. Denise Muth, pp. 37–58. Newark, Del.: International Reading Association, 1989.

Newman, Harold. "Oral Reading Miscue Analysis Is Good, but Not Complete." *The Reading Teacher* 31 (May 1978): 883–86.

Norton, Donna E. *The Impact of Literature-Based Reading.* New York: Merrill, 1992.

Pikulski, John J. "The Assessment of Reading: A Time for Change?" *The Reading Teacher* 43 (October 1989): 80–81.

Pikulski, John. "A Critical Review: Informal Reading Inventories." *The Reading Teacher* 28 (November 1974): 141–51.

Pikulski, John J. "Informal Reading Inventories." *The Reading Teacher* 43 (March 1990): 514–16.

Valmont, William J. "Creating Questions for Informal Reading Inventories." *The Reading Teacher* 25 (March 1972): 509–12.

Winograd, Peter, Paris, Scott, and Bridge, Connie. "Improving the Assessment of Literacy." *The Reading Teacher* 45 (October 1991): 108–16.

PLACEMENT WORD LISTS

STUDENT WORD LIST 1

1. a
2. at
3. back
4. big
5. can
6. do
7. for
8. go
9. have
10. help
11. I
12. in
13. jump
14. of
15. one
16. play
17. said
18. see
19. she
20. that

1. all
2. am
3. any
4. came
5. day
6. find
7. had
8. into
9. now
10. out
11. put
12. ran
13. say
14. soon
15. there
16. two
17. well
18. what
19. with
20. yes

1. after	1. also
2. again	2. always
3. book	3. around
4. boy	4. best
5. come	5. box
6. hand	6. color
7. how	7. fall
8. keep	8. five
9. long	9. grow
10. many	10. head
11. never	11. light
12. next	12. made
13. once	13. part
14. open	14. people
15. room	15. read
16. school	16. same
17. them	17. small
18. think	18. town
19. up	19. turn
20. where	20. wish

1. air
2. cold
3. dear
4. drink
5. every
6. food
7. hold
8. learn
9. move
10. number
11. often
12. several
13. start
14. such
15. table
16. today
17. try
18. wash
19. wrong
20. yellow

1. amused
2. ancient
3. award
4. cemetery
5. echo
6. elastic
7. flock
8. government
9. invade
10. jealous
11. lizard
12. mechanic
13. mysterious
14. portion
15. savage
16. scarlet
17. signal
18. statue
19. stout
20. vicious

1. base
2. border
3. bore
4. detour
5. dismay
6. establish
7. exhausted
8. gallant
9. glimpse
10. haunt
11. hitched
12. ignore
13. impulse
14. lacked
15. marvel
16. rude
17. thicket
18. transaction
19. transparent
20. turban

1. absurd
2. affairs
3. appeal
4. association
5. cavity
6. complicated
7. crucial
8. deliberately
9. despite
10. eternal
11. extinct
12. hesitate
13. inspiration
14. menace
15. precise
16. rehearsal
17. ridiculous
18. routine
19. specific
20. strenuous

1. accumulate
2. apprehension
3. comprehend
4. delegated
5. dense
6. domain
7. execute
8. exited
9. justifiable
10. omen
11. optimistic
12. potential
13. quaint
14. ritual
15. status
16. tampered
17. terrain
18. tranquil
19. versatile
20. vulnerable

1. agile
2. candid
3. convey
4. enumeration
5. gorge
6. immune
7. improvised
8. incredulous
9. intricate
10. neurotic
11. nocturnal
12. petty
13. placid
14. poise
15. reluctantly
16. shiftless
17. tactful
18. tangible
19. toxic
20. unduly

1. alien
2. animation
3. apprentice
4. binoculars
5. burnished
6. chronic
7. discern
8. ecstatic
9. exaggerate
10. ethnic
11. furtive
12. horde
13. ingenious
14. perennial
15. predecessor
16. quarantine
17. scrutinize
18. strategy
19. velocity
20. warp

1. adept
2. analysis
3. benign
4. bizarre
5. chagrin
6. composure
7. diminish
8. falter
9. fanatic
10. gaunt
11. hybrid
12. jostle
13. lethargic
14. parallel
15. predatory
16. reverie
17. simultaneous
18. sustenance
19. taunt
20. valiant

1. affluent
2. anachronism
3. bivouac
4. blithe
5. deteriorate
6. divergent
7. euphoria
8. grimace
9. incongruity
10. legitimate
11. ludicrous
12. monotonous
13. periphery
14. pianissimo
15. rendezvous
16. repatriate
17. shrapnel
18. temerity
19. upholstery
20. wizened

1. abstinence
2. apprentice
3. blasphemy
4. boisterous
5. clandestine
6. coherent
7. diminutive
8. domicile
9. facetious
10. feudalism
11. garrulous
12. irony
13. macabre
14. monologue
15. nuptial
16. paradoxical
17. renaissance
18. synopsis
19. veranda
20. vestibule

PLACEMENT WORD LISTS

TEACHER WORD LIST 1

LIST 1

PREPRIMER ○	PRIMER □	LEVEL 1 ◇	LEVEL 2 ○○	LEVEL 3 □□
1. a ______	1. all ______	1. after ______	1. also ______	1. air ______
2. at ______	2. am ______	2. again ______	2. always ______	2. cold ______
3. back ______	3. any ______	3. book ______	3. around ______	3. dear ______
4. big ______	4. came ______	4. boy ______	4. best ______	4. drink ______
5. can ______	5. day ______	5. come ______	5. box ______	5. every ______
6. do ______	6. find ______	6. hand ______	6. color ______	6. food ______
7. for ______	7. had ______	7. how ______	7. fall ______	7. hold ______
8. go ______	8. into ______	8. keep ______	8. five ______	8. learn ______
9. have ______	9. now ______	9. long ______	9. grow ______	9. move ______
10. help ______	10. out ______	10. many ______	10. head ______	10. number ______
11. I ______	11. put ______	11. never ______	11. light ______	11. often ______
12. in ______	12. ran ______	12. next ______	12. made ______	12. several ______
13. jump ______	13. say ______	13. once ______	13. part ______	13. start ______
14. of ______	14. soon ______	14. open ______	14. people ______	14. such ______
15. one ______	15. there ______	15. room ______	15. read ______	15. table ______
16. play ______	16. two ______	16. school ______	16. same ______	16. today ______
17. said ______	17. well ______	17. them ______	17. small ______	17. try ______
18. see ______	18. what ______	18. think ______	18. town ______	18. wash ______
19. she ______	19. with ______	19. up ______	19. turn ______	19. wrong ______
20. that ______	20. yes ______	20. where ______	20. wish ______	20. yellow ______

0–2 errors—Independent level **3–4 errors**—Instructional level **5+ errors**—Frustration level

LIST 1

LEVEL 4 ◇◇	LEVEL 5 ☆	LEVEL 6 ●	LEVEL 7 ■	LEVEL 8 ◆
1. amused ______	1. base ______	1. absurd ______	1. accumulate ______	1. agile ______
2. ancient ______	2. border ______	2. affairs ______	2. apprehension ______	2. candid ______
3. award ______	3. bore ______	3. appeal ______	3. comprehend ______	3. convey ______
4. cemetery ______	4. detour ______	4. association ______	4. delegated ______	4. enumeration ______
5. echo ______	5. dismay ______	5. cavity ______	5. dense ______	5. gorge ______
6. elastic ______	6. establish ______	6. complicated ______	6. domain ______	6. immune ______
7. flock ______	7. exhausted ______	7. crucial ______	7. execute ______	7. improvised ______
8. government ______	8. gallant ______	8. deliberately ______	8. exited ______	8. incredulous ______
9. invade ______	9. glimpse ______	9. despite ______	9. justifiable ______	9. intricate ______
10. jealous ______	10. haunt ______	10. eternal ______	10. omen ______	10. neurotic ______
11. lizard ______	11. hitched ______	11. extinct ______	11. optimistic ______	11. nocturnal ______
12. mechanic ______	12. ignore ______	12. hesitate ______	12. potential ______	12. petty ______
13. mysterious ______	13. impulse ______	13. inspiration ______	13. quaint ______	13. placid ______
14. portion ______	14. lacked ______	14. menace ______	14. ritual ______	14. poise ______
15. savage ______	15. marvel ______	15. precise ______	15. status ______	15. reluctantly ______
16. scarlet ______	16. rude ______	16. rehearsal ______	16. tampered ______	16. shiftless ______
17. signal ______	17. thicket ______	17. ridiculous ______	17. terrain ______	17. tactful ______
18. statue ______	18. transaction ______	18. routine ______	18. tranquil ______	18. tangible ______
19. stout ______	19. transparent ______	19. specific ______	19. versatile ______	19. toxic ______
20. vicious ______	20. turban ______	20. strenuous ______	20. vulnerable ______	20. unduly ______

0–2 errors—Independent level **3–4 errors**—Instructional level **5+ errors**—Frustration level

LIST 1

LEVEL 9 ●●

1. alien ______
2. animation ______
3. apprentice ______
4. binoculars ______
5. burnished ______
6. chronic ______
7. discern ______
8. ecstatic ______
9. exaggerate ______
10. ethnic ______
11. furtive ______
12. horde ______
13. ingenious ______
14. perennial ______
15. predecessor ______
16. quarantine ______
17. scrutinize ______
18. strategy ______
19. velocity ______
20. warp ______

LEVEL 10 ■■

1. adept ______
2. analysis ______
3. benign ______
4. bizarre ______
5. chagrin ______
6. composure ______
7. diminish ______
8. falter ______
9. fanatic ______
10. gaunt ______
11. hybrid ______
12. jostle ______
13. lethargic ______
14. parallel ______
15. predatory ______
16. reverie ______
17. simultaneous ______
18. sustenance ______
19. taunt ______
20. valiant ______

LEVEL 11 ◆◆

1. affluent ______
2. anachronism ______
3. bivouac ______
4. blithe ______
5. deteriorate ______
6. divergent ______
7. euphoria ______
8. grimace ______
9. incongruity ______
10. legitimate ______
11. ludicrous ______
12. monotonous ______
13. periphery ______
14. pianissimo ______
15. rendezvous ______
16. repatriate ______
17. shrapnel ______
18. temerity ______
19. upholstery ______
20. wizened ______

LEVEL 12 ★

1. abstinence ______
2. apprentice ______
3. blasphemy ______
4. boisterous ______
5. clandestine ______
6. coherent ______
7. diminutive ______
8. domicile ______
9. facetious ______
10. feudalism ______
11. garrulous ______
12. irony ______
13. macabre ______
14. monologue ______
15. nuptial ______
16. paradoxical ______
17. renaissance ______
18. synopsis ______
19. veranda ______
20. vestibule ______

0–2 errors—Independent level **3–4 errors**—Instructional level **5+ errors**—Frustration level

PLACEMENT WORD LISTS

STUDENT WORD LIST 2

1. and	1. about
2. be	2. are
3. but	3. black
4. did	4. give
5. down	5. just
6. get	6. me
7. good	7. new
8. he	8. other
9. here	9. our
10. house	10. saw
11. is	11. some
12. it	12. their
13. like	13. then
14. little	14. they
15. look	15. too
16. no	16. under
17. on	17. was
18. the	18. went
19. we	19. when
20. you	20. would

1. before
2. children
3. could
4. from
5. got
6. hard
7. know
8. night
9. off
10. over
11. something
12. stop
13. take
14. time
15. tree
16. very
17. walk
18. water
19. who
20. work

1. another
2. ask
3. both
4. bring
5. call
6. change
7. first
8. found
9. high
10. last
11. men
12. party
13. pull
14. right
15. should
16. sleep
17. tell
18. these
19. which
20. why

LIST 2

1. carry
2. clean
3. different
4. door
5. draw
6. eight
7. family
8. full
9. half
10. leave
11. money
12. morning
13. o'clock
14. old
15. seven
16. story
17. street
18. together
19. use
20. write

1. assembly
2. captive
3. cartridge
4. disease
5. disturbance
6. foundation
7. gaze
8. harpoon
9. jewel
10. nervous
11. offend
12. prairie
13. relief
14. remote
15. rumor
16. salary
17. serious
18. slope
19. tiresome
20. wilderness

1. astonish
2. contract
3. depressed
4. deprived
5. eagerly
6. evaporate
7. fashion
8. frantic
9. frontier
10. furnish
11. hazel
12. impress
13. indication
14. massive
15. platform
16. pledge
17. poaching
18. skirt
19. starvation
20. summit

1. aggressive
2. appropriate
3. calm
4. clutching
5. enthusiastic
6. extensive
7. furiously
8. hostile
9. intense
10. minimum
11. minor
12. nuisance
13. offensive
14. prominently
15. puny
16. ravine
17. reliable
18. scarcely
19. transplant
20. vow

1. contemplate	1. arrogant
2. crisis	2. belligerent
3. debris	3. contrive
4. divert	4. detection
5. domestic	5. evade
6. fraud	6. foreman
7. impounded	7. indignant
8. indifferent	8. inevitable
9. industrious	9. infinitely
10. intellectual	10. intact
11. inventory	11. intolerant
12. motives	12. manifest
13. obscure	13. migrate
14. ravenous	14. modifications
15. revert	15. oasis
16. ridicule	16. prestige
17. segment	17. sauntered
18. stability	18. serenity
19. subtle	19. stamina
20. vivid	20. sullen

1. authentic
2. biceps
3. certify
4. controversy
5. corsage
6. detrimental
7. empathy
8. ethereal
9. hypocrisy
10. insidious
11. lethal
12. mesmerize
13. nurture
14. relevant
15. trajectory
16. transition
17. utilize
18. vaudeville
19. vicinity
20. wince

1. appraisal
2. arsenal
3. coincide
4. defiant
5. duplicate
6. elaborate
7. feasible
8. intent
9. intrigue
10. meditate
11. morass
12. mutual
13. panorama
14. perpetual
15. retrieve
16. subterranean
17. synthetic
18. vehemence
19. virtual
20. zealous

1. arthritis
2. bereave
3. chronological
4. cryptic
5. docile
6. eminent
7. flagrantly
8. hiatus
9. inexplicable
10. legendary
11. meander
12. oblique
13. pendulous
14. rational
15. scepter
16. statistics
17. tether
18. transient
19. vigilance
20. vulnerability

1. articulate
2. avarice
3. camaraderie
4. celestial
5. delineate
6. elusive
7. equanimity
8. gabardine
9. insignia
10. interrogate
11. laconic
12. languid
13. prodigy
14. querulous
15. reverie
16. solace
17. taciturn
18. trigonometric
19. unctuous
20. vociferous

PLACEMENT WORD LISTS

TEACHER WORD LIST 2

LIST 2

PREPRIMER ○	PRIMER □	LEVEL 1 ◇	LEVEL 2 ○○	LEVEL 3 □□
1. and ____	1. about ____	1. before ____	1. another ____	1. carry ____
2. be ____	2. are ____	2. children ____	2. ask ____	2. clean ____
3. but ____	3. black ____	3. could ____	3. both ____	3. different ____
4. did ____	4. give ____	4. from ____	4. bring ____	4. door ____
5. down ____	5. just ____	5. got ____	5. call ____	5. draw ____
6. get ____	6. me ____	6. hard ____	6. change ____	6. eight ____
7. good ____	7. new ____	7. know ____	7. first ____	7. family ____
8. he ____	8. other ____	8. night ____	8. found ____	8. full ____
9. here ____	9. our ____	9. off ____	9. high ____	9. half ____
10. house ____	10. saw ____	10. over ____	10. last ____	10. leave ____
11. is ____	11. some ____	11. something ____	11. men ____	11. money ____
12. it ____	12. their ____	12. stop ____	12. party ____	12. morning ____
13. like ____	13. then ____	13. take ____	13. pull ____	13. o'clock ____
14. little ____	14. they ____	14. time ____	14. right ____	14. old ____
15. look ____	15. too ____	15. tree ____	15. should ____	15. seven ____
16. no ____	16. under ____	16. very ____	16. sleep ____	16. story ____
17. on ____	17. was ____	17. walk ____	17. tell ____	17. street ____
18. the ____	18. went ____	18. water ____	18. these ____	18. together ____
19. we ____	19. when ____	19. who ____	19. which ____	19. use ____
20. you ____	20. would ____	20. work ____	20. why ____	20. write ____

0–2 errors—Independent level **3–4 errors**—Instructional level **5+ errors**—Frustration level

LIST 2

LEVEL 4 ◇◇

1. assembly ______
2. captive ______
3. cartridge ______
4. disease ______
5. disturbance ______
6. foundation ______
7. gaze ______
8. harpoon ______
9. jewel ______
10. nervous ______
11. offend ______
12. prairie ______
13. relief ______
14. remote ______
15. rumor ______
16. salary ______
17. serious ______
18. slope ______
19. tiresome ______
20. wilderness ______

LEVEL 5 ☆

1. astonish ______
2. contract ______
3. depressed ______
4. deprived ______
5. eagerly ______
6. evaporate ______
7. fashion ______
8. frantic ______
9. frontier ______
10. furnish ______
11. hazel ______
12. impress ______
13. indication ______
14. massive ______
15. platform ______
16. pledge ______
17. poaching ______
18. skirt ______
19. starvation ______
20. summit ______

LEVEL 6 ●

1. aggressive ______
2. appropriate ______
3. calm ______
4. clutching ______
5. enthusiastic ______
6. extensive ______
7. furiously ______
8. hostile ______
9. intense ______
10. minimum ______
11. minor ______
12. nuisance ______
13. offensive ______
14. prominently ______
15. puny ______
16. ravine ______
17. reliable ______
18. scarcely ______
19. transplant ______
20. vow ______

LEVEL 7 ■

1. contemplate ______
2. crisis ______
3. debris ______
4. divert ______
5. domestic ______
6. fraud ______
7. impounded ______
8. indifferent ______
9. industrious ______
10. intellectual ______
11. inventory ______
12. motives ______
13. obscure ______
14. ravenous ______
15. revert ______
16. ridicule ______
17. segment ______
18. stability ______
19. subtle ______
20. vivid ______

LEVEL 8 ◆

1. arrogant ______
2. belligerent ______
3. contrive ______
4. detection ______
5. evade ______
6. foreman ______
7. indignant ______
8. inevitable ______
9. infinitely ______
10. intact ______
11. intolerant ______
12. manifest ______
13. migrate ______
14. modifications ______
15. oasis ______
16. prestige ______
17. sauntered ______
18. serenity ______
19. stamina ______
20. sullen ______

0–2 errors—Independent level **3–4 errors**—Instructional level **5+ errors**—Frustration level

LIST 2

LEVEL 9 ●●

1. authentic ____
2. biceps ____
3. certify ____
4. controversy ____
5. corsage ____
6. detrimental ____
7. empathy ____
8. ethereal ____
9. hypocrisy ____
10. insidious ____
11. lethal ____
12. mesmerize ____
13. nurture ____
14. relevant ____
15. trajectory ____
16. transition ____
17. utilize ____
18. vaudeville ____
19. vicinity ____
20. wince ____

LEVEL 10 ■■

1. appraisal ____
2. arsenal ____
3. coincide ____
4. defiant ____
5. duplicate ____
6. elaborate ____
7. feasible ____
8. intent ____
9. intrigue ____
10. meditate ____
11. morass ____
12. mutual ____
13. panorama ____
14. perpetual ____
15. retrieve ____
16. subterranean ____
17. synthetic ____
18. vehemence ____
19. virtual ____
20. zealous ____

LEVEL 11 ◆◆

1. arthritis ____
2. bereave ____
3. chronological ____
4. cryptic ____
5. docile ____
6. eminent ____
7. flagrantly ____
8. hiatus ____
9. inexplicable ____
10. legendary ____
11. meander ____
12. oblique ____
13. pendulous ____
14. rational ____
15. scepter ____
16. statistics ____
17. tether ____
18. transient ____
19. vigilance ____
20. vulnerability ____

LEVEL 12 ★

1. articulate ____
2. avarice ____
3. camaraderie ____
4. celestial ____
5. delineate ____
6. elusive ____
7. equanimity ____
8. gabardine ____
9. insignia ____
10. interrogate ____
11. laconic ____
12. languid ____
13. prodigy ____
14. querulous ____
15. reverie ____
16. solace ____
17. taciturn ____
18. trigonometric ____
19. unctuous ____
20. vociferous ____

0–2 errors—Independent level **3–4 errors**—Instructional level **5+ errors**—Frustration level

GRADED PASSAGES

STUDENT BOOKLET FORM A

Passages PP to 12

Read this story to find out about Jill's problem.

Jill's Mom said, "It is time for bed."
Jill put the puppy to bed.
She said, "Good night, Puppy.
Sleep well."

Jill and Mom and Dad went to bed.
But the puppy did not sleep.

Jill said, "I hear you, Puppy.
Do not cry, Puppy.
What do you want, my little puppy?
Do you want me to play with you?"

Jill played with the puppy.
She said, "Now you can sleep.
Good night."

Read this story to find out what Paco's problem was.

"Paco, where is your smile?" asked Mom.
"This is a happy day for all of us.
Dad has a birthday!"

"I am not happy," said Paco.
"I do not have a nice big gift for Dad."

"A small gift is nice," said Mom.
"Why not make a small gift?
Dad will like that."

"What can I make?" asked Paco.

"That is up to you," said Mom.
"I have to go in the house now.
You will think of a nice gift."

STUDENT ☐

FORM A

☐ PASSAGE

Paco went in the yard.
He looked at all the things there.
There was his box of rocks.
"But rocks are not a gift Dad will like," he said.
Then there was his box of little play people.
"My play people are not the best gift for Dad," he said.

Paco did not smile at all.

Read this story to find out what a girl in the city wants very much.

I want a pet very, very much.
My mother says I have to wait.
We have had this talk many times, my mother and I.
Dad says I can buy some fish.
They are small and can fit well in my small room.
But my brother has four fish.
I want something different.
I want something of my own.

One day, Grandma showed me flowers hanging in her window.
She had many kinds of flowers.
Grandma told me she would help me grow flowers of my own.
She said that they are not the same as a pet, but that flowers can bring magic to a city home.

Read this story to find out about Pablo's home.

In a valley at the foot of a mountain lived a boy named Pablo. His home was a little brick house with a roof of banana leaves. There were holes in the sides of the house and holes in the roof, but no one cared. The valley was never cold, and it never rained there.

Pablo used to say to himself, "If only it would rain!"

Then the valley would not be dusty and brown. Grass would grow and flowers would bloom. It would be the most beautiful valley in all Mexico. And he could catch the rain in pans and jars. Then he would not have to go to the river for water.

Every day he took two big jars to the river. He filled them with water and brought them home.

STUDENT PASSAGE FORM A

Read this story to find out about what two youngsters decide to do.

It's summer, it's hot, and it's Monday.

"What do you want to do?" asks Slam.

"I do not know," says Dunk. "It's too hot for a game of basketball."

"Do you want to play checkers?" asks Slam.

"No," says Dunk. "We did that for the last six days. Why not go swimming?"

That's when Slam and Dunk go down to the kitchen. Grandpa is there. He has a big grin. He's got something in his hands, but Slam and Dunk cannot see what it is.

"Do not look," says Grandpa. "See if you can think of what I have in my hands."

"A sandwich!" says Slam.

"A cactus!" says Dunk.

"No," says Grandpa. "Look! This is what we will do for fun today!"

"Go fishing!" yell Slam and Dunk. "What a good idea!"

Matthew had been going to the library and reading there because it was a quiet place. Then the library was closed until a new one could be built. Read this story to find out what Matthew did.

On the corner, one block away from the closed library, Matthew saw the long green bookmobile. He walked up to the truck, climbed the three little steps, and walked inside. A girl who looked a little like Claudia took his book from him. The woman from the library was standing next to her, stamping books for people to take home. She smiled when she saw Matthew. "Look at the titles," she said. "I'll come over as soon as I can and help you find a book you'll like."

Matthew smiled back and walked around the bookmobile, looking for the children's section. There were other people walking around, too. They were all close together because there wasn't a lot of room. The books were lined up against the wall on shelves. When you walked around them, you couldn't find a place to be by yourself. Matthew saw that he couldn't stay at the bookmobile the way he could at a real library. So when he came to the children's section, he looked through the shelves and tried to find a book as fast as he could. He looked at the titles and all the bright book covers. His eyes fell on a book with a picture of a boy on it. The boy had brown skin just like Matthew's, and he looked about the same age. Matthew thought it would be nice to read a book about a boy who looked so much like himself. He picked it up and took it to the librarian. She said, "You picked out a really good book." Then she took his card and stamped the book.

Read this story to find out about a harbor seal pup that has a special problem.

In the sea, a harbor seal pup learns to catch and eat fish by watching its mother. By the time it is weaned, at the age of four or five weeks, it is able to feed on its own.

Without a mother, and living temporarily in captivity, Pearson had to be taught what a fish was and how to swallow it. Eventually, he would have to learn to catch one himself.

Holly started his training with a small herring—an oily fish which is a favorite with seals. Gently, she opened his mouth and slipped the fish in headfirst. Harbor seals have sharp teeth for catching fish but no teeth for grinding and chewing. They swallow their food whole.

But Pearson didn't seem to understand what he was supposed to do. He bit down on the fish and then spit it out. Holly tried again. This time, Pearson got the idea. He swallowed the herring in one gulp and looked eagerly for more.

Within a week, he was being hand-fed a pound of fish a day in addition to his formula. This new diet made him friskier than ever. He chased the other pups in the outside pen. He plunged into the small wading pool and rolled in the shallow water, splashing both seals and people.

Read this story to find out about Dave and what he wanted to do.

Dave wanted very much to succeed in athletics, but he was always afraid he would not quite make it. Last winter, in basketball, he had not. He spent more time on the bench than on the floor, much more. So, with spring, he had turned to track. Coach Stevens said he greatly needed a good quarter-miler, and Dave hoped to be that person.

The coach stressed that because Dave's legs were shorter than average he should work on lengthening his stride. To do that, the coach added, would require much practice and an equal amount of desire.

At first, Dave's father ruled out the road beside the railroad tracks for practice, but then he talked with Mr. Johnson. The old man assured the father that it would not be dangerous as long as Dave stayed well away from the tracks and used only the quiet road. Mr. Johnson also promised to "keep an eye" on the boy.

Read the following story to find out about some famous animals that live on Sable Island, which is in the Atlantic Ocean near Nova Scotia.

What did the first horses that came to Sable Island look like? We can only assume that they were much like farm horses anywhere in the world, but the harsh winters on Sable slowly changed the appearance of their descendants. They became smaller and stockier, had short ears, and in winter grew very long hair. Some stallions today have manes and tails so long that they nearly touch the ground.

Most of the horses live in small herds, each consisting of several mares and their foals and a stallion who protects them. The herd is usually led by a mare, but when two herds meet, the stallions trot toward each other, heads held high, tossing their long manes from side to side. Shoulder to shoulder, they push each other and neigh and nip a bit, but then, having proven that they are both powerful and unafraid, they proudly prance back to their herds.

This is what biologists call ritual fighting: it's mostly for show.

Read this story to find out some interesting facts about elephants.

The perfect place to observe elephants is at a water hole, for elephants consume a great deal of water and must drink at least every second day to survive. An adult elephant will drink between forty and eighty gallons of water. If the water holes go dry, the elephants die. However, the elephant is the only creature besides a human being that can dig a water hole. I have witnessed such a feat in the dried-out Letaba River. The elephants wandered into the middle of the riverbed, and the strongest bulls and the largest females began to dig with their tusks and forefeet where they smelled water below. In half an hour, they had dug a four-foot-deep hole. They then inserted their trunks, and by sucking they created a vacuum that sipped up water from below. The water began to flow into their trunks through the soft sand. A new well had been created. We once photographed a whole sector full of elephant-made wells which had saved not only the elephants but all the other animals in the region, who did not possess the intellect and the strength of the resourceful elephants.

Read to find out about a well-known singer from Tennessee, Dolly Parton.

Under showgirl make-up and a head of bleached blonde hair, Dolly is probably the most beautiful of the country singers. She's extremely well liked by the other women, who are fond of saying, "Dolly's even more beautiful on the inside."

Dolly's childhood dreams were to be a country-music star, wear "flashy" clothes and have a tube of lipstick. Now she carries an extensive make-up collection in a tackle box and laughs infectiously at her own image.

"I always felt so ugly when I was little 'cause we never had nothing to fix up with and no pretty clothes. I once saw a lady with a lipstick and I thought she was a millionaire. I never doubted for a minute that I was gonna bring my music to Nashville, and I decided that when I did, I'd be real fancy."

Read this story to find out about a woman who became a famous pilot—Amelia Earhart.

Earhart was away a lot, in his work as a claims agent, and sometimes he took his wife along with him. The result was that Amelia and her younger sister Muriel spent much of their childhood living with their grandparents. Amelia had a rich fantasy life, and lived adventurous summers exploring caves, playing baseball with equipment given to her by her father, reading Scott, Dickens, George Elliot; but she must have learned early on that she was essentially alone.

"I was a horrid little girl," she said later. "Perhaps the fact that I was exceedingly fond of reading made me endurable. With a large library to browse in, I spent many hours not bothering anyone after I once learned to read."

The family moved to Des Moines in 1907, apparently to escape the domination of the grandparents, and on her tenth birthday, Amelia saw her first airplane. That day, her father took her to the Iowa State Fair; it was only five years after the Wright Brothers had first flown at Kitty Hawk (incidentally, with money provided by a Wright sister) and airplanes were a great curiosity. Amelia, however, was not impressed.

Read this story to find out some things Johnny Appleseed did.

There is some disagreement concerning the way in which Johnny went about planting apple trees in the wild frontier country. Some say that he scattered the seed as he went along the edges of marshes or natural clearings in the thick, almost tropical forests, others that he distributed the seeds among the settlers themselves to plant, and still others claim that in the damp land surrounding the marshes he established nurseries where he kept the seedlings until they were big enough to transplant. My Great-Aunt Mattie said that her father, who lived in a rather grand way for a frontier settler, had boxes of apples brought each year from Maryland until his own trees began to bear, and then he always saved the seeds, drying them on the shelf above the kitchen fireplace, to be put later into a box and kept for Johnny Appleseed when he came on one of his overnight visits.

Johnny scattered fennel seed all through our Ohio country, for when the trees were first cleared and the land plowed up, the mosquitoes increased and malaria spread from family to family. Johnny regarded a tea brewed of fennel leaves as a specific against what the settlers called "fever and ague," and he seeded the plant along trails and fence rows over all Ohio.

Read this story to find out all you can about an interesting and unusual man.

Punctually at midday he opened his bag and spread out his professional equipment, which consisted of a dozen cowrie shells, a square piece of cloth with obscure mystic charts on it, a notebook, and a bundle of palmyra writing. His forehead was resplendent with sacred ash and vermillion, and his eyes sparkled with a sharp abnormal gleam which was really an outcome of a continual searching look for customers, but which his simple clients took to be a prophetic light and felt comforted. The power of his eyes was considerably enhanced by their position—placed as they were between the painted forehead and the dark whiskers which streamed down his cheeks: even a half-wit's eyes would sparkle in such a setting. To crown the effect he wound a saffron-colored turban around his head. This color scheme never failed. People were attracted to him as bees are attracted to cosmos or dahlia stalks. He sat under the boughs of a spreading tamarind tree which flanked a path running through the Town Hall Park. It was a remarkable place in many ways: a surging crowd was always moving up and down this narrow road morning till night.

GRADED PASSAGES

TEACHER BOOKLET FORM A

Passages and Questions PP to 12

Summary Forms for Quantitative and Qualitative Analysis

Worksheets

INTRODUCTORY STATEMENT: Read this story to find out about Jill's problem.

Jill's Mom said, "It is time for bed."
Jill put the puppy to bed.
She said, "Good night, Puppy.
Sleep well."

Jill and Mom and Dad went to bed.
But the puppy did not sleep.

Jill said, "I hear you, Puppy.
Do not cry, Puppy.
What do you want, my little puppy?
Do you want me to play with you?"

Jill played with the puppy.
She said, "Now you can sleep.
Good night."

Source: "Good Night, Puppy," in Elizabeth Sulzby and others, *Peek In* (New York: McGraw-Hill School Divison, 1989), pp. 68–69.

[*Note*: Do not count as a miscue mispronunciation of the name Jill. You may pronounce this name for the student if needed.]

SCORING AID
Word Recognition
%–Miscues
99–1
95–3
90–7
85–10
Comprehension
%–Errors
100–0
87.5–1
75–2
62.5–3
50–4
37.5–5
25–6
12.5–7
0–8
68 Words (for Word Recognition)
73 Words (for Rate)
WPM
4380

COMPREHENSION QUESTIONS

____ main idea — 1. What is this story about? (Jill tries to get a puppy to sleep.)

____ vocabulary — 2. What is a puppy? (a young dog)

____ cause and effect/ inference — 3. What caused Jill to put the puppy to bed? (Her mother said, "It is time for bed.")

____ sequence — 4. Who went to bed after the puppy was put to bed? (Jill and Mom and Dad) [Note: All three people must be named, but any order is acceptable. If only one or two are named, ask "Who else?"]

____ inference — 5. What did Jill hear the puppy doing after she went to bed? (crying)

____ inference — 6. What did Jill think the puppy wanted? (to play with Jill)

____ sequence — 7. What did Jill do with the puppy after she asked it what it wanted? (She played with it.)

____ inference — 8. Did Jill think playing with the puppy had solved the problem? (yes) What did the story say that made you think that? (She said, "Now you can sleep.")

☐ TEACHER P ☐

FORM A

☐ P PASSAGE ☐

INTRODUCTORY STATEMENT: Read this story to find out what Paco's problem was.

"Paco, where is your smile?" asked Mom.
"This is a happy day for all of us.
Dad has a birthday!"

"I am not happy," said Paco.
"I do not have a nice big gift for Dad."

"A small gift is nice," said Mom.
"Why not make a small gift?
Dad will like that."

"What can I make?" asked Paco.

"That is up to you," said Mom.
"I have to go in the house now.
You will think of a nice gift."

Paco went in the yard.
He looked at all the things there.
There was his box of rocks.
"But rocks are not a gift Dad will like," he said.
Then there was his box of little play people.
"My play people are not the best gift for Dad," he said.

Paco did not smile at all.

SCORING AID
Word Recognition
%–Miscues
99–2
95–7
90–13
85–20
Comprehension
%–Errors
100–0
87.5–1
75–2
62.5–3
50–4
37.5–5
25–6
12.5–7
0–8
132 Words (for Word Recognition)
137 Words (for Rate)
WPM
8220

Source: "A Gift from Paco," by Gary Bargar, in Leo Fay and others, *Dive In* (Chicago: The Riverside Publishing Company, 1989), pp. 61–63.

[*Note*: Do not count as a miscue mispronunciation of the name Paco. You may pronounce this name for the student if needed.]

COMPREHENSION QUESTIONS

____ main idea	1. What is this story about? (Paco is looking for a nice gift for Dad.)
____ cause and effect/ inference	2. Why didn't Paco smile? (He was unhappy that he did not have a nice gift for his dad.)
____ vocabulary	3. What is a gift? (a present; something that you give to someone)
____ detail	4. What kind of gift did Paco's mom tell him was nice? (a small gift)
____ sequence	5. What did Paco ask after his mother suggested that he make a small gift? (What can I make?)
____ inference	6. Did Paco want to make his gift? (no) What happened in the story that made you believe that? (He kept looking for things to give that he did not have to make.)
____ detail	7. Where did Paco go to look for a gift? (in the yard)
____ detail	8. What were the two things that Paco did not think his dad would like? (rocks and play people)

INTRODUCTORY STATEMENT: Read this story to find out what a girl in the city wants very much.

I want a pet very, very much.
My mother says I have to wait.
We have had this talk many times, my mother and I.
Dad says I can buy some fish.
They are small and can fit well in my small room.
But my brother has four fish.
I want something different.
I want something of my own.

One day, Grandma showed me flowers hanging in her window.
She had many kinds of flowers.
Grandma told me she would help me grow flowers of my own.
She said that they are not the same as a pet, but that flowers can bring magic to a city home.

Source: "City Magic," by Laura Schenone and Pat Garbarini, in Elizabeth Sulzby and others, *Just the Thing* (New York: McGraw-Hill School Division, 1989), pp. 178–179.

[*Note*: Do not count as a miscue mispronunciation of the word Grandma. You may pronounce this word for the student if needed.]

SCORING AID

Word Recognition
%–Miscues
99–1
95–5
90–11
85–16

Comprehension
%–Errors
100–0
87.5–1
75–2
62.5–3
50–4
37.5–5
25–6
12.5–7
0–8

106 Words
(for Word Recognition)

108 Words
(for Rate)

WPM
6480

COMPREHENSION QUESTIONS

____ main idea — 1. What is this story about?
(A girl wants a pet, but her grandmother suggests growing flowers.)

____ inference — 2. How does the girl who is telling the story feel about pets?
(She wants one very much; she would like one.)

____ detail — 3. What kind of pet does her dad say she can buy? (fish)

____ cause and effect/inference — 4. What probably caused him to suggest fish for her pets?
(They are small and would fit well in her small room; they are small.)

____ detail — 5. What does her brother have for his pets? (four fish; fish)

____ detail — 6. Why doesn't the girl want fish?
(She wants something different; she wants something of her own.)
[Accept either statement as correct.]

____ vocabulary — 7. What does the word "different" mean?
(not the same; not like something else)

____ sequence — 8. What did the girl's grandmother tell her after she showed her the flowers?
(She would help her grow flowers of her own; flowers are not the same as a pet, but they can bring magic to a city home.)
[Accept either statement as correct.]

INTRODUCTORY STATEMENT: Read this story to find out about Pablo's home.

In a valley at the foot of a mountain lived a boy named Pablo. His home was a little brick house with a roof of banana leaves. There were holes in the sides of the house and holes in the roof, but no one cared. The valley was never cold, and it never rained there.

Pablo used to say to himself, "If only it would rain!"

Then the valley would not be dusty and brown. Grass would grow and flowers would bloom. It would be the most beautiful valley in all Mexico. And he could catch the rain in pans and jars. Then he would not have to go to the river for water.

Every day he took two big jars to the river. He filled them with water and brought them home.

Source: *The Poppy Seeds*, by Clyde Robert Bulla (New York: Puffin Books, 1983), unnumbered.

[*Note*: Do not count as miscues mispronunciation of the names Pablo and Mexico. You may pronounce these names for the student if necessary.]

SCORING AID

Word Recognition

%–Miscues
99–1
95–6
90–13
85–19

Comprehension

%–Errors
100–0
87.5–1
75–2
62.5–3
50–4
37.5–5
25–6
12.5–7
0–8

130 Words (for Word Recognition)

133 Words (for Rate)

WPM
7980

COMPREHENSION QUESTIONS

____ main idea — 1. What is this story about? (Pablo wishes it would rain and change the valley.)

____ detail — 2. Where did Pablo live? (in a valley at the foot of a mountain) [If the student answers "in Mexico," count the answer as correct and code the question as inference, rather than detail. If the student answers "in a brick house," ask, "Where was the brick house?"]

____ vocabulary — 3. What does the word "foot" mean when the story says "the foot of the mountain"? (the lowest part; the bottom)

____ vocabulary — 4. What is a valley? (low land between hills or mountains)

____ detail — 5. What was the roof of Pablo's home made of? (banana leaves)

____ cause and effect/ inference — 6. Why didn't the people care that there were holes in the sides sides of the house and the roof? (The valley was never cold and never had rain.)

____ cause and effect/ inference — 7. What would rain cause to happen in the valley? (It wouldn't be dusty and brown. Grass would grow. Flowers would bloom. It would become beautiful.) [Accept any two reasons for full credit. Give half credit for only one reason.]

____ sequence — 8. Name in order the three things that Pablo did every day. (took two big jars to the river, filled them with water, and brought them home) [Award half credit for only two things in order. Award no credit if anything is given out of order.]

INTRODUCTORY STATEMENT: Read this story to find out about what two youngsters decide to do.

It's summer, it's hot, and it's Monday.

"What do you want to do?" asks Slam.

"I do not know," says Dunk. "It's too hot for a game of basketball."

"Do you want to play checkers?" asks Slam.

"No," says Dunk. "We did that for the last six days. Why not go swimming?"

That's when Slam and Dunk go down to the kitchen. Grandpa is there. He has a big grin. He's got something in his hands, but Slam and Dunk cannot see what it is.

"Do not look," says Grandpa. "See if you can think of what I have in my hands."

"A sandwich!" says Slam.

"A cactus!" says Dunk.

"No," says Grandpa. "Look! This is what we will do for fun today!"

"Go fishing!" yell Slam and Dunk. "What a good idea!"

Source: *Go to Hawaii*, by Chris Sawyer (Gateway Learning Corporation, 2001), pp. 9–13.

SCORING AID

Word Recognition

%–Miscues
99–1
95–6
90–13
85–19

Comprehension

%–Errors
100–0
90–1
80–2
70–3
60–4
50–5
40–6
30–7
20–8
10–9
0–10

133 Words (for Word Recognition)

133 Words (for Rate)

WPM

7980

COMPREHENSION QUESTIONS

____ main idea — 1. What is this story about? (Slam and Dunk decide what to do.) [If a child says, "Slam and Dunk," ask, "What about Slam and Dunk?"]

____ detail — 2. In what season does the story take place? (summer)

____ cause and effect/detail — 3. What caused Dunk not to want to play basketball? (It was too hot.)

____ inference — 4. What have they done for the last six days? (play checkers)

____ inference — 5. What part of the house were Slam and Dunk in at the beginning of the story? (upstairs)

____ sequence — 6. What room do Slam and Dunk go to after Dunk suggests going swimming? (the kitchen)

____ inference — 7. How does Grandpa feel when Slam and Dunk see him? (pleased; happy)

____ vocabulary — 8. What is a cactus? (A plant that usually has stickers, prickles or spines and grows in dry areas, such as deserts.) [Accept reasonable approximations of this definition.]

____ inference — 9. Which guess about what Grandpa had in his hands was best? Why do you say so? (the sandwich, because a cactus might hurt his hands) [Accept any reasonable rationale for the choice made.]

____ inference — 10. What did Grandpa have in his hands? [Accept a fishing pole, a fishing rod, or fishing gear of any kind.]

INTRODUCTORY STATEMENT: Matthew had been going to the library and reading there because it was a quiet place. Then the library was closed until a new one could be built. Read this story to find out what Matthew did.

On the corner, one block away from the closed library, Matthew saw the long green bookmobile. He walked up to the truck, climbed the three little steps, and walked inside. A girl who looked a little like Claudia took his book from him. The woman from the library was standing next to her, stamping books for people to take home. She smiled when she saw Matthew. "Look at the titles," she said. "I'll come over as soon as I can and help you find a book you'll like."

Matthew smiled back and walked around the bookmobile, looking for the children's section. There were other people walking around, too. They were all close together because there wasn't a lot of room. The books were lined up against the wall on shelves. When you walked around them, you couldn't find a place to be by yourself. Matthew saw that he couldn't stay at the bookmobile the way he could at a real library. So when he came to the children's section, he looked through the shelves and tried to find a book as fast as he could. He looked at the titles and all the bright book covers. His eyes fell on a book with a picture of a boy on it. The boy had brown skin just like Matthew's, and he looked about the same age. Matthew thought it would be nice to read a book about a boy who looked so much like himself. He picked it up and took it to the librarian. She said, "You picked out a really good book." Then she took his card and stamped the book.

Source: "A Quiet Place," by Rose Blue, in Leo Fay and others, *Star Show* (Chicago: The Riverside Publishing Company, 1989), pp. 212–213.

[*Note*: Do not count as miscues mispronunciation of the names Matthew and Claudia. You may pronounce these names for the student if needed.]

SCORING AID

Word Recognition

%–Miscues
99–3
95–13
90–25
85–36

Comprehension

%–Errors
100–0
90–1
80–2
70–3
60–4
50–5
40–6
30–7
20–8
10–9
0–10

237 Words (for Word Recognition)

244 Words (for Rate)

WPM
14640

COMPREHENSION QUESTIONS

____ main idea — 1. What is this story about? (Matthew visits the bookmobile because the library is closed; Matthew makes his first visit to the bookmobile.)

____ detail — 2. Where did Matthew see the bookmobile? (on the corner; one block away from the library)

____ vocabulary — 3. What is a bookmobile? (a library in a truck or bus or van)

____ cause and effect/ inference — 4. Why did Matthew go to the bookmobile? (He had a book to turn in and wanted another one and the library was closed.)

____ inference — 5. Was the librarian friendly? (yes) What did the story say that made you think that? (She smiled at Matthew and offered to help him.)

____ sequence — 6. What was the first thing Matthew looked for after he returned his book? (the children's section)

____ inference — 7. Was the bookmobile crowded? (yes) What did the story say that made you think that? (People were close together; there wasn't a lot of room; there was no place to be by yourself.)

____ detail — 8. What two things did Matthew look at to help him pick out a book? (the titles and the book covers)

____ vocabulary — 9. What does the phrase "his eyes fell on a book" mean? (He saw a book.)

____ inference — 10. What did Matthew look like? (He had brown skin.)

INTRODUCTORY STATEMENT: Read this story to find out about a harbor seal pup that has a special problem.

In the sea, a harbor seal pup learns to catch and eat fish by watching its mother. By the time it is weaned, at the age of four or five weeks, it is able to feed on its own.

Without a mother, and living temporarily in captivity, Pearson had to be taught what a fish was and how to swallow it. Eventually, he would have to learn to catch one himself.

Holly started his training with a small herring—an oily fish which is a favorite with seals. Gently, she opened his mouth and slipped the fish in headfirst. Harbor seals have sharp teeth for catching fish but no teeth for grinding and chewing. They swallow their food whole.

But Pearson didn't seem to understand what he was supposed to do. He bit down on the fish and then spit it out. Holly tried again. This time, Pearson got the idea. He swallowed the herring in one gulp and looked eagerly for more.

Within a week, he was being hand-fed a pound of fish a day in addition to his formula. This new diet made him friskier than ever. He chased the other pups in the outside pen. He plunged into the small wading pool and rolled in the shallow water, splashing both seals and people.

Source: *Pearson, A Harbor Seal Pup*, by Susan Meyers (New York: E. P. Dutton, 1980), pp. 15–16.

[*Note*: Do not count as a miscue mispronunciation of the name Pearson. You may pronounce this name for the student if needed.]

SCORING AID

Word Recognition
%–Miscues
99–3
95–11
90–22
85–33

Comprehension
%–Errors
100–0
90–1
80–2
70–3
60–4
50–5
40–6
30–7
20–8
10–9
0–10

214 Words
(for Word Recognition)

217 Words
(for Rate)

WPM
13020

COMPREHENSION QUESTIONS

____ main idea — 1. What is this story about? (teaching a harbor seal pup to catch and eat fish; teaching Pearson to catch and eat fish)

____ detail — 2. How does a harbor seal pup learn to catch and eat fish in the sea? (by watching its mother)

____ vocabulary — 3. What does the word "temporarily" mean? (for a short time; not permanently)

____ vocabulary — 4. What does the word "captivity" mean? (the condition of being held as a prisoner or captive; confinement; a condition in which a person or animal is not free)

____ cause and effect/ inference — 5. What caused Pearson to need to be taught what a fish was and how to swallow it? (He didn't have a mother to show him.)

____ inference — 6. What is an oily fish that seals like? (herring)

____ cause and effect/ inference — 7. What causes harbor seals to swallow their food whole? (They have no teeth for grinding and chewing.)

____ sequence — 8. Name, in order, the two things that Pearson did the first time Holly put a fish in his mouth. (bit down on the fish and then spit it out)

____ inference — 9. How fast did Pearson learn how to eat a fish? (He learned on the second try.)

____ detail — 10. What made Pearson get friskier? (his new diet of fish and formula; his new diet)

INTRODUCTORY STATEMENT: Read this story to find out about Dave and what he wanted to do.

Dave wanted very much to succeed in athletics, but he was always afraid he would not quite make it. Last winter, in basketball, he had not. He spent more time on the bench than on the floor, much more. So, with spring, he had turned to track. Coach Stevens said he greatly needed a good quarter-miler, and Dave hoped to be that person.

The coach stressed that because Dave's legs were shorter than average he should work on lengthening his stride. To do that, the coach added, would require much practice and an equal amount of desire.

At first, Dave's father ruled out the road beside the railroad tracks for practice, but then he talked with Mr. Johnson. The old man assured the father that it would not be dangerous as long as Dave stayed well away from the tracks and used only the quiet road. Mr. Johnson also promised to "keep an eye" on the boy.

Source: From "Run for the Blue Ribbon," by Rafe Gibbs.

SCORING AID

Word Recognition
%–Miscues
99–2
95–8
90–16
85–24

Comprehension
%–Errors
100–0
90–1
80–2
70–3
60–4
50–5
40–6
30–7
20–8
10–9
0–10

157 Words
(for Word Recognition)

157 Words
(for Rate)

WPM
9420

COMPREHENSION QUESTIONS

____ main idea	1. Using your own words, tell me one sentence that describes what Dave had decided to try to do. (He had decided to try to be a quarter-miler in track.)
____ detail	2. How did Dave feel about athletics and his ability in athletics? (He wanted very much to succeed but was afraid he would not quite make it.)
____ sequence	3. Name, in order, the two sports Dave tried. (basketball and track)
____ inference	4. Was Dave good at basketball? (no) What does the story say that makes you believe that? (He spent more time on the bench than on the floor.)
____ cause and effect/ detail	5. Why did Dave need to work on lengthening his stride? (because his legs were shorter than average)
____ vocabulary	6. What does the phrase "lengthening his stride" mean? (taking longer steps)
____ inference	7. Did the coach believe it would be easy for Dave to lengthen his stride? (no) What did the story say that caused you to believe that? (The coach told him it would take much practice and desire.)
____ detail	8. How did Dave's father feel, at first, about him using the road beside the railroad tracks for practice? (He ruled it out.)
____ cause and effect/ inference	9. What caused Dave's father to change his mind? (talking with Mr. Johnson; Mr. Johnson telling him it would not be dangerous as long as Dave stayed well away from the tracks)
____ detail	10. What did Mr. Johnson promise Dave's father at the end of the story? (to "keep an eye" on Dave)

INTRODUCTORY STATEMENT: Read the following story to find out about some famous animals that live on Sable Island, which is in the Atlantic Ocean near Nova Scotia.

What did the first horses that came to Sable Island look like? We can only assume that they were much like farm horses anywhere in the world, but the harsh winters on Sable slowly changed the appearance of their descendants. They became smaller and stockier, had short ears, and in winter grew very long hair. Some stallions today have manes and tails so long that they nearly touch the ground.

Most of the horses live in small herds, each consisting of several mares and their foals and a stallion who protects them. The herd is usually led by a mare, but when two herds meet, the stallions trot toward each other, heads held high, tossing their long manes from side to side. Shoulder to shoulder, they push each other and neigh and nip a bit, but then, having proven that they are both powerful and unafraid, they proudly prance back to their herds.

This is what biologists call ritual fighting: it's mostly for show.

Source: From "The Wild Horses of Sable Island," by Fred Bruemmer. Reprinted from Owl Magazine with permission of the publisher, Bayard Presse Canada, Inc.

SCORING AID

Word Recognition

%–Miscues

99–2
95–8
90–16
85–25

Comprehension

%–Errors

100–0
90–1
80–2
70–3
60–4
50–5
40–6
30–7
20–8
10–9
0–10

164 Words
(for Word Recognition)

164 Words
(for Rate)

WPM
9840

COMPREHENSION QUESTIONS

____ main idea 1. What is the purpose of this story? (to describe the horses of Sable Island and the way they live)

____ inference 2. Do we know what the first horses that came to Sable Island looked like? (no) What did the story say that caused you to answer this way? (It says, "We can only *assume* that they were much like farm horses anywhere in the world.")

____ cause and effect/ detail 3. What can we assume caused the appearance of the descendants of the first Sable Island horses to change? (the harsh winters)

____ vocabulary 4. What are descendants? (their offspring; later generations of horses)

____ detail 5. How does the author say the horses changed? (They became smaller and stockier, had short ears, and in winter grew very long hair.) [Accept two out of the three changes as an adequate response.]

____ detail 6. How long are the manes and tails of some stallions today? (long enough to nearly touch the ground)

____ vocabulary 7. What is a foal? (a young horse)

____ inference 8. Do the stallions with the small herds really want to fight stallions from other herds? (no) What did the story say that caused you to answer this way? (They only neigh and nip a bit. It is mostly for show.)

____ sequence 9. Name, in order, three things the stallions from different herds do when they meet. (trot toward each other, push each other and neigh and nip a bit, proudly prance back to their herds) [Give full credit for the second step if any part of it is given.]

____ detail 10. What do biologists call this type of fighting? (ritual fighting)

INTRODUCTORY STATEMENT: Read this story to find out some interesting facts about elephants.

The perfect place to observe elephants is at a water hole, for elephants consume a great deal of water and must drink at least every second day to survive. An adult elephant will drink between forty and eighty gallons of water. If the water holes go dry, the elephants die. However, the elephant is the only creature besides a human being that can dig a water hole. I have witnessed such a feat in the dried-out Letaba River. The elephants wandered into the middle of the riverbed, and the strongest bulls and the largest females began to dig with their tusks and forefeet where they smelled water below. In half an hour, they had dug a four-foot-deep hole. They then inserted their trunks, and by sucking they created a vacuum that sipped up water from below. The water began to flow into their trunks through the soft sand. A new well had been created. We once photographed a whole sector full of elephant-made wells which had saved not only the elephants but all the other animals in the region, who did not possess the intellect and the strength of the resourceful elephants.

Source: "My Friends the Elephants," by Ivan Tors, in Leo Fay and others, *On Exhibit* (Chicago: The Riverside Publishing Company, 1989), pp. 145–146.

[*Note*: Do not count as a miscue mispronunciation of the word Letaba. You may pronounce this word for the student if needed.]

SCORING AID

Word Recognition

%–Miscues
99–2
95–10
90–20
85–29

Comprehension

%–Errors
100–0
90–1
80–2
70–3
60–4
50–5
40–6
30–7
20–8
10–9
0–10

191 Words (for Word Recognition)

192 Words (for Rate)

WPM
$\overline{)11520}$

COMPREHENSION QUESTIONS

____ main idea	1. What is the main idea of this story? (Water is very important to elephants; elephants are smart enough to obtain the water they need.)
____ detail	2. How often must elephants drink water to survive? (every second day)
____ vocabulary	3. What does the word "consume" mean in the statement "elephants consume a great deal of water"? (drink up)
____ detail	4. How much water will an adult elephant drink at once? (between forty and eighty gallons)
____ cause and effect/ detail	5. What would result if all the water holes went dry? (The elephants would die, or the elephants would dig wells.) [Accept either answer as correct.]
____ inference	6. How do elephants know where to dig water holes? (They can smell water in the ground.)
____ detail	7. What do elephants use to dig water holes? (their tusks and forefeet)
____ sequence	8. Name, in order, the next two things that the elephants in this story did after they dug a four-foot-deep hole. (They put their trunks in it and sucked the water through the sand.)
____ vocabulary	9. What does the word "created" mean? (made)
____ inference	10. Did animals besides elephants drink at the well? (yes) What did the story say that made you believe that? (They saved all the other animals in the region.)

INTRODUCTORY STATEMENT: Read to find out about a well-known singer from Tennessee, Dolly Parton.

Under showgirl make-up and a head of bleached blonde hair, Dolly is probably the most beautiful of the country singers. She's extremely well liked by other women, who are fond of saying, "Dolly's even more beautiful on the inside."

Dolly's childhood dreams were to be a country-music star, wear "flashy" clothes and have a tube of lipstick. Now she carries an extensive make-up collection in a tackle box and laughs infectiously at her own image.

"I always felt so ugly when I was little 'cause we never had nothing to fix up with and no pretty clothes. I once saw a lady with a lipstick and I thought she was a millionaire. I never doubted for a minute that I was gonna bring my music to Nashville, and I decided that when I did, I'd be real fancy."

Source: "Country Music's New Women," by Joan Drew, *Redbook Magazine*, January 1975.

SCORING AID

Word Recognition

%–Miscues

99–1
95–7
90–13
85–21

Comprehension

%–Errors

100–0
90–1
80–2
70–3
60–4
50–5
40–6
30–7
20–8
10–9
0–10

138 Words
(for Word Recognition)

138 Words
(for Rate)

WPM
8280

COMPREHENSION QUESTIONS

____ main idea	1. What is the main idea of this selection? (Dolly Parton achieved her childhood dreams; Dolly Parton is beautiful and successful.)
____ detail	2. How do other women feel about Dolly Parton? (They like her. They think she is "beautiful on the inside.")
____ vocabulary	3. What does "beautiful on the inside" mean as it is used in this selection? (a good person)
____ detail	4. What were Dolly's three childhood dreams? (to be a country-music star, wear flashy clothes, and have a tube of lipstick)
____ vocabulary	5. What does the word "extensive" mean in the phrase "extensive make-up collection"? (made up of many items)
____ detail	6. In what does Dolly carry her make-up collection? (tackle box)
____ vocabulary	7. What is the meaning of the word "infectiously" in the phrase "laughs infectiously"? (tending to spread easily or catch on)
____ cause and effect/ detail	8. Why did Dolly feel ugly as a child? (She had nothing to fix up with and had no pretty clothes.)
____ cause and effect/ detail	9. Why did Dolly think the lady was a millionaire? (She had lipstick.)
____ inference	10. Was Dolly sure that she would be a successful country-music star? (yes) What in the story caused you to answer that way? (She said, "I never doubted for a minute. . . .")

INTRODUCTORY STATEMENT: Read this story to find out about a woman who became a famous pilot—Amelia Earhart.

Earhart was away a lot, in his work as a claims agent, and sometimes he took his wife along with him. The result was that Amelia and her younger sister Muriel spent much of their childhood living with their grandparents. Amelia had a rich fantasy life, and lived adventurous summers exploring caves, playing baseball with equipment given to her by her father, reading Scott, Dickens, George Eliot; but she must have learned early on that she was essentially alone.

"I was a horrid little girl," she said later. "Perhaps the fact that I was exceedingly fond of reading made me endurable. With a large library to browse in, I spent many hours not bothering anyone after I once learned to read."

The family moved to Des Moines in 1907, apparently to escape the domination of the grandparents, and on her tenth birthday, Amelia saw her first airplane. That day, her father took her to the Iowa State Fair; it was only five years after the Wright Brothers had first flown at Kitty Hawk (incidentally, with money provided by a Wright sister) and airplanes were a great curiosity. Amelia, however, was not impressed.

Source: Reprinted from *Ms.* magazine with the permission of the author.

SCORING AID

Word Recognition

%–Miscues

99–3
95–10
90–20
85–29

Comprehension

%–Errors

100–0
90–1
80–2
70–3
60–4
50–5
40–6
30–7
20–8
10–9
0–10

192 Words
(for Word Recognition)

192 Words
(for Rate)

WPM
11520

COMPREHENSION QUESTIONS

____ main idea	1.	What is the purpose of this story? (to describe Amelia Earhart's early life and what she was like)
____ inference	2.	What was Amelia's father's occupation? (claims agent)
____ cause and effect/ inference	3.	Why did Amelia and her younger sister spend much of their childhood living with their grandparents? (Her father sometimes took her mother with him in his travels as a claims agent.)
____ inference	4.	Did Amelia have a good imagination? (yes) What did the story say that made you believe that? (She had a rich fantasy life.)
____ detail	5.	What kind of equipment did Amelia's father give her? (baseball equipment)
____ vocabulary	6.	What does the term "endurable" mean? (bearable; tolerable)
____ cause and effect/ detail	7.	Why did the family move to Des Moines in 1907? (apparently to escape the domination of the grandparents)
____ sequence	8.	What happened five years after the Wright Brothers first flew at Kitty Hawk? (Amelia saw her first airplane at the Iowa State Fair; Amelia's father took her to the Iowa State Fair) [If the second response is given, ask "What happened there?" Students should respond, "She saw her first airplane."]
____ detail	9.	Who supplied the money for the Wright Brother's first flight? (a Wright sister)
____ detail	10.	How did Amelia feel about the first airplane she saw? (She was not impressed.)

INTRODUCTORY STATEMENT: Read this story to find out some things Johnny Appleseed did.

There is some disagreement concerning the way in which Johnny went about planting apple trees in the wild frontier country. Some say that he scattered the seed as he went along the edges of marshes or natural clearings in the thick, almost tropical forests, others that he distributed the seeds among the settlers themselves to plant, and still others claim that in the damp land surrounding the marshes he established nurseries where he kept the seedlings until they were big enough to transplant. My Great-Aunt Mattie said that her father, who lived in a rather grand way for a frontier settler, had boxes of apples brought each year from Maryland until his own trees began to bear, and then he always saved the seeds, drying them on the shelf above the kitchen fireplace, to be put later into a box and kept for Johnny Appleseed when he came on one of his overnight visits.

Johnny scattered fennel seed all through our Ohio country, for when the trees were first cleared and the land plowed up, the mosquitoes increased and malaria spread from family to family. Johnny regarded a tea brewed of fennel leaves as a specific against what the settlers called "fever and ague," and he seeded the plant along trails and fence rows over all Ohio.

Source: "Johnny Appleseed and Aunt Mattie," by Louis Bromfield, in *Pleasant Valley* (New York: Harper and Row, 1945).

SCORING AID

Word Recognition
%–Miscues
99–3
95–12
90–22
85–33

Comprehension
%–Errors
100–0
90–1
80–2
70–3
60–4
50–5
40–6
30–7
20–8
10–9
0–10

217 Words
(for Word Recognition)

217 Words
(for Rate)

WPM
|13020

COMPREHENSION QUESTIONS

____ main idea — 1. What is the main idea of this story? (Johnny Appleseed planted apple trees and fennel seed.)

____ detail — 2. In what kind of country did Johnny plant trees? (wild frontier country; marshes; thick forests)

____ vocabulary — 3. What does the word "distributed" mean? (handed out to different people)

____ vocabulary — 4. What are the nurseries mentioned in the story? (places where trees, shrubs, and vines are grown until they are large enough to transplant)

____ inference — 5. Was Great-Aunt Mattie's father rich or poor? (rich) What in the story caused you to answer that way? (He lived in a grand way for a frontier settler and had boxes of apples brought from Maryland until his own trees began to bear.)

____ detail — 6. What did Great-Aunt Mattie's father save for Johnny? (seeds from his apples)

____ sequence — 7. Name, in order, the two things Great-Aunt Mattie's father did with the seeds. (He dried them on the shelf above the kitchen fireplace and then put them in a box.)

____ cause and effect/ inference — 8. What caused the spread of malaria through Ohio? (The increase in mosquitoes when the trees were first cleared and the land plowed up.)

____ inference — 9. What did the settlers call malaria? (fever and ague)

____ inference — 10. What did Johnny believe would help malaria sufferers? (a tea brewed of fennel leaves)

INTRODUCTORY STATEMENT: Read this story to find out all you can about an interesting and unusual man.

Punctually at midday he opened his bag and spread out his professional equipment, which consisted of a dozen cowrie shells, a square piece of cloth with obscure mystic charts on it, a notebook, and a bundle of palmyra writing. His forehead was resplendent with sacred ash and vermillion, and his eyes sparkled with a sharp abnormal gleam which was really an outcome of a continual searching look for customers, but which his simple clients took to be a prophetic light and felt comforted. The power of his eyes was considerably enhanced by their position—placed as they were between the painted forehead and the dark whiskers which streamed down his cheeks: even a half-wit's eyes would sparkle in such a setting. To crown the effect he wound a saffron-colored turban around his head. This color scheme never failed. People were attracted to him as bees are attracted to cosmos or dahlia stalks. He sat under the boughs of a spreading tamarind tree which flanked a path running through the Town Hall Park. It was a remarkable place in many ways: a surging crowd was always moving up and down this narrow road morning till night.

Source: "An Astrologer's Day," by R. K. Narayan, in *Tales from Modern India* (New York: Macmillan, 1973).

SCORING AID

Word Recognition

%–Miscues

99–2
95–10
90–20
85–30

Comprehension

%–Errors

100–0
90–1
80–2
70–3
60–4
50–5
40–6
30–7
20–8
10–9
0–10

195 Words
(for Word Recognition)

195 Words
(for Rate)

WPM
11700

COMPREHENSION QUESTIONS

____ main idea — 1. What is the main idea of this story?
(People are attracted to the fortune teller; people are attracted to the mystic.)

____ detail — 2. When did the man open his bag and spread out his professional equipment? (at midday)

____ vocabulary — 3. What does the word "resplendent" mean?
(shining brilliantly; lustrous; splendid)

____ cause and effect/detail — 4. What caused his eyes to sparkle with a sharp abnormal gleam?
(continually searching for customers)

____ vocabulary — 5. What does the word "enhanced" mean?
(intensified; added to the effectiveness of)

____ inference — 6. What attracted people to the man?
(the gleam in his eyes and the color scheme he used)

____ detail — 7. Where did the man sit?
(under the boughs of a tamarind tree beside a path)

____ detail — 8. What did the man wear on his head? (a saffron-colored turban; a turban)

____ inference — 9. Was the man in an isolated place? (no)
What did the story say that caused you to answer in that way?
("A surging crowd was always moving up and down this narrow road.")

____ vocabulary — 10. What does the word "surging" mean in the phrase "a surging crowd"?
(sweeping forward; rushing forward)

SUMMARY OF QUANTITATIVE ANALYSIS

Student's Name ______________________ **Grade** ______ **Date** ________ **Administrator** ______________________

Forms Used: Word Lists, Form ______ Oral Passages, Form ______ Silent Passages, Form ______ Listening Comprehension, Form ______

Performance Levels Based on Full Inventory (Oral & Silent): Independent ______ Instructional ______ Frustration ______ Listening Comprehension ______

Performance Levels Based on Oral Passages: Independent ______ Instructional ______ Frustration ______ Listening Comprehension ______

Performance Levels Based on Silent Passages: Independent ______ Instructional ______ Frustration ______ Listening Comprehension ______

Optional Comparison Levels: Independent ______ Instructional ______ Frustration ______ **Rate of Reading:** High ______ Average ______ Low ______

Performance Levels Based on Graded Word Lists: Placement ______ Independent ______ Instructional ______ Frustration ______

Types of Miscues in Context

	Mispronunciation	Substitution	Insertion	Omission	Reversal	Repetition	Refusal to Pronounce	Row Totals
Total								
Meaning changed								
Self-corrected								

Comprehension Skill Analysis Chart

Skill	Number of Questions	Number of Errors	Percent of Errors
Main idea			
Detail			
Sequence			
Cause and effect			
Inference			
Vocabulary			

Summary Table of Percentages

Level	Word Recognition	Oral Comprehension	Silent Comprehension	Average Comprehension	Listening Comprehension
PP					
P					
1					
2					
3					
4					
5					
6					
7					
8					
9					
10					
11					
12					

SUMMARY OF QUALITATIVE ANALYSIS

Summary of Strengths and Weaknesses in Word Recognition

(Include all of the important data that have been collected on word recognition skills.)

Summary of Strengths and Weaknesses in Comprehension

(Include all of the important data that have been collected about comprehension.)

Checklist of Reading Behaviors

(Place a [+] by areas that are strong and a [–] by areas that are weak.)

1. Reads in phrases _____
2. Reads with expression _____
3. Attends to punctuation _____
4. Pronounces words correctly _____
5. Sounds out unfamiliar words _____
6. Uses structure clues, when available, to recognize unfamiliar words _____
7. Uses context clues _____
8. Makes strategic attempts to recognize unfamiliar words (applies word recognition skills flexibly) _____
9. Keeps place in material being read _____
10. Shows few signs of tension when reading _____
11. Holds book at appropriate distance from face when reading _____
12. Self-corrects errors without prompting _____

WORKSHEET FOR WORD RECOGNITION MISCUE TALLY CHART

Miscue		PP	P	1	2	3	4	5	6	7	8	9	10	11	12	Totals
Mispronunciation	**A**															**A**
	MC															**MC**
	SC															**SC**
Substitution	**A**															**A**
	MC															**MC**
	SC															**SC**
Insertion	**A**															**A**
	MC															**MC**
	SC															**SC**
Omission	**A**															**A**
	MC															**MC**
	SC															**SC**
Reversal	**A**															**A**
	MC															**MC**
	SC															**SC**
Repetition	**A**															**A**
Refusal to pronounce	**A**															**A**
Totals	**A**															**A**
	MC															**MC**
	SC															**SC**

A = All miscues of that type (excluding ones that were self-corrected)
MC = Miscues that resulted in a meaning change
SC = Self-corrected miscues

Miscue Analysis of Phonic and Structural Analysis Skills

(Tally total miscues on appropriate lines.)

Miscue	For Words in Isolation	For Words in Context
Single consonants	______	______
Consonant blends	______	______
Single vowels	______	______
Vowel digraphs	______	______
Consonant digraphs	______	______
Diphthongs	______	______
Prefixes	______	______
Suffixes	______	______
Special combinations	______	______
Word beginnings	______	______
Word middles	______	______
Word endings	______	______
Compound words	______	______
Inflectional endings	______	______
Syllabication	______	______
Accent	______	______

(*Note*: In order to fill out the analysis for words in context, it is helpful to make a list of expected reader responses and unexpected responses for easy comparison as to graphic similarity, syntactic acceptability, and semantic acceptability. See page 108 for a good way to record this information.)

WORKSHEET FOR QUALITATIVE ANALYSIS OF UNCORRECTED MISCUES IN CONTEXT

(Include mispronunciations, substitutions, insertions, omissions, and reversals.)

Passage	Type of Miscue	Expected Response	Unexpected Response	Graphic Similarity	Syntactic Acceptability	Semantic Acceptability

GRADED PASSAGES

STUDENT BOOKLET FORM B

Passages PP to 12

Read this story to find out what Jane did.

Jane saw a dog.
He was big.
He was black.
"Here, dog!" said Jane.
"Play with me."

Jane threw a ball.
The dog ran after it.
He took the ball to Jane.
Jane laughed.
"This is fun," she said.

The dog barked.
Then he ran away.

"Do not go," Jane called.
But the dog went on.
Then Jane was sad.

Read this story to find out a problem that a girl has and what she decides to do.

Mother said, “Don’t leave the yard.”

I saw Pam. She came over. We played. Then she had to go.

“Come with me,” she said.

I did. I wanted to play. I left the yard. Bad idea.

Mother called me. I didn’t hear. I was not there.

I was with Pam. We were playing.

I made a mistake. I’m sorry. But it’s too late.

Now I can’t play with Pam. She can’t come over.

I’ll do better. Mother will see.

I’ll be good. I’ll follow rules.

Mother will be glad. She will change her mind.

Read this story to find out what a little girl named Beatrice did while she waited in the library for her brother, Henry, to come after her.

A woman started to read, "Alfred Mouse lived in a new house."

Beatrice looked out the window next to her.

The woman read some more, "Alfred Mouse had new skates."

Beatrice liked to skate.

"But Alfred's mother didn't like it when he skated in the house," read the woman.

The children laughed.

Beatrice thought about the time she had skated in her house.

Then at last Beatrice laughed.

She wanted to know all about Alfred.

When the story was over, Beatrice asked, "May I see that book?"

"Oh, yes," said the woman.
Beatrice looked at the book.

Henry came to get Beatrice.
"Time to go," he said to her.
Beatrice didn't stop reading.

This is a story about Ellie and her family. Read the story to find out what happened one day.

For Ellie, there was always Gram. It was Gram who was watching for Ellie when she got home from school. It was Gram who sat with her while she had her after-school snack. It was Gram who played with her and let her help get dinner ready.

When Mom came home from work, she was tired. And Ellie's big sister Lily always had homework to do.

But Gram was always there.

Then one day Mom sat down and talked with Ellie. "Gram is sick," said Mom. "She's in the hospital."

Gram sick? Gram was never sick!

"I don't want Gram to be sick!" Ellie cried. "I don't want her to be in the hospital. I want Gram to be home."

Read this story to find out what Tooter Pepperday and her family are doing.

"Bye, old house."

Chuckie waved as they drove off. He rode in the truck with his mother.

Tooter and her father followed in the car. Tooter did not wave. She did not even look. She grumped in the backseat.

The Pepperdays were moving to Aunt Sally's farm, two states and three hundred miles away. They were moving because they could live for free at Aunt Sally's.

Living for free was a good idea, because the Pepperdays did not have much money. Mr. Pepperday had quit his job, and Mrs. Pepperday did not earn much driving a school bus.

Aunt Sally had said they would all be "happy as hogs in slop."

Mr. Pepperday was happy. Now he could spend all his time writing books for children.

Mrs. Pepperday was happy. Now she could live on a farm.

Aunt Sally was happy. Now she would have help with the chores. And she could give more time to her beekeeping.

And Chuckie was happy. Now he would get to sleep with Harvey. Harvey was Aunt Sally's rusty, shaggy dog.

"I'm a hog in slop!" Chuckie kept laughing.

Everybody was happy but Tooter.

Sally Ride was America's first woman in space. Read this story to find out about one of her experiences.

The lift-off went well. The 100-ton blue and white ship flew up like a bird. Sally tried not to sound excited on the radio. But she said that her upward flight was like a trip to Disneyland.

Then it came time for everybody to go to work. The *Challenger* had to prove itself. It was like a truck that shipped things. Some of its customers were governments of other countries: Canada, Indonesia, and Germany.

Sally's most important job was to work with a long robot arm. With the arm she moved a packaged German laboratory out of the ship. Later, she reached out and caught it. Then she carefully pulled it back in again.

The group also did important work for Americans. They mixed metals that won't go together on earth. They made glass in sound waves. They started seeds to see how plants would grow. They even tried to learn whether the habits of ants would change in space.

Six days later, the ship landed. All over the world people cheered. Hundreds of news stories were written about Sally. She was asked to appear on many TV shows.

Read this selection to find out about one activity that is common in New Zealand.

New Zealand has a mild and rainy climate. This makes it a good place for sheep ranching. Even the steep sides of the mountains are used. Here, sure-footed sheep can graze where farm machinery cannot go.

New Zealand has about eighteen times as many sheep as it has people. The sheep are raised on large ranches called stations. During the summer, the sheep feed on the lush grass in the mountains. In late fall, they must be rounded up, or mustered. Then they are herded down to spend the winter months on the warmer lower slopes.

On a large station, thousands of sheep may be scattered over many mountain acres. The musterers cannot use horses on the steep mountainsides. With the help of well-trained dogs, they herd the flock, or mob, on foot.

The real work, however, begins in spring. Once again, the sheep are mustered. This time the mobs are herded down from the lower slopes to fenced-in pens. The lambs to be fattened for meat are separated from the others. The remaining thousands are moved into sheds where their thick wool is clipped, or sheared. This job is done by workers called shearers.

Link is a city boy who has come to the wilderness with his Aunt Harriet. He has been asked to do some photography for his uncle while he is there. Read the story to find out what Link does and how he feels about his situation.

He went to his room, got out his Uncle Albert's camera, and picked a 105 mm lens. There were only four exposures left on the roll of film, so he went outside and used them up taking pictures of the cabin. Then he reloaded the camera, tucked his aunt's bird guide in his pocket, and started off through the woods. There might be a sandhill crane at the old beaver pond. "Wet areas," Harriet had said. He might be lucky and get his pictures right away. If he did, he wouldn't say anything but wait until he got the developed slides back. He could put up with another week or so buried in the woods. Then Harriet wouldn't feel she had completely wasted her money having the cabin repaired.

He spent the next hour crouched beside the pond, trying to sit quietly, but it was almost impossible. Tiny insects buzzed around his face, crawled down his collar, and generally made him miserable. At first he tried to swat them but decided this was a waste of time. Finally he crawled underneath a low shrub and, with the leaves almost brushing his face, managed to find a little peace.

Read this selection to find out who the Anasazi are.

The story of the Anasazi at Mesa Verde begins before the Christian era. These early people were hunters and gatherers. The men hunted small game while the women gathered many varieties of plants and food. They roamed over the land searching for rabbits, piñon nuts, and other foods that the land had to offer. These people built small shelters and wove baskets in which to carry their possessions.

By A.D. 1 a great transformation had begun to take place. The Anasazi started to grow beans and squash. They no longer had to search all the time for food and could stay longer in one place. They constructed houses called pit houses on top of Mesa Verde or in the rock shelters along the canyon floor. The pit houses were not only to live in but were places in which to worship. Each house had a small hole in the floor called a sipapu. This was a very holy place, as it was where their ancestors emerged to live upon the earth.

Read this story to find out about a problem that developed during the Civil War.

The deserters came in droves. The Point Prospect campground was said to be swarming with soldiers who made forays on chicken coops, pigpens, and smokehouses where winter meat was hung. In the spring and summer, vegetable gardens, cornfields, and fruit orchards were robbed. No one dared to approach the camp. Even the U.S. agents from the cities upstate appeared to be in no hurry for a visit; it was known that the deserters carried their arms and that they were desperate. For a neighbor to have recognized a face among them might well have been sufficient reason for getting a bullet between the eyes; these men meant to take no chances with an informer.

The stories varied; some said there were a hundred men at Point Prospect; others put the number at nearer five hundred. In the early months of '63, the theft of food was their only crime against the community; by March, however, a killing took place.

Read to find out about some boys at work.

I was a delivery boy for Mr. Sasaki then. I had seen clerks come and go, and although they were of various sorts of temperaments and conducts, all of them had the technique of waiting on the customers or acquired one eventually. You could never tell about a new one, however, and to be on the safe side, I said nothing and watched our boss readily take on this young man. Anyhow we were glad to have an extra hand.

Mr. Sasaki undoubtedly remembered last year's rush when Tommy, Mr. Sasaki, and I had to do everything and had our hands tied behind our backs for having so many things to do at one time. He wanted to be ready this time. "Another clerk and we'll be all set for any kind of business," he used to tell us. When Teruo came around looking for a job, he got it, and Morning Glory Flower Shop was all set for the year as far as our boss was concerned.

When Teruo reported for work the following morning Mr. Sasaki left him in Tommy's hands. Tommy was our number one clerk for a long time.

Read this story to learn about an adventure three youths had over two hundred years ago.

First to discover what must stand as one of the greatest engineering achievements of its time were Jack Smith, Tony Vaughn, and Daniel McGinnis, three youths from nearby Lunenberg on Nova Scotia.

This trio landed from their canoe one day in 1795 and soon noticed, about four hundred feet from shore, a majestic oak from which a long lower limb projected over a depressed square of earth. The limb showed signs of block-and-tackle pressure; the depressed ground indicated that there had once been an excavation.

Next day the three returned to Oak Island equipped with shovels, axes, and picks. They began to dig. Ten feet down they hit something hard. It turned out to be a platform of six-inch-thick oak planks. Why was it there? To protect a golden treasure? The boys' imaginations were fired. Ten feet farther they hit another oaken barrier. Thirty feet down, a similar platform halted their progress.

The youths returned week after week to probe deeper into the pit until exhaustion forced them to postpone further digging. Back in Nova Scotia, they began asking guarded questions about the isle.

Read this story to learn about a boy's feelings for his father.

Slumped in his seat, he glared out of the window as the suburban bus jerked and shook its way through the downtown traffic. The usual hurrying shoppers pushed along, arms filled with packages; the usual harried policemen watched over the intersections; the usual drivers inched through the crowds to make their turns. All were preoccupied with the business of shopping for Christmas.

Ming wondered, and reproached himself even as he wondered, if he really cared any more than those strangers did that his father had died. This father of his had been little more than an old man with iron-gray hair that he saw occasionally on his Sunday trips home. Then it was nearly always only, "Hello, Pa," answered by an almost inaudible grunt as the old man hurried in from the restaurant to spend his two-hour rest period in bed. The dishwashing was bad for his rheumatism, Ming had heard him say many times, but you had to work when there were six children and a woman to feed. Really, there were only five since Ming was out working as a houseboy, but Ming had never corrected him.

Rosie was a Japanese-American girl whose mother started writing *haiku* poetry and even took the pen name Umé Hanazono. Read the story to find out how this affected Rosie's family life.

Umé Hanazono, who came to life after the dinner dishes were done, was an earnest, muttering stranger who often neglected speaking when spoken to and stayed busy at the parlor table as late as midnight scribbling with pencil on scratch paper or carefully copying characters on good paper with her fat, pale-green Parker.

This new interest had some repercussions on the household routine. Before, Rosie had been accustomed to her parents and herself taking their hot baths early and going to bed almost immediately afterwards, unless her parents challenged each other to a game of flower cards or unless company dropped in. Now, if her father wanted to play cards, he had to resort to solitaire (at which he always cheated fearlessly), and if a group of friends came over, it was bound to contain someone who was also writing *haiku,* and the small assemblage would be split in two, her father entertaining the non-literary members and her mother comparing ecstatic notes with the visiting poet.

GRADED PASSAGES

TEACHER BOOKLET FORM B

Passages and Questions
PP to 12

Summary Forms for Quantitative and Qualitative Analysis

Worksheets

INTRODUCTORY STATEMENT: Read this story to find out what Jane did.

Jane saw a dog.
He was big.
He was black.
"Here, dog!" said Jane.
"Play with me."

Jane threw a ball.
The dog ran after it.
He took the ball to Jane.
Jane laughed.
"This is fun," she said.

The dog barked.
Then he ran away.

"Do not go," Jane called.
But the dog went on.
Then Jane was sad.

[*Note*: Do not count as a miscue mispronunciation of the name Jane. You may pronounce this name for the student if necessary.]

SCORING AID

Word Recognition
%–Miscues
99–0
95–2
90–5
85–8

Comprehension
%–Errors
100–0
87.5–1
75–2
62.5–3
50–4
37.5–5
25–6
12.5–7
0–8

53 Words
(for Word Recognition)

60 Words
(for Rate)

WPM
3600

COMPREHENSION QUESTIONS

____ main idea	1. What is this story about? (Jane plays with a dog.)
____ detail	2. What did Jane see? (a dog)
____ detail	3. What did the dog look like? (He was big and black.)
____ inference	4. What did Jane and the dog play with? (a ball)
____ sequence	5. What did the dog do just after Jane threw the ball? (ran after it and brought it back to her) [Accept either part of this answer for full credit.]
____ inference	6. Did Jane enjoy playing with the dog? (yes) What does the story say that lets you know that? (She laughed; she said it was fun; she didn't want him to go.) [Any one part of the possible answer is sufficient for the answer to be considered correct.]
____ vocabulary	7. What does the word "barked" mean in this story? (the sound a dog makes) [Accept the imitation of the sound as correct.]
____ cause and effect/ inference	8. What caused Jane to be sad? (The dog went away.)

INTRODUCTORY STATEMENT: Read this story to find out a problem that a girl has and what she decides to do.

Mother said, "Don't leave the yard."
I saw Pam. She came over. We played. Then she had to go.
"Come with me," she said.
I did. I wanted to play. I left the yard. Bad idea.
Mother called me. I didn't hear. I was not there.
I was with Pam. We were playing.
I made a mistake. I'm sorry. But it's too late.
Now I can't play with Pam. She can't come over.
I'll do better. Mother will see.
I'll be good. I'll follow rules.
Mother will be glad. She will change her mind.

[*Note*: Do not count as a miscue mispronunciation of the name Pam. You may pronounce this name for the student if necessary.]

SCORING AID

Word Recognition
%–Miscues
99–1
95–5
90–9
85–14

Comprehension
%–Errors
100–0
87.5–1
75–2
62.5–3
50–4
37.5–5
25–6
12.5–7
0–8

91 Words
(for Word Recognition)

94 Words
(for Rate)

WPM
5640

COMPREHENSION QUESTIONS

____ main idea	1. What is this story about? (A girl makes a mistake; a girl disobeys her mother.)
____ sequence	2. What was the first thing that happened in the story? (The girl's mother told her not to leave the yard.)
____ cause and effect/ inference	3. Why did the girl leave the yard? (She wanted to play with Pam; Pam asked the girl to come with her.)
____ sequence	4. What happened when the girl's mother called her? (She didn't hear.)
____ detail	5. How did the girl feel about what she had done? (She was sorry.)
____ vocabulary	6. What is a mistake? (an error; something that a person does that is wrong)
____ inference	7. What was the girl's punishment? (She can't play with Pam, and Pam can't come over.)
____ cause and effect/ inference	8. What caused the girl to decide to follow rules? (She wanted her mother to change her mind; she wanted to see Pam again.)

INTRODUCTORY STATEMENT: Read this story to find out what a little girl named Beatrice did while she waited in the library for her brother, Henry, to come after her.

A woman started to read, "Alfred Mouse lived in a new house."
Beatrice looked out the window next to her.

The woman read some more, "Alfred Mouse had new skates."
Beatrice liked to skate.
"But Alfred's mother didn't like it when he skated in the house," read the woman.
The children laughed.

Beatrice thought about the time she had skated in her house.
Then at last Beatrice laughed.
She wanted to know all about Alfred.

When the story was over, Beatrice asked, "May I see that book?"

"Oh, yes," said the woman.
Beatrice looked at the book.

Henry came to get Beatrice.
"Time to go," he said to her.
Beatrice didn't stop reading.

SCORING AID

Word Recognition
%–Miscues
99–1
95–5
90–10
85–15

Comprehension
%–Errors
100–0
87.5–1
75–2
62.5–3
50–4
37.5–5
25–6
12.5–7
0–8

98 Words
(for Word Recognition)

113 Words
(for Rate)

WPM
6780

Source: "Beatrice," by Laura Joffe Numeroff, in William K. Durr and others, *Carousels* (Boston: Houghton Mifflin Company, 1989), pp. 20–22.

[*Note*: Do not count as miscues mispronunciation of the names Beatrice, Alfred Mouse, and Henry. You may pronounce these names for the student if needed.]

COMPREHENSION QUESTIONS

____ main idea
1. What is this story about? (Beatrice gets interested in reading; Beatrice wants to read; Beatrice wants to read [or reads] about Alfred Mouse.)

____ inference
2. Was Beatrice interested in the story about Alfred Mouse when the woman first started to read it? (no)
What did the story say that made you believe that?
(She was looking out the window.)

____ vocabulary
3. What are skates?
(shoes that have wheels on them, or wheels that you put on your shoes)

____ inference
4. What part of the story made Beatrice want to listen to the woman read?
(the part about skating)

____ sequence
5. What did the children do just after the woman read that Alfred's mother didn't like it when he skated in the house? (They laughed.)

____ cause and effect/ inference
6. What finally caused Beatrice to laugh?
(She thought about the time she had skated in her house.)

____ sequence
7. What did Beatrice do first after the story that the woman read was over?
(She asked the woman if she could see the book.)

____ detail
8. What did Henry say to Beatrice when he came to get her?
("Time to go.")

INTRODUCTORY STATEMENT: This is a story about Ellie and her family. Read the story to find out what happened one day.

For Ellie, there was always Gram. It was Gram who was watching for Ellie when she got home from school. It was Gram who sat with her while she had her after-school snack. It was Gram who played with her and let her help get dinner ready.

When Mom came home from work, she was tired. And Ellie's big sister Lily always had homework to do.

But Gram was always there.

Then one day Mom sat down and talked with Ellie. "Gram is sick," said Mom. "She's in the hospital."

Gram sick? Gram was never sick!

"I don't want Gram to be sick!" Ellie cried. "I don't want her to be in the hospital. I want Gram to be home."

Source: From *I Love Gram*, by Ruth A. Sonneborn, 1971.

[*Note*: Do not count as miscues mispronunciation of the names Ellie, Lily, and Gram. You may pronounce these names for the student if necessary.]

SCORING AID

Word Recognition

%–Miscues

99–1
95–5
90–10
85–16

Comprehension

%–Errors

100–0
87.5–1
75–2
62.5–3
50–4
37.5–5
25–6
12.5–7
0–8

104 Words
(for Word Recognition)

120 Words
(for Rate)

WPM
7200

COMPREHENSION QUESTIONS

____ main idea	1. What is this story about? (Ellie is upset when Gram gets sick; Gram is important to Ellie.)
____ inference	2. Who did the most things with Ellie? (Gram)
____ sequence	3. What was the first thing that Gram did with Ellie after she got home from school? (sat with her while she had her after-school snack)
____ vocabulary	4. What is a snack? (a little bit of food; a small meal; something to eat between meals)
____ cause and effect/ inference	5. Why was Mom tired in the evening? (because she had worked all day)
____ detail	6. What did Lily always have to do? (homework)
____ inference	7. Was Gram away from home often? (no) What did the story say that made you believe that? (It said, "Gram was always there.")
____ detail	8. Who told Ellie that Gram was sick? (Mom)

INTRODUCTORY STATEMENT: Read this story to find out what Tooter Pepperday and her family are doing.

"Bye, old house."

Chuckie waved as they drove off. He rode in the truck with his mother.

Tooter and her father followed in the car. Tooter did not wave. She did not even look. She grumped in the backseat.

The Pepperdays were moving to Aunt Sally's farm, two states and three hundred miles away. They were moving because they could live for free at Aunt Sally's.

Living for free was a good idea, because the Pepperdays did not have much money. Mr. Pepperday had quit his job, and Mrs. Pepperday did not earn much driving a school bus.

Aunt Sally had said they would all be "happy as hogs in slop."

Mr. Pepperday was happy. Now he could spend all his time writing books for children.

Mrs. Pepperday was happy. Now she could live on a farm.

Aunt Sally was happy. Now she would have help with the chores. And she could give more time to her beekeeping.

And Chuckie was happy. Now he would get to sleep with Harvey. Harvey was Aunt Sally's rusty, shaggy dog.

"I'm a hog in slop!" Chuckie kept laughing.

Everybody was happy but Tooter.

Source: *Tooter Pepperday*, by Jerry Spinelli (New York: Random House, 1995), pp. 7–8.

[*Note*: Do not count as miscues mispronunciation of the names Chuckie, Tooter, Pepperday (or Pepperdays), or Harvey. You may pronounce these names for the student if necessary.]

SCORING AID

Word Recognition

%–Miscues
99–1
95–8
90–17
85–26

Comprehension

%–Errors
100–0
90–1
80–2
70–3
60–4
50–5
40–6
30–7
20–8
10–9
0–10

176 Words
(for Word Recognition)

190 Words
(for Rate)

WPM
11400

COMPREHENSION QUESTIONS

____ main idea 1. What is the main idea of this story? (Tooter's family is moving, and she is unhappy about it.)

____ sequence 2. When did Chuckie wave goodbye? (at the beginning of the story; as they drove away from their old home.) [Accept either answer for full credit.]

____ inference 3. What mood was Tooter in? (bad; grumpy)

____ cause and effect/ detail 4. Why did the Pepperdays not have much money? (Mr. Pepperday had quit his job, and Mrs. Pepperday did not earn much driving a school bus.) [Both reasons must be given for full credit. If a student gives only one, ask, "Anything else?" Give half credit for either one alone.]

____ vocabulary 5. What does "as happy as hogs in slop" mean? (very happy)

____ cause and effect/ inference 6. What caused Mr. Pepperday to be happy? (He could spend his time writing books for children.)

____ inference 7. Had the Pepperdays lived on a farm before they moved? (no) How did you know? (The story says that now Mrs. Pepperday could live on a farm.)

____ inference 8. Who lived on Aunt Sally's farm before Tooter's family moved in? (just Aunt Sally or Aunt Sally and Harvey) [Count either of these answers for full credit.]

____ detail 9. Who was Harvey? (Aunt Sally's dog)

____ detail 10. What did Harvey look like? (He was rusty and shaggy.)

INTRODUCTORY STATEMENT: Sally Ride was America's first woman in space. Read this story to find out about one of her experiences.

The lift-off went well. The 100-ton blue and white ship flew up like a bird. Sally tried not to sound excited on the radio. But she said that her upward flight was like a trip to Disneyland.

Then it came time for everybody to go to work. The *Challenger* had to prove itself. It was like a truck that shipped things. Some of its customers were governments of other countries: Canada, Indonesia, and Germany.

Sally's most important job was to work with a long robot arm. With the arm she moved a packaged German laboratory out of the ship. Later, she reached out and caught it. Then she carefully pulled it back in again.

The group also did important work for Americans. They mixed metals that won't go together on earth. They made glass in sound waves. They started seeds to see how plants would grow. They even tried to learn whether the habits of ants would change in space.

Six days later, the ship landed. All over the world people cheered. Hundreds of news stories were written about Sally. She was asked to appear on many TV shows.

Source: "Sally Ride," by Marie Cocinero, in Elizabeth Sulzby and others, *This We Wish* (New York: McGraw-Hill School Division, 1989), pp. 363–364.

[*Note*: Do not count as a miscue mispronunciation of the word Indonesia. You may pronounce this word for the student if needed.]

SCORING AID

Word Recognition

%–Miscues
99–2
95–10
90–19
85–29

Comprehension

%–Errors
100–0
90–1
80–2
70–3
60–4
50–5
40–6
30–7
20–8
10–9
0–10

188 Words (for Word Recognition)

189 Words (for Rate)

WPM
11340

COMPREHENSION QUESTIONS

____ main idea 1. What is this story about? (Sally Ride goes on a trip into space on the *Challenger*; astronauts work during a trip into space on the *Challenger*.)

____ vocabulary 2. What does the term "lift-off" mean? (leaving the ground; rising up into the air)

____ detail 3. How heavy was the blue and white ship? (100 tons)

____ inference 4. Was the lift-off exciting? (yes) What did the story say that made you think that? (She tried not to sound excited. It was like a trip to Disneyland.)

____ sequence 5. What was the first thing that happened after the lift-off? (Everybody had to go to work.)

____ detail 6. What was Sally's most important job? (working with a robot arm)

____ sequence 7. Name, in order, three things Sally did with the robot arm. (moved a packaged German laboratory out of the ship, then reached out and caught it, then carefully pulled it back in)

____ detail 8. What did they do with metals? (They mixed ones that won't go together on earth.)

____ inference 9. How long did the space flight last? (six days)

____ cause and effect/ inference 10. Why did people cheer when the ship landed? (because the space travelers had returned safely; because travel in space is dangerous)

INTRODUCTORY STATEMENT: Read this selection to find out about one activity that is common in New Zealand.

New Zealand has a mild and rainy climate. This makes it a good place for sheep ranching. Even the steep sides of the mountains are used. Here, sure-footed sheep can graze where farm machinery cannot go.

New Zealand has about eighteen times as many sheep as it has people. The sheep are raised on large ranches called stations. During the summer, the sheep feed on the lush grass in the mountains. In late fall, they must be rounded up, or mustered. Then they are herded down to spend the winter months on the warmer lower slopes.

On a large station, thousands of sheep may be scattered over many mountain acres. The musterers cannot use horses on the steep mountainsides. With the help of well-trained dogs, they herd the flock, or mob, on foot.

The real work, however, begins in spring. Once again, the sheep are mustered. This time the mobs are herded down from the lower slopes to fenced-in pens. The lambs to be fattened for meat are separated from the others. The remaining thousands are moved into sheds where their thick wool is clipped, or sheared. This job is done by workers called shearers.

Source: "New Zealand," in William K. Durr and others, *Explorations* (Boston: Houghton Mifflin Company, 1989), pp. 388–389.

SCORING AID

Word Recognition
%–Miscues
99–3
95–10
90–20
85–30

Comprehension
%–Errors
100–0
90–1
80–2
70–3
60–4
50–5
40–6
30–7
20–8
10–9
0–10

195 Words
(for Word Recognition)

195 Words
(for Rate)

WPM
$\overline{)11700}$

COMPREHENSION QUESTIONS

____ main idea — 1. What is the purpose of this story? (to tell what sheep ranching in New Zealand is like)

____ detail — 2. What kind of climate does New Zealand have? (mild and rainy)

____ vocabulary — 3. What does the word "stations" mean in this article? (large ranches where sheep are raised)

____ vocabulary — 4. What does the word "mustered" mean in this article? (rounded up)

____ inference — 5. What is the temperature like high in the mountains? (It is cooler than it is on the lower slopes.)

____ cause and effect/ inference — 6. What causes the workers to muster the sheep on foot? (Horses can't keep their footing on the steep mountainsides.)

____ detail — 7. What kind of help do the musterers have in herding the sheep? (well-trained dogs; dogs)

____ vocabulary — 8. What is a flock of sheep sometimes called? (a mob)

____ sequence — 9. Name, in order, three things that happen when the sheep are mustered in the spring. (They are herded into pens; then lambs to be fattened for meat are separated from the others; the others are moved into sheds; then they are sheared.) [Accept any three of the four items as long as they are in order.]

____ detail — 10. Who clips the sheep's thick wool? (workers called shearers; shearers)

INTRODUCTORY STATEMENT: Link is a city boy who has come to the wilderness with his Aunt Harriet. He has been asked to do some photography for his uncle while he is there. Read the story to find out what Link does and how he feels about his situation.

He went to his room, got out his Uncle Albert's camera, and picked a 105 mm lens. There were only four exposures left on the roll of film, so he went outside and used them up taking pictures of the cabin. Then he reloaded the camera, tucked his aunt's bird guide in his pocket, and started off through the woods. There might be a sandhill crane at the old beaver pond. "Wet areas," Harriet had said. He might be lucky and get his pictures right away. If he did, he wouldn't say anything but wait until he got the developed slides back. He could put up with another week or so buried in the woods. Then Harriet wouldn't feel she had completely wasted her money having the cabin repaired.

He spent the next hour crouched beside the pond, trying to sit quietly, but it was almost impossible. Tiny insects buzzed around his face, crawled down his collar, and generally made him miserable. At first he tried to swat them but decided this was a waste of time. Finally he crawled underneath a low shrub and, with the leaves almost brushing his face, managed to find a little peace.

Source: From *In Search of a Sandhill Crane*, by Keith Robertson.

SCORING AID

Word Recognition

%–Miscues
99–2
95–10
90–20
85–30

Comprehension

%–Errors
100–0
90–1
80–2
70–3
60–4
50–5
40–6
30–7
20–8
10–9
0–10

198 Words (for Word Recognition)

198 Words (for Rate)

WPM
11880

COMPREHENSION QUESTIONS

____ main idea — 1. What is the main idea of this story? (Link tries to get a picture of a sandhill crane; Link tries to take pictures in the woods.)

____ detail — 2. Whose camera was Link using? (his Uncle Albert's; his uncle's)

____ sequence — 3. What was the next thing Link did after he picked a lens? (went outside and took pictures of the cabin)

____ cause and effect/ inference — 4. Why did Link use up the four pictures on the cabin? (He wanted to take the camera to the woods with a full load of film.)

____ detail — 5. What did Link put in his pocket before he started for the woods? (his aunt's bird guide)

____ inference — 6. Why would Link want to take a bird book with him? (so he could recognize a sandhill crane; so he could recognize different kinds of birds)

____ inference — 7. Did Link like the woods? (no) What did the story say that made you believe that? (He thought he could put up with another week or so "buried in the woods." The insects made him miserable.)

____ inference — 8. Was Link considerate of his Aunt Harriet? (yes) What did the story say that made you believe that? (He was going to put up with the woods for another week or so, so that she wouldn't feel she had wasted her money.)

____ vocabulary — 9. What does the word "crouched" mean? (stooped down; bent down low)

____ inference — 10. Did swatting the insects keep them away? (no) What did the story say that made you believe that? (He decided that swatting them was a waste of time.)

INTRODUCTORY STATEMENT: Read this selection to find out who the Anasazi are.

The story of the Anasazi at Mesa Verde begins before the Christian era. These early people were hunters and gatherers. The men hunted small game while the women gathered many varieties of plants and food. They roamed over the land searching for rabbits, piñon nuts, and other foods that the land had to offer. These people built small shelters and wove baskets in which to carry their possessions.

By A.D. 1 a great transformation had begun to take place. The Anasazi started to grow beans and squash. They no longer had to search all the time for food and could stay longer in one place. They constructed houses called pit houses on top of Mesa Verde or in the rock shelters along the canyon floor. The pit houses were not only to live in but were places in which to worship. Each house had a small hole in the floor called a sipapu. This was a very holy place, as it was where their ancestors emerged to live upon the earth.

Source: "The People of Mesa Verde," by Gregory R. Campbell, in Elizabeth Sulzby and others, *Star to Star* (New York: McGraw-Hill Publishing Company, 1989), pp. 124–125.

[*Note*: Do not count as miscues mispronunciation of the words Anasazi, Mesa Verde, and sipapu. You may pronounce these words for the student if needed.]

SCORING AID

Word Recognition
%–Miscues

99–2
95–9
90–17
85–25

Comprehension
%–Errors

100–0
90–1
80–2
70–3
60–4
50–5
40–6
30–7
20–8
10–9
0–10

165 Words
(for Word Recognition)

172 Words
(for Rate)

WPM
10320

COMPREHENSION QUESTIONS

____ main idea	1.	What is the main idea of this selection? (The Anasazi changed from hunters and gatherers to farmers.)
____ sequence	2.	What did the Anasazi start to make after they started to grow crops? (pit houses; houses)
____ detail	3.	Who did the hunting? (the men)
____ vocabulary	4.	What does the term "small game" mean in the statement "The men hunted small game"? (small animals to be used for food; small animals)
____ inference	5.	What were some of the foods that the Anasazi ate when they were gatherers? (rabbits and piñon nuts)
____ inference	6.	Who collected the piñon nuts for the people? (the women)
____ cause and effect/ inference	7.	Why did the Anasazi stop roaming from place to place as much? (because they learned to grow food)
____ detail	8.	What crops did the Anasazi start to grow? (beans and squash)
____ detail	9.	What purpose did the pit houses serve besides being places to live? (They were places of worship.)
____ vocabulary	10.	What are ancestors? (forefathers; parents, grandparents, etc.)

INTRODUCTORY STATEMENT: Read this story to find out about a problem that developed during the Civil War.

The deserters came in droves. The Point Prospect campground was said to be swarming with soldiers who made forays on chicken coops, pigpens, and smokehouses where winter meat was hung. In the spring and summer, vegetable gardens, cornfields, and fruit orchards were robbed. No one dared to approach the camp. Even the U.S. agents from the cities upstate appeared to be in no hurry for a visit; it was known that the deserters carried their arms and that they were desperate. For a neighbor to have recognized a face among them might well have been sufficient reason for getting a bullet between the eyes; these men meant to take no chances with an informer.

The stories varied; some said there were a hundred men at Point Prospect; others put the number at nearer five hundred. In the early months of '63, the theft of food was their only crime against the community; by March, however, a killing took place.

Source: From *Across Five Aprils*, by Irene Hunt. © 1991 by Modern Curriculum Press, Simon & Schuster Education Group. Used by permission.

SCORING AID

Word Recognition

%–Miscues
99–2
95–10
90–20
85–29

Comprehension

%–Errors
100–0
90–1
80–2
70–3
60–4
50–5
40–6
30–7
20–8
10–9
0–10

159 Words (for Word Recognition)

159 Words (for Rate)

WPM
9540

COMPREHENSION QUESTIONS

____ main idea — 1. What is the main idea of this story? (The deserters were dangerous; the deserters committed crimes and frightened people.)

____ vocabulary — 2. What are deserters? (people who run away from service in the army without intending to return)

____ vocabulary — 3. What does the word "droves" mean in this story? (large groups of people)

____ detail — 4. Where did the deserters stay? (the Point Prospect campground)

____ detail — 5. How did the soldiers get their food? (They stole it.)

____ cause and effect/ inference — 6. Why did people stay away from the camp? (because they were afraid of being killed)

____ vocabulary — 7. What does the word "arms" in the phrase "deserters carried their arms" mean? (weapons)

____ inference — 8. Were the deserters glad to see people that they knew? (no) What does the story say that caused you to believe that? ("For a neighbor to have recognized a face among them might well have been sufficient reason for getting a bullet between the eyes; these men meant to take no chances with an informer.") [It is not necessary for the student to use the exact words.]

____ detail — 9. How many men did people say were at Point Prospect? (Some said 100; others put the number at nearer 500.)

____ sequence — 10. What was the last crime of the deserters against the community that is mentioned in the story? (a killing)

INTRODUCTORY STATEMENT: Read to find out about some boys at work.

I was a delivery boy for Mr. Sasaki then. I had seen clerks come and go, and although they were of various sorts of temperaments and conducts, all of them had the technique of waiting on the customers or acquired one eventually. You could never tell about a new one, however, and to be on the safe side, I said nothing and watched our boss readily take on this young man. Anyhow we were glad to have an extra hand.

Mr. Sasaki undoubtedly remembered last year's rush when Tommy, Mr. Sasaki, and I had to do everything and had our hands tied behind our backs for having so many things to do at one time. He wanted to be ready this time. "Another clerk and we'll be all set for any kind of business," he used to tell us. When Teruo came around looking for a job, he got it, and Morning Glory Flower Shop was all set for the year as far as our boss was concerned.

When Teruo reported for work the following morning Mr. Sasaki left him in Tommy's hands. Tommy was our number one clerk for a long time.

Source: "Say it With Flowers," by Toshio Mori, from *Yokohama, California* (Caldwell, Idaho: Caxton Printers, 1949).

[*Note*: Do not count as miscues mispronunciation of the names Sasaki or Teruo. These names may be pronounced for the student if needed.]

SCORING AID

Word Recognition

%–Miscues
99–2
95–10
90–19
85–29

Comprehension

%–Errors
100–0
90–1
80–2
70–3
60–4
50–5
40–6
30–7
20–8
10–9
0–10

187 Words (for Word Recognition)

193 Words (for Rate)

WPM
/11580

COMPREHENSION QUESTIONS

____ main idea — 1. What is the main idea of this story? (Mr. Sasaki hires a new clerk; a new clerk is hired at the flower shop.)

____ detail — 2. What was the writer's job? (delivery boy)

____ inference — 3. Had there been several other clerks for Mr. Sasaki? (yes) What in the story caused you to answer that way? (The writer said he had seen clerks come and go.)

____ vocabulary — 4. What is the meaning of the word "temperaments" in the phrase "various sorts of temperaments and conducts"? (disposition; personality)

____ detail — 5. What did all clerks know or learn? (technique of waiting on customers)

____ vocabulary — 6. What is the meaning of the word "eventually"? (at last; finally)

____ sequence — 7. What did the writer do after a new clerk was hired? (said nothing; watched the boss with him)

____ cause and effect/detail — 8. Why did Tommy, Mr. Sasaki, and the writer have their "hands tied behind their backs"? (They had so many things to do at one time.)

____ inference — 9. What was Mr. Sasaki's business? (flower shop)

____ inference — 10. Why did Mr. Sasaki assign Teruo to Tommy? (Tommy was the number one clerk.)

INTRODUCTORY STATEMENT: Read this story to learn about an adventure three youths had over two hundred years ago.

First to discover what must stand as one of the greatest engineering achievements of its time were Jack Smith, Tony Vaughn, and Daniel McGinnis, three youths from nearby Lunenberg on Nova Scotia.

This trio landed from their canoe one day in 1795 and soon noticed, about four hundred feet from shore, a majestic oak from which a long lower limb projected over a depressed square of earth. The limb showed signs of block-and-tackle pressure; the depressed ground indicated that there had once been an excavation.

Next day the three returned to Oak Island equipped with shovels, axes, and picks. They began to dig. Ten feet down they hit something hard. It turned out to be a platform of six-inch-thick oak planks. Why was it there? To protect a golden treasure? The boys' imaginations were fired. Ten feet farther they hit another oaken barrier. Thirty feet down, a similar platform halted their progress.

The youths returned week after week to probe deeper into the pit until exhaustion forced them to postpone further digging. Back in Nova Scotia, they began asking guarded questions about the isle.

Source: Adapted from "The Buried Treasure of Oak Island," by Ralph H. Major, Jr., *Coronet*, July 1954. Adapted from "The Mystery of Oak Island" by Ron Rosenbaum. First published in *Esquire* Magazine.

SCORING AID

Word Recognition

%–Miscues
99–3
95–10
90–19
85–28

Comprehension

%–Errors
100–0
90–1
80–2
70–3
60–4
50–5
40–6
30–7
20–8
10–9
0–10

184 Words (for Word Recognition)

184 Words (for Rate)

WPM
11040

COMPREHENSION QUESTIONS

____ main idea — 1. What is the main idea of this story? (Three boys dig for a treasure; three boys hope to find treasure on Oak Island.)

____ detail — 2. Where did the three youths live? (Nova Scotia)

____ vocabulary — 3. What does the word "depressed" mean in the phrase "the depressed ground"? (pressed down; sunken)

____ vocabulary — 4. What does the word "excavation" mean? (dug out or hollowed out area; an area from which dirt had been removed)

____ detail — 5. What kinds of equipment did the youths use? (shovels, axes, picks) [Accept two of the three for full credit; accept one of the three for half credit.]

____ cause and effect/ detail — 6. What caused the boys to think they might have found a buried treasure? (They hit oaken barriers or platforms of oak planks.)

____ detail — 7. How many feet down did the boys hit the third platform? (thirty feet)

____ sequence — 8. What was the last thing the boys did in this story? (began asking questions about the isle)

____ vocabulary — 9. What does the word "guarded" mean in the term "guarded questions"? (watchful; careful; cautious)

____ inference — 10. Did the boys seem to be planning to return to the island? (yes) What facts in the story caused you to answer that way? (They asked questions about the island. They only postponed further digging, which indicates they hadn't given up.)

INTRODUCTORY STATEMENT: Read this story to learn about a boy's feelings for his father.

Slumped in his seat, he glared out of the window as the suburban bus jerked and shook its way through the downtown traffic. The usual hurrying shoppers pushed along, arms filled with packages; the usual harried policemen watched over the intersections; the usual drivers inched through the crowds to make their turns. All were preoccupied with the business of shopping for Christmas.

Ming wondered, and reproached himself even as he wondered, if he really cared any more than those strangers did that his father had died. This father of his had been little more than an old man with iron-gray hair that he saw occasionally on his Sunday trips home. Then it was nearly always only, "Hello, Pa," answered by an almost inaudible grunt as the old man hurried in from the restaurant to spend his two-hour rest period in bed. The dishwashing was bad for his rheumatism, Ming had heard him say many times, but you had to work when there were six children and a woman to feed. Really, there were only five since Ming was out working as a houseboy, but Ming had never corrected him.

Source: Number One Son, by Monfoon Leong (San Francisco, Calif.: Donaldina Cameron House, 1975).

SCORING AID

Word Recognition
%–Miscues
99–2
95–10
90–19
85–29

Comprehension
%–Errors
100–0
90–1
80–2
70–3
60–4
50–5
40–6
30–7
20–8
10–9
0–10

190 Words
(for Word Recognition)

190 Words
(for Rate)

WPM
$\overline{)11400}$

COMPREHENSION QUESTIONS

____ main idea	1.	What is the main idea of this story? (Ming thinks about his father; Ming considers his feelings about his father.)
____ inference	2.	Was Ming happy at the beginning of this story? (no) What in the story caused you to answer that way? (Ming slumped in his seat, glared out the window, and wondered about his father's death.)
____ vocabulary	3.	What does the word "harried" mean in the phrase "harried policemen"? (worried, annoyed, harassed)
____ detail	4.	Why were there many people downtown? (Christmas shopping)
____ vocabulary	5.	What does the word "reproached" mean in the phrase "reproached himself"? (blamed, rebuked, chided)
____ inference	6.	Were Ming and his father close friends? (no) What in the story caused you to answer that way? (Ming wondered if he cared about his father's death; when they were together, they didn't talk much.)
____ inference	7.	Did Ming live with his father? (no) What in the story caused you to answer that way? (He saw him only on his Sunday trips home; he was out working as a houseboy.)
____ vocabulary	8.	What does the word "inaudible" mean in the phrase "inaudible grunt"? (not heard)
____ sequence	9.	What would Ming's father do immediately after coming in from the restaurant? (He'd rest in bed.)
____ cause and effect/ detail	10.	What did Ming's father say caused his rheumatism to be bad? (dishwashing)

TEACHER 12 ★

INTRODUCTORY STATEMENT: Rosie was a Japanese-American girl whose mother started writing *haiku* poetry and even took the pen name Umé Hanazono. Read the story to find out how this affected Rosie's family life.

Umé Hanazono, who came to life after the dinner dishes were done, was an earnest, muttering stranger who often neglected speaking when spoken to and stayed busy at the parlor table as late as midnight scribbling with pencil on scratch paper or carefully copying characters on good paper with her fat, pale-green Parker.

This new interest had some repercussions on the household routine. Before, Rosie had been accustomed to her parents and herself taking their hot baths early and going to bed almost immediately afterwards, unless her parents challenged each other to a game of flower cards or unless company dropped in. Now, if her father wanted to play cards, he had to resort to solitaire (at which he always cheated fearlessly), and if a group of friends came over, it was bound to contain someone who was also writing *haiku,* and the small assemblage would be split in two, her father entertaining the non-literary members and her mother comparing ecstatic notes with the visiting poet.

Source: From "Seventeen Syllables," by Hisaye Yamamoto.

[*Note*: Do not count as a miscue mispronunciation of the name Umé Hanazono. You may pronounce this name for the student if needed.]

SCORING AID

Word Recognition

%–Miscues

99–2
95–9
90–17
85–25

Comprehension

%–Errors

100–0
90–1
80–2
70–3
60–4
50–5
40–6
30–7
20–8
10–9
0–10

164 Words
(for Word Recognition)

166 Words
(for Rate)

WPM
9960

COMPREHENSION QUESTIONS

____ main idea — 1. What is the main idea of this story? (Rosie's mother [Umé Hanazono] was totally wrapped up in her poetry after the dinner dishes were done in the evening.)

____ sequence — 2. What did Umé Hanazono do immediately after the dinner dishes were done? (sat at the parlor table and wrote)

____ inference — 3. What was Umé Hanazono writing at the parlor table after dinner? (*haiku*)

____ inference — 4. Did Rosie's mother act like her usual self after dinner? (no) What did the story say that caused you to answer in that way? (It said she was a stranger.)

____ detail — 5. How late did Umé Hanazono often stay up? (midnight)

____ sequence — 6. Name in order the two things the family had usually done after dinner before Rosie's mother developed her new interest. (taken hot baths early and gone to bed immediately afterwards)

____ vocabulary — 7. What does the word "repercussions" mean in this story? (disruptive effect; effect)

____ cause and effect/inference — 8. What caused Rosie's father to have to resort to playing solitaire? (Rosie's mother wrote at night and wasn't available to play cards with him.)

____ detail — 9. What did Rosie's father always do when he played solitaire? (He cheated.)

____ vocabulary — 10. What does the word "ecstatic" mean? (delighted; joyous)

FORM B

★ 12 PASSAGE

SUMMARY OF QUANTITATIVE ANALYSIS

Student's Name ______________________ **Grade** ______ **Date** ______ **Administrator** ______________________

Forms Used: Word Lists, Form ______ Oral Passages, Form ______ Silent Passages, Form ______ Listening Comprehension, Form ______

Performance Levels Based on Full Inventory (Oral & Silent): Independent ______ Instructional ______ Frustration ______ Listening Comprehension ______

Performance Levels Based on Oral Passages: Independent ______ Instructional ______ Frustration ______ Listening Comprehension ______

Performance Levels Based on Silent Passages: Independent ______ Instructional ______ Frustration ______ Listening Comprehension ______

Optional Comparison Levels: Independent ______ Instructional ______ Frustration ______ **Rate of Reading:** High ______ Average ______ Low ______

Performance Levels Based on Graded Word Lists: Placement ______ Independent ______ Instructional ______ Frustration ______

Types of Miscues in Context

	Mispronunciation	Substitution	Insertion	Omission	Reversal	Repetition	Refusal to Pronounce	Row Totals
Total								
Meaning changed								
Self-corrected								

Comprehension Skill Analysis Chart

Skill	Number of Questions	Number of Errors	Percent of Errors
Main idea			
Detail			
Sequence			
Cause and effect			
Inference			
Vocabulary			

Summary Table of Percentages

Level	Word Recognition	Oral Comprehension	Silent Comprehension	Average Comprehension	Listening Comprehension
PP					
P					
1					
2					
3					
4					
5					
6					
7					
8					
9					
10					
11					
12					

SUMMARY OF QUALITATIVE ANALYSIS

Summary of Strengths and Weaknesses in Word Recognition

(Include all of the important data that have been collected on word recognition skills.)

Summary of Strengths and Weaknesses in Comprehension

(Include all of the important data that have been collected about comprehension.)

Checklist of Reading Behaviors

(Place a [+] by areas that are strong and a [–] by areas that are weak.)

1. Reads in phrases _____
2. Reads with expression _____
3. Attends to punctuation _____
4. Pronounces words correctly _____
5. Sounds out unfamiliar words _____
6. Uses structure clues, when available, to recognize unfamiliar words _____
7. Uses context clues _____
8. Makes strategic attempts to recognize unfamiliar words (applies word recognition skills flexibly) _____
9. Keeps place in material being read _____
10. Shows few signs of tension when reading _____
11. Holds book at appropriate distance from face when reading _____
12. Self-corrects errors without prompting _____

WORKSHEET FOR WORD RECOGNITION MISCUE TALLY CHART

Miscue		PP	P	1	2	3	4	5	6	7	8	9	10	11	12	Totals
Mispronunciation	**A**															**A**
	MC															**MC**
	SC															**SC**
Substitution	**A**															**A**
	MC															**MC**
	SC															**SC**
Insertion	**A**															**A**
	MC															**MC**
	SC															**SC**
Omission	**A**															**A**
	MC															**MC**
	SC															**SC**
Reversal	**A**															**A**
	MC															**MC**
	SC															**SC**
Repetition	**A**															**A**
Refusal to pronounce	**A**															**A**
Totals	**A**															**A**
	MC															**MC**
	SC															**SC**

A = All miscues of that type (excluding ones that were self-corrected)
MC = Miscues that resulted in a meaning change
SC = Self-corrected miscues

Miscue Analysis of Phonic and Structural Analysis Skills

(Tally total miscues on appropriate lines.)

Miscue	For Words in Isolation	For Words in Context
Single consonants	______	______
Consonant blends	______	______
Single vowels	______	______
Vowel digraphs	______	______
Consonant digraphs	______	______
Diphthongs	______	______
Prefixes	______	______
Suffixes	______	______
Special combinations	______	______
Word beginnings	______	______
Word middles	______	______
Word endings	______	______
Compound words	______	______
Inflectional endings	______	______
Syllabication	______	______
Accent	______	______

(*Note*: In order to fill out the analysis for words in context, it is helpful to make a list of expected reader responses and unexpected responses for easy comparison as to graphic similarity, syntactic acceptability, and semantic acceptability. See page 144 for a good way to record this information.)

WORKSHEET FOR QUALITATIVE ANALYSIS OF UNCORRECTED MISCUES IN CONTEXT

(Include mispronunciations, substitutions, insertions, omissions, and reversals.)

Passage	Type of Miscue	Expected Response	Unexpected Response	Graphic Similarity	Syntactic Acceptability	Semantic Acceptability

GRADED PASSAGES

STUDENT BOOKLET FORM C

Passages PP to 12

Read this story to find out what Nancy has.

My name is Nancy.
I have a cat.
My cat is white.
Her name is Fluffy.
Fluffy is little.
I play with her.
Jack plays with her, too.

Fluffy runs with us.
She runs from dogs.
She hides in a box.
She hides in a tree.
Then she cannot get down.

We call Dad.
Dad gets Fluffy down.
We are happy.
Fluffy is happy, too.

Read this story to find out about two boys and their visitor.

"Come in, Ned," said Jack.
"I am happy to see you.
I don't have a thing to do."

"That's what I'm here for," said Ned.
"What can we do?"

"A woman is at the door," said Ned.

Jack went to the door.

"Hello, Mrs. Little," said Jack.
"Can I help you?"

"Hello, Jack," said Mrs. Little.
"Is your mom home?"

"No," said Jack.
"But I'm here."

"Oh," said Mrs. Little.
"I want to see your mom.
I want her to care for my dog."

Nate is trying to help his friend Annie find a missing picture of her dog. He goes into her room to look for it. Everything in the room is yellow. Read the story to see what Nate says he did.

I looked all over the room.
I looked on the table.
And under the table.
No picture.

I looked on the bed.
And under the bed.
Still no picture.

I looked in the wastebasket.
I found a picture of a dog.

"Is this it?" I asked.

"No," Annie said.
"My picture of Fang is yellow."

"I should have known," I said.
"Now tell me.
Who has seen your picture?"

"My friend Rosamond has seen it, and my brother Harry—and Fang."

"Let me see Fang," I said.

Annie took me outside.
"Hmm," I said.
"Look at Fang hiding that bone.
He could hide a picture, too."

"Why would he hide a picture?" Annie asked.
"Maybe it wasn't a good picture of him," I said.

This story is about a family. Read it to find out about the family.

Once there was a little girl named Lydia. She lived with her father, who grew flowers, and Andy, who was her brother.

Every day Lydia's father was busy in his greenhouse, where the plants got so big they needed holes in the roof.

Every day Lydia was busy painting pictures, reading books, and making things. Lydia was so busy doing so many things she never finished anything.

Andy could do some things, but some things he didn't know how to do. If he asked Lydia to help him do something, she always said, "No-no-no-no! I haven't got time!"

Whenever her father heard Lydia say that, he always said, "Oh, no? Oh, ho! If you take time, you can have time."

But Lydia was too busy to listen.

This is a story about a girl named Megan and her father. Read the story to find out what their life was like.

For a long time Megan had not even known that she was blind. Outside the house, Mike's strong hand had taught her how to move from place to place. Inside the house, she knew just where everything was. She could easily find her way from her own small bedroom to all the other rooms of the house.

Mike was Megan's father. He had a leather shop at the front of the house. He made fine leather belts, shoes, and bags to sell in his shop. The new leather was smooth and smelled better than almost anything.

Megan liked to help Mike as he worked. She made sandwiches for their lunch and swept up the bits of leather that fell to the floor.

Often on Sunday afternoons, Megan and Mike would walk down to the beach. Hand in hand, they would make a trail with their bare feet in the wet sand.

"Nobody lives a better life than we do," Mike always said. And Megan would smile up at him and agree.

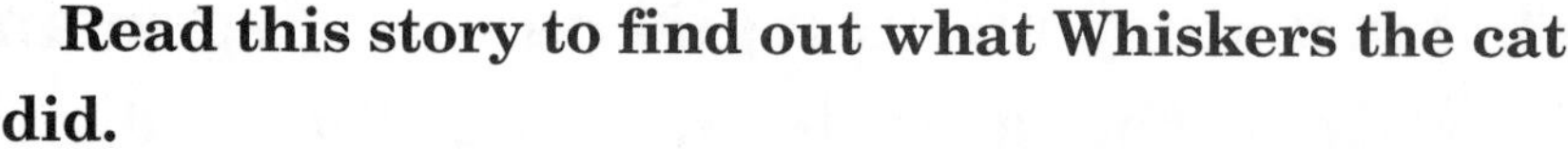

Read this story to find out what Whiskers the cat did.

Soon after Whiskers sharpened his claws, he saw some blades of grass move to and fro. A human being might have said to himself, "That grass is moving against the breeze. There must be a mouse on the ground!" But Whiskers could not talk, to himself or anyone else, and he did not take time to think things out. Instead, he crouched down and began to creep forward and pounced upon it.

Dogs and wolves bite their prey and hold it, but Whiskers did not bite. He struck the mouse with one paw and then backed away. When the mouse got up and tried to escape, Whiskers struck it again. He did this several times until the mouse was dead. Then the cat picked it up and carried it to the house. When his mistress opened the door to let him in, he laid the dead mouse at her feet.

Read this story to find out how a student felt about something that he saw happen.

The day they started taking the school down, our teacher said that we were very lucky. We had watched the new school being built, she said, and now we'd see the old school being demolished. She said we ought to learn all we could about how a building is wrecked.

I was still feeling pretty sad just thinking about it. Then the action began. BANG!

It was the scrap-metal collectors yanking out radiators and throwing them into a truck.

Other people came. They took away some of the big, heavy old chalkboards. The next day workers were up on the roof removing slates so they could be used on another building. It was good to know that some parts of our old school wouldn't just be thrown away or melted down.

Read this story to find out about something that happened on a trip in space.

Apollo 13, its crew huddled in one end, hurtled on through space. The ship curved around the back side of the moon, out of sight of the Earth. The gray lunar surface, pocked with craters, unrolled beneath the ship at about ten times the speed of a fast jet plane on Earth. Then Earth, a blue-green ball, appeared again. It was time to see whether the small rocket on Aquarius could blast the whole ship into a good course back home to Earth. If the course adjustment failed, Apollo could miss Earth completely. The crew wouldn't survive long, and the ship would carry their bodies on an endless trip through space.

"Mark!" said a man in Texas, telling Lovell he had forty seconds to go before firing. Lovell put his hand on the firing button. "Five . . . four . . . three . . . two . . . one." At exactly the right time, the rocket began to fire, pushing the whole ship into line. It fired on, a four-minute explosion. Then a computer took over to turn the rocket off at precisely the right instant.

The astronauts in space and the mission control on the ground anxiously checked the course. The rocket had done its job. The ship was aimed for a landing in the Pacific Ocean, a quarter of a million miles away. At least the ship was headed in the right direction. Whether it would splash down safely, no one knew.

Read this story to find out an experience that a man named Olaudah (oh-law′ dah), who was a slave, had in Philadelphia in the 1700s.

One thing I overheard that was not about politics was talk of a wise woman who was known for her power to predict things. A man in front of the Exchange was telling such an extraordinary story about her that the crowded listeners kept interrupting him with noises of amazement. I couldn't hear the story but went back to some shopkeepers I'd met that morning to ask about her. She did exist, they said, and told me where she lived. That night I dreamed of her. It was an ordinary dream, the kind you forget when you wake and remember later in the day only if something reminds you. So, as I made plans to see her that evening—a jingled-jeweled gypsy in bright colors—I remembered with a shock what I'd dreamed. In my dream she was not a gypsy at all but a small woman dressed in the quiet gray of the Quakers.

Read this selection to learn about two unusual creatures.

Flying squirrels are fond of fruits and nuts, but enticing them to a windowsill for closer acquaintance requires both skill and luck. The shelf must be at a level to which they can leap from a tree and then away again, for unlike bats, these nocturnal midget squirrels can only glide, not flap or fly. At times they do visit feeding stations built for the daytime birds. They will clean up a little pile of dry rolled oats—relishing them as a delicacy preferred to sunflower seeds or apple.

In darkness a wide variety of insect life is on the wing. A glowworm can be found in almost any city garden, vacant lot, or park. Wherever fallen leaves and rotting wood accumulate, these insects search out smaller creatures they can subdue and eat. Usually a glowworm proves to be the wingless female of a special firefly, *Phengodes.* In the dark it shines with rows of bright points along the sides of its three-quarter-inch length. Smaller and less spectacular facsimiles turn out to be the immature stages of other kinds of fireflies.

Read this story to learn about a special job.

Surveying the scene from high wooden stands set fifty feet apart were Nauset's lifeguards.

The lifeguards, youthful, muscular, and deeply tanned, are used to being surrounded by a horde of admiring youngsters and teased by jokes such as, "You mean to tell me you guys actually get paid just to sit up there all day and watch . . . ?"

"That's the way it looks," admitted guard Lee Anderson, "but on a busy day when there are 3,000 people on this beach, we concentrate so hard we wind up practically cross-eyed. On this job, you don't sit around and wait for somebody to yell for help. People who are drowning actually haven't got an ounce of breath left to call out. They're choking, gasping, and paralyzed by fear and exhaustion. You watch for them and you keep an eye on the ocean, trying to anticipate trouble. You take a special interest because when you're in the water with a panic-stricken, drowning person, it's your life as well as his that's on the line."

Read this story to learn as much as you can about what happened at a historic spot.

The O'Brien home was one of the few examples of solid-style wooden structures that hadn't been demolished in Boston's urban-renewal campaign at the turn of the century. The family had been able to avoid this because of its wealth and political influence and the house was passed on through several generations to the present. Old man O'Brien had no heirs, so when he died the family home went up for auction, and the Urban Center bought it. When local officials arrived for an appraisal, they discovered that the house had a backyard, which is forbidden by zoning restrictions.

In the yard was a live tree—an oak was what Mom called it.

When the news of the tree's discovery leaked out, quite a few sightseers stopped by to have a look at it, and the local government, realizing the money-making potential, began charging admission and advertising the place. By now it had become a favorite spot for school field trips and family excursions such as ours.

This story tells of an experience that astronaut Buzz Aldrin had during EVA (extravehicular activity) on the moon. Read the story to find out about it.

Aldrin was now working to set up the solar wind experiment, a sheet of aluminum foil hung on a stand. For the next hour and a half, the foil would be exposed to the solar wind, an invisible, unfelt, but high-velocity flow of noble gases from the sun like argon, krypton, neon, and helium. For the astronauts, it was the simplest of procedures, no more difficult than setting up a piece of sheet music on a music stand. At the end of the EVA, however, the aluminum foil would be rolled up, inserted in the rock box and delivered eventually to a laboratory in Switzerland uniquely equipped for the purpose. There any noble gases which had been trapped in the atomic lattice of the aluminum would be baked out in virtuoso procedures of quantitative analysis, and a closer knowledge of the components of the solar wind would be gained. Since the solar wind, it may be recalled, was diverted by the magnetosphere away from the earth, it had not hitherto been available for casual study.

Pius, an African man, won money from the football pools and suddenly had visitors arrive at his home. Read the story to find out what happened at his home.

Behind the hut—Pius had no proper kitchen—gallons of tea were being boiled, whilst several of the female cousins were employed in ruthlessly hacking down the bunches of *matoke* from his meagre plantains, to cook food for everybody. One woman—she had introduced herself as Cousin Sarah—discovered Pius's hidden store of banana beer, and dished it out to all and sundry as though it were her own. Pius had become very wary of Cousin Sarah. He didn't like the way in which she kept loudly remarking that he needed a woman about the place, and he was even more seriously alarmed when suddenly Salongo gave him a painful dig in the ribs and muttered, "You'll have to watch that one—she's a sticker!"

Everybody who came wanted to see the telegram that announced Pius's win. When it had arrived at the Ggombolola Headquarters—the postal address of everyone living within a radius of fifteen miles—Musisi had brought it out personally, delighted to be the bearer of such good tidings.

GRADED PASSAGES

TEACHER BOOKLET FORM C

Passages and Questions
PP to 12

Summary Forms for Quantitative and Qualitative Analysis

Worksheets

INTRODUCTORY STATEMENT: Read this story to find out what Nancy has.

My name is Nancy.
I have a cat.
My cat is white.
Her name is Fluffy.
Fluffy is little.
I play with her.
Jack plays with her, too.

Fluffy runs with us.
She runs from dogs.
She hides in a box.
She hides in a tree.
Then she cannot get down.

We call Dad.
Dad gets Fluffy down.
We are happy.
Fluffy is happy, too.

[*Note*: Do not count as miscues the mispronunciation of the names Nancy, Fluffy, and Jack. You may pronounce these names for the student if needed.]

SCORING AID

Word Recognition

%–Miscues

99–0
95–3
90–6
85–9

Comprehension

%–Errors

100–0
87.5–1
75–2
62.5–3
50–4
37.5–5
25–6
12.5–7
0–8

58 Words
(for Word Recognition)

65 Words
(for Rate)

WPM
3900

COMPREHENSION QUESTIONS

____ detail	1. What color is Nancy's cat? (white)
____ detail	2. What is Nancy's cat's name? (Fluffy)
____ detail	3. Who plays with Fluffy? (Nancy and Jack) [If only one name is given, ask "Who else?"]
____ inference	4. Is Fluffy a girl cat or a boy cat? (girl) What in the story lets you know this? (When it talks about Fluffy, it says "she.")
____ inference	5. Where does Fluffy hide that causes trouble for her? (in a tree)
____ sequence	6. What happens after Fluffy can't get down from the tree? (Jack and Nancy call Dad.)
____ main idea	7. What does Dad do? (Dad rescues Fluffy from the tree.)
____ cause and effect/ inference	8. What causes Nancy to be happy at the end of the story? (Fluffy is safe; Fluffy is rescued.)

INTRODUCTORY STATEMENT: Read this story to find out about two boys and their visitor.

"Come in, Ned," said Jack.
"I am happy to see you.
I don't have a thing to do."

"That's what I'm here for," said Ned.
"What can we do?"

"A woman is at the door," said Ned.

Jack went to the door.

"Hello, Mrs. Little," said Jack.
"Can I help you?"

"Hello, Jack," said Mrs. Little.
"Is your mom home?"

"No," said Jack.
"But I'm here."

"Oh," said Mrs. Little.
"I want to see your mom.
I want her to care for my dog."

SCORING AID

Word Recognition
%–Miscues
99–1
95–4
90–8
85–12

Comprehension
%–Errors
100–0
87.5–1
75–2
62.5–3
50–4
37.5–5
25–6
12.5–7
0–8

76 Words
(for Word Recognition)

84 Words
(for Rate)

WPM
5040

Source: "Pet-Sitters," by Leo Fay, Ramon R. Ross, and Margaret LaPray, Rand McNally Reading Program, in *Magic Rings and Funny Things*, Level 5 (Chicago: The Riverside Publishing Company, 1978), pp. 7–9.

[*Note*: Do not count as miscues mispronunciation of the names Ned and Jack. You may pronounce these words for the student if needed.]

COMPREHENSION QUESTIONS

____ inference	1. What was the name of Jack's friend? (Ned)
____ cause and effect/ detail	2. What made Jack happy? (seeing Ned)
____ sequence	3. Was Jack busy when Ned arrived? (no) What did the story say that caused you to answer that way? (He didn't have a thing to do.)
____ detail	4. What did Ned ask Jack? ("What can we do?")
____ sequence	5. Who came to the door after Ned arrived? (Mrs. Little)
____ inference	6. Did Ned know Mrs. Little? (no) What in the story made you say that? (He said a woman was at the door; he didn't call her by name.)
____ detail	7. What did Jack ask Mrs. Little? ("Can I help you?")
____ main idea	8. What did Mrs. Little want Jack's mother to do? (She wanted her to care for her dog.)

INTRODUCTORY STATEMENT: Nate is trying to help his friend Annie find a missing picture of her dog. He goes into her room to look for it. Everything in the room is yellow. Read the story to see what Nate says he did.

I looked all over the room.
I looked on the table.
And under the table.
No picture.

I looked on the bed.
And under the bed.
Still no picture.

I looked in the wastebasket.
I found a picture of a dog.

"Is this it?" I asked.

"No," Annie said.
"My picture of Fang is yellow."

"I should have known," I said.
"Now tell me.
Who has seen your picture?"

"My friend Rosamond has seen it, and my brother Harry—and Fang."

"Let me see Fang," I said.

Annie took me outside.
"Hmm," I said.
"Look at Fang hiding that bone.
He could hide a picture, too."

"Why would he hide a picture?" Annie asked.
"Maybe it wasn't a good picture of him," I said.

SCORING AID

Word Recognition
%–Miscues

99–1
95–6
90–12
85–17

Comprehension
%–Errors

100–0
87.5–1
75–2
62.5–3
50–4
37.5–5
25–6
12.5–7
0–8

115 Words
(for Word Recognition)

124 Words
(for Rate)

WPM
7440

Source: From *Nate the Great*, by Marjorie Weinman Sharmat.

[*Note*: Do not count as miscues the mispronunciation of the names Annie, Fang, Harry, and Rosamond. You may pronounce these names for the student if necessary.]

COMPREHENSION QUESTIONS

____ main idea	1.	What is this story about? (Nate doesn't find the picture; Nate tries to find the picture.)
____ sequence	2.	Where was the first place Nate looked in the room? (on the table) [Accept just "the table."]
____ inference	3.	Did Nate find the picture under the bed? (no) What did the story say that helped you to know that? (It said, "Still no picture.")
____ vocabulary	4.	What is a wastebasket? (a place to throw away things you don't want)
____ detail	5.	What did Nate find in the wastebasket? (a picture of a dog)
____ detail	6	What color was Annie's picture of Fang? (yellow)
____ cause and effect/ inference	7.	Why did Annie take Nate outside? (to show him Fang)
____ cause and effect/ detail	8.	Why did Nate think Fang might have hidden the picture? (It might not have been a good picture of him; if he could hide a bone, he could hide a picture.)

INTRODUCTORY STATEMENT: This story is about a family. Read it to find out about the family.

Once there was a little girl named Lydia. She lived with her father, who grew flowers, and Andy, who was her brother.

Every day Lydia's father was busy in his greenhouse, where the plants got so big they needed holes in the roof.

Every day Lydia was busy painting pictures, reading books, and making things. Lydia was so busy doing so many things she never finished anything.

Andy could do some things, but some things he didn't know how to do. If he asked Lydia to help him do something, she always said, "No-no-no-no! I haven't got time!"

Whenever her father heard Lydia say that, he always said, "Oh, no? Oh, ho! If you take time, you can have time."

But Lydia was too busy to listen.

Source: From *Do You Have the Time, Lydia?* by Evaline Ness.

[*Note*: Do not count as a miscue mispronunciation of the name Lydia. You may pronounce this name for the student if necessary.]

SCORING AID

Word Recognition

%–Miscues

99–1
95–6
90–12
85–18

Comprehension

%–Errors

100–0
87.5–1
75–2
62.5–3
50–4
37.5–5
25–6
12.5–7
0–8

120 Words
(for Word Recognition)

127 Words
(for Rate)

WPM
7620

COMPREHENSION QUESTIONS

____ main idea — 1. What is this story about? (Lydia stays busy; Lydia doesn't have time.)

____ detail — 2. What did Lydia's father do? (grew flowers)

____ vocabulary — 3. What is a greenhouse? (a place where you grow plants indoors)

____ inference or detail — 4. How tall were the plants Lydia's father grew? (taller than the roof [inference] or so big they needed holes in the roof [detail]) [If the student says "very tall," ask for more information about their height.]

____ detail — 5. What did Lydia do every day? (painted pictures, read books, made things) [Accept any two of the three for full credit; accept one for half credit.]

____ sequence — 6. What would Lydia say after Andy asked her to help him do something? ("No-no-no-no! I haven't got time!") [Accept either part for full credit.]

____ inference — 7. Did Lydia's father agree that Lydia was really too busy to play with her brother? (no)
What did he say that makes you think this?
("If you take time, you can have time.")

____ cause and effect/inference — 8. What caused Lydia not to listen to her father? (She was too busy to listen.)

TEACHER 3 □□

FORM C

□□ 3 PASSAGE

INTRODUCTORY STATEMENT: This is a story about a girl named Megan and her father. Read the story to find out what their life was like.

For a long time Megan had not even known that she was blind. Outside the house, Mike's strong hand had taught her how to move from place to place. Inside the house, she knew just where everything was. She could easily find her way from her own small bedroom to all the other rooms of the house.

Mike was Megan's father. He had a leather shop at the front of the house. He made fine leather belts, shoes, and bags to sell in his shop. The new leather was smooth and smelled better than almost anything.

Megan liked to help Mike as he worked. She made sandwiches for their lunch and swept up the bits of leather that fell to the floor.

Often on Sunday afternoons, Megan and Mike would walk down to the beach. Hand in hand, they would make a trail with their bare feet in the wet sand.

"Nobody lives a better life than we do," Mike always said. And Megan would smile up at him and agree.

Source: Adapted from *A Bowl of Sun*, by Frances Wosmek.

[*Note*: Do not count as a miscue mispronunciation of the name Megan. You may pronounce this name for the student if necessary.]

SCORING AID

Word Recognition

%–Miscues

99–2

95–9

90–17

85–25

Comprehension

%–Errors

100–0

90–1

80–2

70–3

60–4

50–5

40–6

30–7

20–8

10–9

0–10

166 Words
(for Word Recognition)

171 Words
(for Rate)

WPM

10260

COMPREHENSION QUESTIONS

____ main idea	1.	What kind of life did Megan and Mike have? (They had a good life.)
____ inference	2.	What couldn't Megan do that most people can do? (see)
____ cause and effect/ inference	3.	Why had Megan not even known she was blind for a long time? (because she could move around outside and find her way around inside too; because nobody had told her and she could do what she needed to do)
____ inference	4.	How did Mike earn money? (He made and sold leather things.)
____ detail	5.	Where was Mike's leather shop? (at the front of the house)
____ detail	6.	How did the new leather feel? (smooth)
____ inference	7.	Did Mike and Megan live near the water? (yes) What did the story say that made you think this? (It said they often walked down to the beach on Sunday afternoons.)
____ detail	8.	What did Megan and Mike do at the beach on Sunday afternoons? (made a trail in the sand with their bare feet)
____ sequence	9.	What would Megan do just after Mike said that nobody lived a better life than they did? (smile at him and agree) [Accept either part for full credit.]
____ vocabulary	10.	What does the word "agree" mean? (say yes; feel the same way) [Accept a nod for "yes" as an answer, if it is clear that it is meant for an answer.]

TEACHER 4

FORM C

4 PASSAGE

INTRODUCTORY STATEMENT: Read this story to find out what Whiskers the cat did.

Soon after Whiskers sharpened his claws, he saw some blades of grass move to and fro. A human being might have said to himself, "That grass is moving against the breeze. There must be a mouse on the ground!" But Whiskers could not talk, to himself or anyone else, and he did not take time to think things out. Instead, he crouched down and began to creep forward and pounced upon it.

Dogs and wolves bite their prey and hold it, but Whiskers did not bite. He struck the mouse with one paw and then backed away. When the mouse got up and tried to escape, Whiskers struck it again. He did this several times until the mouse was dead. Then the cat picked it up and carried it to the house. When his mistress opened the door to let him in, he laid the dead mouse at her feet.

Source: Adapted from *Animals That Help Us: The Story of Domestic Animals*, Rev. Ed., by Carroll Lane Fenton and Herminie B. Kitchen (New York: John Day, 1973). Copyright © 1973 by Mildred Adams Fenton and the Estate of Herminie B. Kitchen. Copyright © 1959 by Carroll Lane Fenton and Herminie B. Kitchen. Used with the permission of Harper & Row, Publishers.

SCORING AID

Word Recognition

%–Miscues

99–2
95–8
90–15
85–23

Comprehension

%–Errors

100–0
90–1
80–2
70–3
60–4
50–5
40–6
30–7
20–8
10–9
0–10

150 Words
(for Word Recognition)

150 Words
(for Rate)

WPM
9000

COMPREHENSION QUESTIONS

____ main idea	1. What is this story about? (Whiskers catches a mouse.)
____ cause and effect/ inference	2. What caused the blades of grass to move to and fro? (a mouse)
____ sequence	3. What was the first thing Whiskers did when he saw the blades of grass move? (He crouched down and began to creep forward.)
____ vocabulary	4. What does the word "crouched" mean? (bent his body down close to the ground)
____ vocabulary	5. What does the word "creep" mean in the sentence "He crouched down and began to creep forward"? (to move slowly in a sneaky way)
____ vocabulary	6. What does the word "pounced" mean? (leaped on)
____ sequence	7. What was the first thing Whiskers did to the mouse when he caught it? (struck it with his paw)
____ inference	8. Was the mouse killed when Whiskers hit it the first time? (no) What fact in the story caused you to answer that way? (It got up and tried to escape.)
____ detail	9. Where did Whiskers carry the dead mouse? (to the house)
____ detail	10. Who opened the door to let Whiskers in? (his mistress)

INTRODUCTORY STATEMENT: Read this story to find out how a student felt about something that he saw happen.

The day they started taking the school down, our teacher said that we were very lucky. We had watched the new school being built, she said, and now we'd see the old school being demolished. She said we ought to learn all we could about how a building is wrecked.

I was still feeling pretty sad just thinking about it. Then the action began. BANG!

It was the scrap-metal collectors yanking out radiators and throwing them into a truck.

Other people came. They took away some of the big, heavy old chalkboards. The next day workers were up on the roof removing slates so they could be used on another building. It was good to know that some parts of our old school wouldn't just be thrown away or melted down.

Source: "How to Wreck a Building," by Elinor Lander Horwitz, in Leo Fay and others, *Grand Tour* (Chicago: The Riverside Publishing Company, 1989), p. 193. Condensed from *How to Wreck a Building*, by Elinor Lander Horwitz, © 1982 by Pantheon Books, a Division of Random House, Inc.

SCORING AID

Word Recognition
%–Miscues
99–2
95–7
90–13
85–20

Comprehension
%–Errors
100–0
90–1
80–2
70–3
60–4
50–5
40–6
30–7
20–8
10–9
0–10

131 Words
(for Word Recognition)

131 Words
(for Rate)

WPM
131 ⟌ 7860

COMPREHENSION QUESTIONS

____ main idea — 1. What is the main idea of this story? (Students see workers tear down their old school; students see their old school being demolished.)

____ sequence — 2. Name, in order, the two things that the teacher said the children were getting to see. (the new school being built and the old school being demolished or torn down)

____ vocabulary — 3. What does the word "demolished" mean? (torn down)

____ detail — 4. What did the teacher tell the students they ought to learn? (all they could about how a building is wrecked)

____ detail — 5. How did the student telling the story feel about the old school being wrecked? (sad)

____ cause and effect/ detail — 6. What caused the noise that the children heard? (the scrap-metal collectors yanking out radiators and throwing them in a truck)

____ inference — 7. Why did people come to take the chalkboards away? (so that they could be used again somewhere else)

____ sequence — 8. What happened after the chalkboards were taken away? (Workers removed slates from the roof.)

____ cause and effect/ detail — 9. Why did the workers remove the slates from the roof? (so they could be used on another building)

____ inference — 10. How did the student telling the story feel about the chalkboards and slates being removed from the school? (glad that they were not going to be thrown away or melted down)

TEACHER 6 · FORM C · 6 PASSAGE

INTRODUCTORY STATEMENT: Read this story to find out about something that happened on a trip in space.

Apollo 13, its crew huddled in one end, hurtled on through space. The ship curved around the back side of the moon, out of sight of the Earth. The gray lunar surface, pocked with craters, unrolled beneath the ship at about ten times the speed of a fast jet plane on Earth. Then Earth, a blue-green ball, appeared again. It was time to see whether the small rocket on Aquarius could blast the whole ship into a good course back home to Earth. If the course adjustment failed, Apollo could miss Earth completely. The crew wouldn't survive long, and the ship would carry their bodies on an endless trip through space.

"Mark!" said a man in Texas, telling Lovell he had forty seconds to go before firing. Lovell put his hand on the firing button. "Five . . . four . . . three . . . two . . . one." At exactly the right time, the rocket began to fire, pushing the whole ship into line. It fired on, a four-minute explosion. Then a computer took over to turn the rocket off at precisely the right instant.

The astronauts in space and the mission control on the ground anxiously checked the course. The rocket had done its job. The ship was aimed for a landing in the Pacific Ocean, a quarter of a million miles away. At least the ship was headed in the right direction. Whether it would splash down safely, no one knew.

Source: "Lifeboat in Space," by Gurney Williams, in William K. Durr and others, *Celebrations* (Boston: Houghton Mifflin Company, 1989), pp. 509–510.

SCORING AID

Word Recognition

%–Miscues
99–3
95–13
90–24
85–36

Comprehension

%–Errors
100–0
90–1
80–2
70–3
60–4
50–5
40–6
30–7
20–8
10–9
0–10

234 Words (for Word Recognition)

234 Words (for Rate)

WPM: 14040

COMPREHENSION QUESTIONS

____ main idea — 1. What is the main idea of this story? (Astronauts are getting ready to try to return to Earth.)

____ vocabulary — 2. What does the word "hurtled" mean in the phrase "hurtled on through space"? (moved fast)

____ inference — 3. What did the surface of the moon look like? (It was gray and had pits [or craters] in it.)

____ inference — 4. How fast was Apollo 13 moving past the moon? (about ten times the speed of a fast jet plane on Earth)

____ cause and effect/ inference — 5. What caused Earth to appear again to the astronauts? (The ship came out from behind the moon.)

____ detail — 6. What would happen if the course adjustment failed? (Apollo could miss Earth completely. The crew wouldn't survive long. The ship would keep on carrying them through space endlessly.) [Accept any one of these answers.]

____ sequence — 7. What did Lovell do immediately after the man in Texas said, "Mark"? (He put his hand on the firing button; he had the countdown.)

____ sequence — 8. What happened immediately after the rocket fired? (The ship was pushed into line; a computer took over to turn the rocket off.)

____ vocabulary — 9. What is an astronaut? (a person trained to fly or participate in the flight of a spacecraft)

____ detail — 10. Where was the ship aimed for a landing? (the Pacific Ocean)

INTRODUCTORY STATEMENT: Read this story to find out an experience that a man named Olaudah (oh-law' dah), who was a slave, had in Philadelphia in the 1700s.

One thing I overheard that was not about politics was talk of a wise woman who was known for her power to predict things. A man in front of the Exchange was telling such an extraordinary story about her that the crowded listeners kept interrupting him with noises of amazement. I couldn't hear the story but went back to some shopkeepers I'd met that morning to ask about her. She did exist, they said, and told me where she lived. That night I dreamed of her. It was an ordinary dream, the kind you forget when you wake and remember later in the day only if something reminds you. So, as I made plans to see her that evening—a jingled-jeweled gypsy in bright colors—I remembered with a shock what I'd dreamed. In my dream she was not a gypsy at all but a small woman dressed in the quiet gray of the Quakers.

Source: From *The Slave Who Bought His Freedom*, adapted by Karen Kennerly.

SCORING AID

Word Recognition

%–Miscues
99–2
95–8
90–15
85–23

Comprehension

%–Errors
100–0
90–1
80–2
70–3
60–4
50–5
40–6
30–7
20–8
10–9
0–10

155 Words (for Word Recognition)

155 Words (for Rate)

WPM
9300

COMPREHENSION QUESTIONS

____ main idea
1. What is the main idea of this story? (Olaudah discovers a woman who can predict things; Olaudah finds out about a fortune teller and dreams about her.)

____ detail
2. Where was the man who was overheard talking about a wise woman who could predict things? (in front of the Exchange)

____ inference
3. Were many people listening to the man who was telling about the wise woman? (yes) What does the story say that caused you to answer this way? (It mentions the "crowded listeners.")

____ vocabulary
4. What does the word "extraordinary" mean? (beyond the ordinary; unusual)

____ cause and effect/ inference
5. What caused the listeners to interrupt the story about the wise woman? (They were amazed by what was being told; they were surprised at the things they heard.)

____ sequence
6. What did Olaudah do immediately after he overheard the story? (He went back to some shopkeepers he had met that morning to ask about her.)

____ inference
7. Did Olaudah want to know about the future? (yes) What did the story say that caused you to answer this way? (The woman had power to predict things, and he planned to go see her.)

____ inference
8. When he was awake, how did Olaudah picture the woman he planned to see? (as a gypsy with jewels and bright colors)

____ inference
9. Why was Olaudah shocked to remember his dream? (The woman in his dream was very different from the woman he had pictured when he was awake.)

____ detail
10. What did the woman look like in Olaudah's dream? (small, and dressed in the quiet gray of the Quakers)

INTRODUCTORY STATEMENT: Read this selection to learn about two unusual creatures.

Flying squirrels are fond of fruits and nuts, but enticing them to a windowsill for closer acquaintance requires both skill and luck. The shelf must be at a level to which they can leap from a tree and then away again, for unlike bats, these nocturnal midget squirrels can only glide, not flap or fly. At times they do visit feeding stations built for the daytime birds. They will clean up a little pile of dry rolled oats—relishing them as a delicacy preferred to sunflower seeds or apple.

In darkness a wide variety of insect life is on the wing. A glowworm can be found in almost any city garden, vacant lot, or park. Wherever fallen leaves and rotting wood accumulate, these insects search out smaller creatures they can subdue and eat. Usually a glowworm proves to be the wingless female of a special firefly, *Phengodes*. In the dark it shines with rows of bright points along the sides of its three-quarter-inch length. Smaller and less spectacular facsimiles turn out to be the immature stages of other kinds of fireflies.

Source: "In the City," by Louis J. Milne and Margery J. Milne, in *The World of Night* (New York: Harper and Row, 1956)

[*Note*: Do not count as a miscue mispronunciation of the proper noun *Phengodes*. You may pronounce this word for the student if needed.]

SCORING AID

Word Recognition

%–Miscues
99–2
95–9
90–18
85–27

Comprehension

%–Errors
100–0
90–1
80–2
70–3
60–4
50–5
40–6
30–7
20–8
10–9
0–10

180 Words (for Word Recognition)

181 Words (for Rate)

WPM
$\overline{)10860}$

COMPREHENSION QUESTIONS

____ main idea	1. What is the purpose of this selection? (to tell about flying squirrels and glowworms; to tell about two night animals)
____ vocabulary	2. What does the word "enticing" in the phrase "enticing them to a windowsill" mean? (luring; attracting; tempting)
____ inference	3. Can bats flap their wings and fly? (yes) What did the story say that caused you to answer this way? (It says *unlike* bats these squirrels cannot flap and fly.)
____ detail	4. How do flying squirrels move through the air? (They leap and glide.)
____ cause and effect/ inference	5. Why do flying squirrels visit feeding stations built for daytime birds? (They like the things people feed to the birds, like dry rolled oats.)
____ vocabulary	6. What does the word "relishing" mean in the phrase "relishing them as a delicacy"? (enjoying)
____ vocabulary	7. What does the word "accumulate" mean in the phrase "wherever fallen leaves and rotting wood accumulate"? (pile up)
____ vocabulary	8. What does the word "subdue" mean in the statement: "these insects search out smaller creatures they can subdue and eat"? (overcome, conquer)
____ detail	9. What does a glowworm usually prove to be? (the wingless female of a special firefly)
____ detail	10. What does the selection tell about the immature stages of fireflies other than the *Phengodes*? (They are smaller and less spectacular than the female of the *Phengodes*.)

INTRODUCTORY STATEMENT: Read this story to learn about a special job.

Surveying the scene from high wooden stands set fifty feet apart were Nauset's lifeguards.

The lifeguards, youthful, muscular, and deeply tanned, are used to being surrounded by a horde of admiring youngsters and teased by jokes such as, "You mean to tell me you guys actually get paid just to sit up there all day and watch . . . ?"

"That's the way it looks," admitted guard Lee Anderson, "but on a busy day when there are 3,000 people on this beach, we concentrate so hard we wind up practically cross-eyed. On this job, you don't sit around and wait for somebody to yell for help. People who are drowning actually haven't got an ounce of breath left to call out. They're choking, gasping, and paralyzed by fear and exhaustion. You watch for them and you keep an eye on the ocean, trying to anticipate trouble. You take a special interest because when you're in the water with a panic-stricken, drowning person, it's your life as well as his that's on the line."

Source: "The Day the Sea Went Down the Drain," by Evan McLeod Wylie, *Yankee*, July 1974. Copyright © 1974 by Evan McLeod Wylie and reprinted by permission.

[*Note:* Do not count as a miscue mispronunciation of the name Nauset. You may pronounce this word for the student if necessary.]

SCORING AID

Word Recognition
%–Miscues
99–2
95–9
90–17
85–26

Comprehension
%–Errors
100–0
90–1
80–2
70–3
60–4
50–5
40–6
30–7
20–8
10–9
0–10

169 Words
(for Word Recognition)

170 Words
(for Rate)

WPM
10200

COMPREHENSION QUESTIONS

____ main idea 1. What is the main idea of this story? (A lifeguard's job is dangerous; rescuing drowning people is dangerous.)

____ vocabulary 2. What is the meaning of the word "surveying" in the phrase "surveying the scene"? (looking over, viewing closely)

____ detail 3. Who sat in the high wooden stands? (lifeguards)

____ detail 4. What were the lifeguards like? (youthful, muscular, deeply tanned) [Accept any two of the three for full credit; accept one for half credit.]

____ vocabulary 5. What is the meaning of the word "horde" in the phrase "horde of admiring youngsters"? (throng; large group)

____ detail 6. How many people visit the beach on a busy day? (3,000)

____ cause and effect/detail 7. What happens when the guards concentrate very hard on the beach? (They become practically cross-eyed.)

____ cause and effect/detail 8. According to the story, why aren't drowning people able to call out? (lack of breath due to choking and gasping, fear, exhaustion) [Two of the reasons earn full credit; one earns half credit.]

____ vocabulary 9. What is the meaning of the word "anticipate" in the phrase "anticipate trouble"? (foresee, expect)

____ inference 10. Could lifeguards die trying to rescue a drowning person? (yes) What did the story say that gave you this idea? (It said your life is also on the line.)

INTRODUCTORY STATEMENT: Read this story to learn as much as you can about what happened at a historic spot.

The O'Brien home was one of the few examples of solid-style wooden structures that hadn't been demolished in Boston's urban-renewal campaign at the turn of the century. The family had been able to avoid this because of its wealth and political influence and the house was passed on through several generations to the present. Old man O'Brien had no heirs, so when he died the family home went up for auction, and the Urban Center bought it. When local officials arrived for an appraisal, they discovered that the house had a backyard, which is forbidden by zoning restrictions.

In the yard was a live tree—an oak was what Mom called it.

When the news of the tree's discovery leaked out, quite a few sightseers stopped by to have a look at it, and the local government, realizing the money-making potential, began charging admission and advertising the place. By now it had become a favorite spot for school field trips and family excursions such as ours.

Source: "Autumntime," by A. Lentini, *Galaxy Magazine*, November 1971.

SCORING AID

Word Recognition

%–Miscues
99–2
95–8
90–17
85–25

Comprehension

%–Errors
100–0
90–1
80–2
70–3
60–4
50–5
40–6
30–7
20–8
10–9
0–10

166 Words (for Word Recognition)

166 Words (for Rate)

WPM
9960

COMPREHENSION QUESTIONS

____ main idea 1. What is the main idea of this story? (An old home becomes a tourist attraction; a house with a tree in the backyard becomes a tourist attraction.)

____ vocabulary 2. What is the meaning of the word "demolished" in this story? (torn down; razed, destroyed)

____ detail 3. Where was the O'Brien home? (Boston)

____ cause and effect/ detail 4. What prevented the O'Brien home from being demolished? (family wealth and political influence)

____ sequence 5. What happened to the house after old man O'Brien died? (It went up for auction.)

____ detail 6. Who bought the home? (the Urban Center)

____ vocabulary 7. What does the word "appraisal" mean in the clause "when local officials arrived for an appraisal"? (estimate of property value; evaluation of the situation)

____ inference 8. Do you think there were many trees in the urban area? (no) What facts in the story caused you to answer that way? (The oak tree was an attraction.)

____ cause and effect/ inference 9. Why did the local government advertise the home? (to make money from sightseers who wanted to see the tree)

____ vocabulary 10. What is an excursion? (a trip)

INTRODUCTORY STATEMENT: This story tells of an experience that astronaut Buzz Aldrin had during EVA (extravehicular activity) on the moon. Read the story to find out about it.

Aldrin was now working to set up the solar wind experiment, a sheet of aluminum foil hung on a stand. For the next hour and a half, the foil would be exposed to the solar wind, an invisible, unfelt, but high-velocity flow of noble gases from the sun like argon, krypton, neon, and helium. For the astronauts, it was the simplest of procedures, no more difficult than setting up a piece of sheet music on a music stand. At the end of the EVA, however, the aluminum foil would be rolled up, inserted in the rock box and delivered eventually to a laboratory in Switzerland uniquely equipped for the purpose. There any noble gases which had been trapped in the atomic lattice of the aluminum would be baked out in virtuoso procedures of quantitative analysis, and a closer knowledge of the components of the solar wind would be gained. Since the solar wind, it may be recalled, was diverted by the magnetosphere away from the earth, it had not hitherto been available for casual study.

Source: From *Of a Fire on the Moon*, by Norman Mailer.

SCORING AID	
Word Recognition	**Comprehension**
%–Miscues	**%–Errors**
99–2	100–0
95–9	90–1
90–17	80–2
85–20	70–3
	60–4
	50–5
	40–6
	30–7
	20–8
	10–9
	0–10

175 Words (for Word Recognition)

175 Words (for Rate)

WPM
10500

COMPREHENSION QUESTIONS

____ main idea — 1. What is the main idea of this story? (Aldrin works on the solar wind experiment.)

____ detail — 2. What equipment was used for the solar wind experiment? (a sheet of aluminum foil hung on a stand)

____ detail — 3. How long would the foil be exposed to the solar wind? (for an hour and a half)

____ inference — 4. Is solar wind like wind on earth? (no) What did the story say that made you believe that? (It says it is unfelt. It is made up of gases from the sun like argon, krypton, neon, and helium.) [Accept either statement as appropriate backing for the answer.]

____ vocabulary — 5. What does the term "high-velocity" mean? (high-speed)

____ detail — 6. How difficult was it for the astronauts to set up the solar wind experiment? (very easy; no harder than setting a piece of sheet music on a music stand)

____ sequence — 7. Name, in order, the two things that the astronauts would do with the aluminum foil at the end of the EVA. (roll it up and insert it in the rock box)

____ detail — 8. Where would the aluminum foil be delivered eventually? (to a laboratory in Switzerland)

____ cause and effect/ inference — 9. Why were the noble gases that had been trapped in the aluminum going to be baked out in the laboratory? (because scientists wanted to find out more about the components of solar wind)

____ cause and effect/ detail — 10. Why had the solar wind not been available for casual study? (because it was diverted away from the earth by the magnetosphere)

INTRODUCTORY STATEMENT: Pius, an African man, won money from the football pools and suddenly had visitors arrive at his home. Read the story to find out what happened at his home.

Behind the hut—Pius had no proper kitchen—gallons of tea were being boiled, whilst several of the female cousins were employed in ruthlessly hacking down the bunches of *matoke* from his meagre plantains, to cook food for everybody. One woman—she had introduced herself as Cousin Sarah—discovered Pius's hidden store of banana beer, and dished it out to all and sundry as though it were her own. Pius had become very wary of Cousin Sarah. He didn't like the way in which she kept loudly remarking that he needed a woman about the place, and he was even more seriously alarmed when suddenly Salongo gave him a painful dig in the ribs and muttered, "You'll have to watch that one—she's a sticker!"

Everybody who came wanted to see the telegram that announced Pius's win. When it had arrived at the Ggombolola Headquarters—the postal address of everyone living within a radius of fifteen miles—Musisi had brought it out personally, delighted to be the bearer of such good tidings.

Source: From *Kalasanda*, by Barbara Kimenye, published by Oxford University Press in Three Crowns Books.

[*Note*: Do not count as miscues mispronunciation of Pius, *matoke*, Salongo, Ggombolola, and Musisi. You may pronounce these words for the student if necessary.]

SCORING AID

Word Recognition

%–Miscues
99–2
95–9
90–17
85–25

Comprehension

%–Errors
100–0
90–1
80–2
70–3
60–4
50–5
40–6
30–7
20–8
10–9
0–10

164 Words (for Word Recognition)

172 Words (for Rate)

WPM
10320

COMPREHENSION QUESTIONS

____ main idea — 1. What is the main idea of this story? (There was a party with food and drink to help Pius celebrate his win.)

____ detail — 2. What was Pius's house like? (It was a hut with no proper kitchen.)

____ vocabulary — 3. What does the word "meagre" mean? (scanty; not enough; scarce)

____ inference — 4. Was it likely that Pius wanted to pass out his banana beer to the crowd? (no) What did the story say that made you believe this? (It was his hidden store, and he wasn't the one who passed it out.)

____ vocabulary — 5. What does the word "wary" mean? (suspicious; apprehensive)

____ cause and effect/ inference — 6. What made Pius wary of Cousin Sarah? (the way she kept saying he needed a woman around the house)

____ inference — 7. What did Salongo think Cousin Sarah had in mind? (sticking with Pius; marrying Pius)

____ detail — 8. What did all of the visitors want to see? (the telegram that announced Pius's win)

____ inference — 9. Did Pius have a personal mailbox? (no) What did the story say that made you believe this? (The place where the telegram arrived was the postal address of everyone living within a fifteen-mile radius.)

____ sequence — 10. What did Musisi do with the telegram after it arrived? (He delivered it personally.)

SUMMARY OF QUANTITATIVE ANALYSIS

Student's Name ______________________ **Grade** ______ **Date** ________ **Administrator** ______________________

Forms Used: Word Lists, Form _____ Oral Passages, Form _____ Silent Passages, Form _____ Listening Comprehension, Form _____

Performance Levels Based on Full Inventory (Oral & Silent): Independent _____ Instructional _____ Frustration _____ Listening Comprehension _____

Performance Levels Based on Oral Passages: Independent _____ Instructional _____ Frustration _____ Listening Comprehension _____

Performance Levels Based on Silent Passages: Independent _____ Instructional _____ Frustration _____ Listening Comprehension _____

Optional Comparison Levels: Independent _____ Instructional _____ Frustration _____ **Rate of Reading:** High _____ Average _____ Low _____

Performance Levels Based on Graded Word Lists: Placement _____ Independent _____ Instructional _____ Frustration _____

Types of Miscues in Context

	Mispronunciation	Substitution	Insertion	Omission	Reversal	Repetition	Refusal to Pronounce	Row Totals
Total								
Meaning changed								
Self-corrected								

Comprehension Skill Analysis Chart

Skill	Number of Questions	Number of Errors	Percent of Errors
Main idea			
Detail			
Sequence			
Cause and effect			
Inference			
Vocabulary			

Summary Table of Percentages

Level	Word Recognition	Oral Comprehension	Silent Comprehension	Average Comprehension	Listening Comprehension
PP					
P					
1					
2					
3					
4					
5					
6					
7					
8					
9					
10					
11					
12					

SUMMARY OF QUALITATIVE ANALYSIS

Summary of Strengths and Weaknesses in Word Recognition

(Include all of the important data that have been collected on word recognition skills.)

Summary of Strengths and Weaknesses in Comprehension

(Include all of the important data that have been collected about comprehension.)

Checklist of Reading Behaviors

(Place a [+] by areas that are strong and a [–] by areas that are weak.)

1. Reads in phrases _____
2. Reads with expression _____
3. Attends to punctuation _____
4. Pronounces words correctly _____
5. Sounds out unfamiliar words _____
6. Uses structure clues, when available, to recognize unfamiliar words _____
7. Uses context clues _____
8. Makes strategic attempts to recognize unfamiliar words (applies word recognition skills flexibly) _____
9. Keeps place in material being read _____
10. Shows few signs of tension when reading _____
11. Holds book at appropriate distance from face when reading _____
12. Self-corrects errors without prompting _____

WORKSHEET FOR WORD RECOGNITION MISCUE TALLY CHART

Miscue		PP	P	1	2	3	4	5	6	7	8	9	10	11	12	Totals
Mispronunciation	A															A
	MC															MC
	SC															SC
Substitution	A															A
	MC															MC
	SC															SC
Insertion	A															A
	MC															MC
	SC															SC
Omission	A															A
	MC															MC
	SC															SC
Reversal	A															A
	MC															MC
	SC															SC
Repetition	A															A
Refusal to pronounce	A															A
Totals	A															A
	MC															MC
	SC															SC

A = All miscues of that type (excluding ones that were self-corrected)
MC = Miscues that resulted in a meaning change
SC = Self-corrected miscues

Miscue Analysis of Phonic and Structural Analysis Skills

(Tally total miscues on appropriate lines.)

Miscue	For Words in Isolation	For Words in Context
Single consonants	______	______
Consonant blends	______	______
Single vowels	______	______
Vowel digraphs	______	______
Consonant digraphs	______	______
Diphthongs	______	______
Prefixes	______	______
Suffixes	______	______
Special combinations	______	______
Word beginnings	______	______
Word middles	______	______
Word endings	______	______
Compound words	______	______
Inflectional endings	______	______
Syllabication	______	______
Accent	______	______

(*Note*: In order to fill out the analysis for words in context, it is helpful to make a list of expected reader responses and unexpected responses for easy comparison as to graphic similarity, syntactic acceptability, and semantic acceptability. See page 180 for a good way to record this information.)

WORKSHEET FOR QUALITATIVE ANALYSIS OF UNCORRECTED MISCUES IN CONTEXT

(Include mispronunciations, substitutions, insertions, omissions, and reversals.)

Passage	Type of Miscue	Expected Response	Unexpected Response	Graphic Similarity	Syntactic Acceptability	Semantic Acceptability

GRADED PASSAGES

STUDENT BOOKLET FORM D

Passages PP to 12

Read this story to find out what a girl says to a friend about going to the lake.

To the lake! Here I go.
Come with me. Please!
Dad will. Spot will.
You can too.
Dad holds my hand.
I wade. I splash. I get wet.
Dad laughs. I laugh. Spot barks.
We get out. We dry off.
That was fun.
Spot wades. He gets wet.
Spot gets out. He barks. He shakes.
Water hits me. Water hits Dad. We laugh.
We sit. We look around.
Boats sail. Birds fly.
Ducks swim. Fish jump.
Spot digs. We smile.
We go home.

Read this story to find out about Jack and his problem.

David was gone.
Jack looked and looked for him.
"David!" he called.
"David! Where are you?"

But David was not to be found.
"Oh, boy," said Jack.
"I have to find David.
What will I say to Mom and Dad?"

Then Jack went to Harriet's house.
Harriet was painting a picture.

"Where is David?" asked Jack.
"Is he here?
Did you see him?"

"No," said Harriet.
"Isn't he with you?"

“No,” said Jack.
“I don’t know where he is.
I got mad at him.
And he ran away.
Where can he be?”

Jack ran to Pat’s house.
“Pat!” he said.
“Did you see David?
I got mad at him, and he ran away.
I have to find him!”

Read this story to find out what happened to a boy named Herman one day.

Little Herman went to see his Aunt Gert.
He took the bus to the last stop.
But he still had a short walk to her house.

It was very cold.

And to keep warm, Herman pulled on his long furry coat.
And he pulled on his furry hat, which came down over his head.

He looked just like a bear, which is just what a bear thought he looked like.

"You must be my cousin Julius!" said the bear.
Grabbing Herman by the hand, the bear ran with him to his cave.

"Look who I found in the woods!" the bear cried.

All the bears ran to see Herman.
"Cousin Julius, Cousin Julius!" they cried.

Read this story to find out about the activities of some of Peter's friends.

Up in a tree, Peter's friend, the little bluebird, was singing away. "All is well! All is well! All is well!" he sang.

Peter, like all boys will do, had left the garden gate open. Soon the fat little duck followed him through the gate and into the meadow. She saw the pond. "Aha!" she thought. "What a fine place for a swim." And into the pond she went.

The bird had been watching the duck. When the duck dived into the water, the bird could not believe his eyes. He flew down for a closer look.

"Hey, you!" he called to the duck. "What are you supposed to be—some kind of a bird?"

"Of course, I'm a bird!" the duck called back.

"You're no bird," the bluebird answered. "Why, you can't even fly."

"What makes you think you're a bird?" the duck called. "You can't even swim!"

This story takes place in Japan with a man named Hamaguchi. Read it to find out about his village and what was happening there.

It was the time of harvest. Hundreds of rice stacks lined Hamaguchi's fields. It had been a fine harvest, and tonight down in the village everyone was having a good time.

Hamaguchi sat outside his house and looked down into the village. He would have liked to join the other villagers, but he was too tired—the day had been very hot. So he stayed at home with his little grandson, Tada. They could see the flags and the paper lanterns that hung across the streets of the village, and see the people getting ready for the dance. The low sun lighted up all the moving bits of color below.

It was still very hot, though a strong breeze was beginning to blow in from the sea. Suddenly the hillside shook—just a little, as if a wave were rolling slowly under it. The house creaked and rocked gently for a moment. Then all became still again.

"An earthquake," thought Hamaguchi, "but not very near. The worst of it seems far away."

Read this story to find out as much as you can about caring for a certain kind of pet.

Kittens are almost always born in a dark place. The mother cat seems to know that a strong light hurts their eyes. At first their eyes are closed. When their eyes open, in about ten days, they are a light gray color, but the kittens cannot yet see. Not until they are about three weeks old can they see clearly. By this time they can walk in a tumbling fashion out into the light, and their teeth are coming through. All this time the mother nurses them.

After kittens have been walking for a few days, it is time for them to start being weaned. Half milk, half water, and a tiny bit of baby cereal is heated and put on the floor in a low dish. Kittens don't have any idea what this is for, so they have to be shown.

Read this story to find out as much as you can about the wind.

Wind does many jobs that help us. It scatters the seeds of plants in new locations. It drives windmills and moves clouds, which are made up of water vapor, to bring rain and snow.

Wind that moves very fast, however, is dangerous. Windstorms can blow down buildings, tear up trees, and cause huge waves to crash on shores. The wildest winds of all are tornadoes. A tornado is a spinning wind that reaches down to the ground. Scientists believe that some tornadoes revolve at speeds of up to 300 miles an hour. These whirling winds tear and claw at everything they touch.

There are tornadoes of many sizes. Some touch the ground for only a few feet, but the average tornado leaves a path one mile long and fifty yards wide.

Read this story to find out about a girl and boy as they prepare to go to school.

Richard and I waved out the window as Ma and Dad drove down the driveway. Then we cleaned up the breakfast table a little and I brushed my hair one more time and we put on our raincoats. Mine is old and too short in the sleeves, and I was sorry I had to wear it on the first day at Jefferson School. We fixed the latch on the front door so it would lock behind us, and went out.

Richard said, "Here we go, up the road, to a birthday party," which are the words to a song we learned in nursery school. We always say that when we're going someplace we worry about, like the dentist.

It was funny to walk down the driveway on the first day of school and not have anyone to look back at and wave to.

Daedalus had made wings for himself and his son, and they had learned to fly. Read this story to find out what happened.

Daedalus kept a watchful eye on the boy, even as a mother bird does when she has brought a fledgling out of its nest in the treetops and launched it in the air. It was early morning; few people were about. But here and there a plowman in the field or a fisherman tending his nets caught sight of them.

"They must be gods!" the simple toilers cried, and they bent their bodies in reverent worship.

Father and son flew far out over the sea. Daedalus was no longer worried about Icarus, who managed his wings as easily as a bird. Already the islands of Delos and Paros were behind them. Calymne, rich in honey, was on their hand. But now Icarus began to yield to the full delight of his newfound powers; he wanted to soar and swoop. How thrilling it was to rise to a height, close his wings, and speed down, like a thunderbolt, then turn and rise again!

Time after time Icarus tried it, each time daring greater heights. Then, forgetting his father's warning, he soared higher still, far up into the cloudless sky.

During the Civil War, Jethro Creighton, who was too young to enlist, worked his family's farm. Read this story to find out about an experience he had.

By the first of March the weather was warm, and the higher fields were dry enough for plowing. Jethro carried a rifle with him when he went down to John's place to work. It was always possible that he might bring down some kind of wild game for the table or that he would have need to defend himself against a desperate deserter.

The field he plowed that day in early March was bordered on the east by dense woods, and Jethro became conscious that each time he approached the woods side of the field, the sharp, harsh call of a wild turkey would sound out with a strange kind of insistence—almost as if some stupid bird demanded that he stop and listen. Once when he halted his team and walked a little distance toward the woods, the calls came furiously, one after the other; then when he returned to his team and moved toward the west, they stopped until he had made the round of the field.

After several repetitions of this pattern, Jethro tethered his team and, taking up his rifle, walked into the woods.

Maurice and Maralyn Bailey were sailing in their yacht when a whale crashed into it and made a hole that caused it to sink. They were left adrift with a dinghy, a life raft, and some things they managed to save from the sinking yacht. Read the following story to find out what Maurice said about their 104th day adrift.

The thunderstorms came and went with increasing frequency. Then the wind increased and low, dark clouds scudded quickly across the sky foretelling the coming of another storm. Apprehensively we watched the waves heighten between periods of torrential driving rain. More and more our discomfort grew with the violently increasing motion; rain was now an ever present facet of our daily routine. It was difficult for us to imagine what it had been like to be warm and dry. My salt water sores were becoming daily more unbearable. The pain from these sapped my spirit and I found little contentment in living. I was in a state of abject misery. Rest had been a luxury that we had both forgotten. Now all our efforts went towards survival. There was no prospect of fishing in those conditions and we expended our energy ridding the raft of water. Even when it was not raining, waves would send water crashing over us and we would start all over again.

Each hour went by slowly and with tedious monotony. I wondered just how we could survive the next hour.

After fourteen years of separation, Joe Dagget has returned to marry Louisa Ellis, to whom he had been engaged during the long separation. Read the story to find out how Louisa felt about Joe's return.

Louisa's first emotion when Joe Dagget came home (he had not apprised her of his coming) was consternation, although she would not admit it to herself, and he never dreamed of it. Fifteen years ago she had been in love with him—at least she considered herself to be. Just at that time, gently acquiescing with and falling into the natural drift of girlhood, she had seen marriage ahead as a reasonable feature and a probable desirability of life. She had listened with calm docility to her mother's views upon the subject. Her mother was remarkable for her cool sense and sweet, even temperament. She talked wisely to her daughter when Joe Dagget presented himself, and Louisa accepted him with no hesitation. He was the first love she had ever had.

She had been faithful to him all these years. She had never dreamed of the possibility of marrying anyone else. Her life, especially for the last seven years, had been full of a pleasant peace; she had never felt discontented nor impatient over her love's absence; still, she had always looked forward to his return and their marriage as the inevitable conclusion of things.

This is a story of two men. Read to find out about them.

Of all the eager young men working on the Verrazano-Narrows Bridge under Hard Nose Murphy in the fall of 1963, few seemed better suited to the work or happier on the bridge job than the two men working together atop the cable 385 feet over the water behind the Brooklyn Tower.

One was very small, the other very large. The small man, standing five feet seven inches and weighing only 138 pounds—but very sinewy and tough—was named Edward Iannielli. He was called "The Rabbit" by the other men because he jumped the beams and ran across wires, and everybody said of the twenty-seven-year-old Iannielli that he would never live to be thirty.

The big boy was named Gerard McKee. He was a handsome, wholesome boy, about two hundred pounds and six feet three and one-half inches. He had been a Coney Island lifeguard, had charm with women and a gentle disposition, and all the men on the bridge immediately took to him, although he was not as friendly and forward as Iannielli.

Read this story to learn about two men as they embark upon an adventure.

Beneath their feet the diesel engine thudded slowly, sending a thrust of power trembling through the deck. Across Tauranga Harbor, against the wharf at Mount Maunganui, a Japanese timber ship lifted her long black hull fretfully on the tide, dragging at the hawser with a dark, clumsy impatience. Farrer looked away, out to the harbor mouth, mentally checking off Matakana Island, impatient to be past it, as though the approaching bird sanctuary barred their passage to the open sea and the things he knew awaited him there. The sun, still rising, spread hot, multifingered hands across the waters.

Conversation between the two men was desultory, as it is between total strangers, but the bond of mutual interest was there. Reminiscent, unembellished reflection forged a slow tie, and each saw the other through the light of his own experience and was willing to draw upon his stored knowledge of the sea's creatures.

And then, when they were long past Mayor Island, and the horizon had taken and absorbed it, leaving them alone with the sea's vastness, they saw the kahawai frantically surfacing in deafening crescendo, panic-stricken.

GRADED PASSAGES

TEACHER BOOKLET FORM D

Passages and Questions
PP to 12

Summary Forms for Quantitative and Qualitative Analysis

Worksheets

INTRODUCTORY STATEMENT: Read this story to find out what a girl says to a friend about going to the lake.

To the lake! Here I go.
Come with me. Please!
Dad will. Spot will.
You can too.
Dad holds my hand.
I wade. I splash. I get wet.
Dad laughs. I laugh. Spot barks.
We get out. We dry off.
That was fun.
Spot wades. He gets wet.
Spot gets out. He barks. He shakes.
Water hits me. Water hits Dad. We laugh.
We sit. We look around.
Boats sail. Birds fly.
Ducks swim. Fish jump.
Spot digs. We smile.
We go home.

SCORING AID

Word Recognition

%–Miscues
99–1
95–4
90–8
85–12

Comprehension

%–Errors
100–0
87.5–1
75–2
62.5–3
50–4
37.5–5
25–6
12.5–7
0–8

83 Words (for Word Recognition)

83 Words (for Rate)

WPM
4980

COMPREHENSION QUESTIONS

____ main idea — 1. What is this story about?
(Going to the lake is fun.)
[If a child only says, "the lake," ask, "What about the lake?"]

____ inference — 2. Does the girl who is telling the story want to go to the lake alone? (no)
What does the story say that makes you believe that?
(She wants a friend to go. She likes it that her dad and dog go.)
[Accept either reason for full credit.]

____ vocabulary — 3. What does *wade* mean? (walk in the water)

____ inference — 4. How does the girl feel about getting wet?
(She likes it. She doesn't mind. She thinks it is funny.)
[Accept any of these answers for full credit.]

____ sequence — 5. What two things does Spot do just after he gets out?
(He barks. He shakes.) [Give half credit for one of these answers.]

____ cause and effect/ inference — 6. When Spot shakes, what happens to Dad and the little girl?
(They get wet from the water he shakes off.)

____ detail — 7. What do the girl and her dad do while they sit?
(They look around, or they watch things.)
[Count either answer as correct.]

____ sequence — 8. What is the last thing they do in the story? (They go home.)

TEACHER P ☐

INTRODUCTORY STATEMENT: **Read this story to find out about Jack and his problem.**

David was gone.
Jack looked and looked for him.
"David!" he called.
"David! Where are you?"

But David was not to be found.
"Oh, boy," said Jack.
"I have to find David.
What will I say to Mom and Dad?"

Then Jack went to Harriet's house.
Harriet was painting a picture.

"Where is David?" asked Jack.
"Is he here?
Did you see him?"

"No," said Harriet.
"Isn't he with you?"

"No," said Jack.
"I don't know where he is.
I got mad at him.
And he ran away.
Where can he be?"

Jack ran to Pat's house.
"Pat!" he said.
"Did you see David?
I got mad at him, and he ran away.
I have to find him!"

SCORING AID

Word Recognition

%–Miscues
99–1
95–5
90–10
85–15

Comprehension

%–Errors
100–0
87.5–1
75–2
62.5–3
50–4
37.5–5
25–6
12.5–7
0–8

102 Words (for Word Recognition)

118 Words (for Rate)

WPM
7080

Source: "David Paints a Picture," by Leo Fay, Ramon R. Ross, and Margaret LaPray, Rand McNally Reading Program, in *Magic Rings and Funny Things*, Level 5 (Chicago: The Riverside Publishing Company, 1978), pp. 69–72.

[*Note*: Do not count as miscues mispronunciation of the names David, Jack, and Harriet. You may pronounce these words for the student if needed.]

COMPREHENSION QUESTIONS

____ main idea — 1. What was Jack's problem? (David had run away, and Jack needed to find him.)

____ sequence — 2. Whose house did Jack go to first? (Harriet's)

____ detail — 3. What was Harriet doing? (She was painting a picture.)

____ detail — 4. What did Harriet ask Jack about David? ("Isn't he with you?")

____ cause and effect/detail — 5. Why did David run away? (because Jack was mad at him)

____ inference — 6. What do you think Jack was supposed to be doing when David ran away? (taking care of David) What did the story say that caused you to answer that way? (Jack said, "What will I say to Mom and Dad?")

____ vocabulary — 7. What does the word "mad" mean in the sentence "I got mad at him"? (angry, upset, frustrated, etc.)

____ sequence — 8. Whose house did Jack go to last? (Pat's)

FORM D

☐ P PASSAGE

INTRODUCTORY STATEMENT: Read this story to find out what happened to a boy named Herman one day.

Little Herman went to see his Aunt Gert.
He took the bus to the last stop.
But he still had a short walk to her house.

It was very cold.

And to keep warm, Herman pulled on his long furry coat.
And he pulled on his furry hat, which came down over his head.

He looked just like a bear, which is just what a bear thought he looked like.

"You must be my cousin Julius!" said the bear.
Grabbing Herman by the hand, the bear ran with him to his cave.

"Look who I found in the woods!" the bear cried.

All the bears ran to see Herman.
"Cousin Julius, Cousin Julius!" they cried.

SCORING AID

Word Recognition
%–Miscues
99–1
95–5
90–10
85–16

Comprehension
%–Errors
100–0
87.5–1
75–2
62.5–3
50–4
37.5–5
25–6
12.5–7
0–8

103 Words
(for Word Recognition)

115 Words
(for Rate)

WPM
6900

Source: "Not This Bear," by Bernice Myers, in Elizabeth Sulzby and others, *Just the Thing* (New York: McGraw-Hill School Division, 1989), pp. 86–88.

[*Note*: Do not count as miscues mispronunciation of the names Herman, Aunt Gert, and Cousin Julius. You may pronounce these names for the student if needed.]

COMPREHENSION QUESTIONS

____ main idea	1. What is this story about? (Herman is mistaken for a bear; bears think Herman is their cousin.)
____ detail	2. Who was Herman going to see? (Aunt Gert; his aunt)
____ sequence	3. Name, in order, the two things he had to do to get to his aunt's house. (take the bus to the last stop and walk a short way; take the bus and then walk)
____ cause and effect/ detail	4. What caused Herman to pull on his long furry coat and his furry hat? (It was very cold; he wanted to keep warm.)
____ vocabulary	5. What does the word "furry" mean? (covered with fur; hairy, like an animal's coat)
____ detail	6. What did Herman look like with his coat and hat on? (a bear)
____ detail	7. Where did the bear take him? (to the bear's cave)
____ inference	8. Did Herman fool any of the other bears? (yes) What did the story say that made you believe that? (The bears all called him Cousin Julius.)

INTRODUCTORY STATEMENT: Read this story to find out about the activities of some of Peter's friends.

Up in a tree, Peter's friend, the little bluebird, was singing away. "All is well! All is well! All is well!" he sang.

Peter, like all boys will do, had left the garden gate open. Soon the fat little duck followed him through the gate and into the meadow. She saw the pond. "Aha!" she thought. "What a fine place for a swim." And into the pond she went.

The bird had been watching the duck. When the duck dived into the water, the bird could not believe his eyes. He flew down for a closer look.

"Hey, you!" he called to the duck. "What are you supposed to be—some kind of a bird?"

"Of course, I'm a bird!" the duck called back.

"You're no bird," the bluebird answered. "Why, you can't even fly."

"What makes you think you're a bird?" the duck called. "You can't even swim!"

SCORING AID

Word Recognition

%–Miscues

99–2
95–8
90–15
85–23

Comprehension

%–Errors

100–0
87.5–1
75–2
62.5–3
50–4
37.5–5
25–6
12.5–7
0–8

149 Words
(for Word Recognition)

149 Words
(for Rate)

WPM
8940

Source: "Peter and the Wolf," by Leo Ray, Ramon R. Ross and Margaret LaPray, Rand McNally Reading Program, in *Cartwheels and Caterpillars*, Level 8 (Chicago: The Riverside Publishing Company, 1978), pp. 140–141.

COMPREHENSION QUESTIONS

____ main idea	1.	What is this story about? (A bluebird finds out about a duck; a duck and a bluebird argue about who is a bird.)
____ detail	2.	Who was singing up in a tree? (the little bluebird)
____ detail	3.	Who followed Peter through the gate? (the fat little duck)
____ detail	4.	Why was she able to follow him? (He had left the garden gate open.)
____ cause and effect/ detail	5.	What did the duck do when she saw the pond? (She jumped in for a swim.)
____ vocabulary	6.	What does the word "dived" mean in this story? (jumped headfirst into the water)
____ sequence	7.	What did the bird do after the duck dived into the water? (He flew down for a closer look.)
____ inference	8.	Was the bluebird a boy or a girl? (a boy) What in the story makes you say so? (In the story the bluebird is called "he.")

INTRODUCTORY STATEMENT: This story takes place in Japan with a man named Hamaguchi. Read it to find out about his village and what was happening there.

It was the time of harvest. Hundreds of rice stacks lined Hamaguchi's fields. It had been a fine harvest, and tonight down in the village everyone was having a good time.

Hamaguchi sat outside his house and looked down into the village. He would have liked to join the other villagers, but he was too tired—the day had been very hot. So he stayed at home with his little grandson, Tada. They could see the flags and the paper lanterns that hung across the streets of the village, and see the people getting ready for the dance. The low sun lighted up all the moving bits of color below.

It was still very hot, though a strong breeze was beginning to blow in from the sea. Suddenly the hillside shook—just a little, as if a wave were rolling slowly under it. The house creaked and rocked gently for a moment. Then all became still again.

"An earthquake," thought Hamaguchi, "but not very near. The worst of it seems far away."

Source: "The Burning of the Rice Fields," by Lafcadio Hearn.

[*Note*: Do not count as miscues mispronunciation of the names Hamaguchi and Tada. You may pronounce these names for the student if necessary.]

SCORING AID

Word Recognition

%–Miscues

99–2
95–9
90–17
85–26

Comprehension

%–Errors

100–0
90–1
80–2
70–3
60–4
50–5
40–6
30–7
20–8
10–9
0–10

168 Words (for Word Recognition)

172 Words (for Rate)

WPM

10320

COMPREHENSION QUESTIONS

____ main idea — 1. What is this story about? (An earthquake happens during the harvest celebration; an earthquake comes while Hamaguchi watches the harvest fun.)

____ vocabulary — 2. What does the word "harvest" mean? (the season's crops; gathering in the crops)

____ detail — 3. What lined Hamaguchi's fields? (hundreds of rice stacks)

____ cause and effect/ inference — 4. Why were the people in the village having a good time and holding a celebration? (They felt good about the fine harvest.)

____ inference — 5. Where was Hamaguchi's house from the village? (up on a hill; higher than the village) [If the student says, "nearby," ask, "How did you know that?" Count the response as correct if the student indicates that the story said that he could look down at the village from his house.]

____ cause and effect/ detail — 6. Why didn't Hamaguchi join the other villagers? (because he was too tired)

____ detail — 7. What hung across the streets of the village? (flags and paper lanterns)

____ detail — 8. What kind of celebration were the people getting ready for? (a dance)

____ sequence — 9. What happened after the house creaked and rocked gently? (All became still; Hamaguchi thought it was an earthquake.) [Accept either answer for full credit.]

____ inference — 10. Was Hamaguchi worried about the earthquake? (no) What did the story say that made you believe this? (He said it wasn't very near. He said the worst of it seemed far away.)

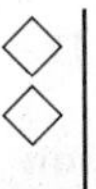

INTRODUCTORY STATEMENT: Read this story to find out as much as you can about caring for a certain kind of pet.

Kittens are almost always born in a dark place. The mother cat seems to know that a strong light hurts their eyes. At first their eyes are closed. When their eyes open, in about ten days, they are a light gray color, but the kittens cannot yet see. Not until they are about three weeks old can they see clearly. By this time they can walk in a tumbling fashion out into the light, and their teeth are coming through. All this time the mother nurses them.

After kittens have been walking for a few days, it is time for them to start being weaned. Half milk, half water, and a tiny bit of baby cereal is heated and put on the floor in a low dish. Kittens don't have any idea what this is for, so they have to be shown.

Source: *Pets*, by Frances N. Chrystie (Boston: Little, Brown, 1964).

SCORING AID

Word Recognition

%–Miscues

99–2
95–7
90–14
85–21

Comprehension

%–Errors

100–0
90–1
80–2
70–3
60–4
50–5
40–6
30–7
20–8
10–9
0–10

142 Words
(for Word Recognition)

142 Words
(for Rate)

WPM
8520

COMPREHENSION QUESTIONS

____ main idea	1. What is the purpose of this story? (to tell about the first weeks in the lives of baby kittens)
____ cause and effect/ inference	2. Why are kittens almost always born in a dark place? (The mother cat seems to know that a strong light hurts their eyes.)
____ detail	3. When do the kittens' eyes open? (in about ten days)
____ detail	4. How old are the kittens when they can see clearly? (about three weeks)
____ detail	5. What color are the kittens' eyes? (light gray)
____ vocabulary	6. What does the word "nurses" mean in the sentence "All this time the mother nurses them"? (gives them milk from her body)
____ sequence	7. What happens after the kittens have been walking for a few days? (They are weaned.)
____ vocabulary	8. What does the word "weaned" mean? (taken off the mother's milk and fed from a dish)
____ inference	9. Does the mother cat do the weaning in this story? (no) Why do you say that? (A cat couldn't heat food and put it in a dish.)
____ detail	10. How do the kittens find out what the food in the dish is for? (They have to be shown.)

INTRODUCTORY STATEMENT: Read this story to find out as much as you can about the wind.

Wind does many jobs that help us. It scatters the seeds of plants in new locations. It drives windmills and moves clouds, which are made up of water vapor, to bring rain and snow.

Wind that moves very fast, however, is dangerous. Windstorms can blow down buildings, tear up trees, and cause huge waves to crash on shores. The wildest winds of all are tornadoes. A tornado is a spinning wind that reaches down to the ground. Scientists believe that some tornadoes revolve at speeds of up to 300 miles an hour. These whirling winds tear and claw at everything they touch.

There are tornadoes of many sizes. Some touch the ground for only a few feet, but the average tornado leaves a path one mile long and fifty yards wide.

Source: "Tornadoes: Killer Storms," by George Laycock, in Leo Fay and others, *Grand Tour* (Chicago: The Riverside Publishing Company, 1989), p. 387.

SCORING AID

Word Recognition
%–Miscues
99–2
95–7
90–13
85–20

Comprehension
%–Errors
100–0
90–1
80–2
70–3
60–4
50–5
40–6
30–7
20–8
10–9
0–10

131 Words
(for Word Recognition)

131 Words
(for Rate)

WPM
$\overline{)7860}$

COMPREHENSION QUESTIONS

____ main idea — 1. What is the main idea of this story? (Although wind can be helpful, fast-moving winds like tornadoes can be dangerous.)

____ detail — 2. What are two things that wind does to help us? (scatters seeds of plants to new locations, drives windmills, moves clouds) [Accept any two of the three for full credit; accept one for half credit.]

____ vocabulary — 3. What does the word "drives" mean in the statement, "It drives windmills"? (makes them turn; makes them work)

____ cause and effect/ inference — 4. Why does the wind moving clouds help to bring rain and snow? (because there is water vapor in the clouds)

____ cause and effect/ detail — 5. What problems can windstorms cause on shores? (They can cause huge waves to crash on them.)

____ inference — 6. Can people be sure of safety in buildings during windstorms? (no) What did the story say that made you believe that? (Windstorms can blow down buildings.)

____ vocabulary — 7. What is a tornado? (a spinning wind that reaches down to the ground)

____ vocabulary — 8. What does "revolve" mean in this selection? (to turn around a center area) [Note: Accept a hand movement that indicates understanding of how the wind moves.]

____ detail — 9. How fast do some tornadoes revolve? (up to 300 miles an hour)

____ detail — 10. How long is the path of the average tornado? (one mile)

INTRODUCTORY STATEMENT: Read this story to find out about a girl and boy as they prepare to go to school.

Richard and I waved out the window as Ma and Dad drove down the driveway. Then we cleaned up the breakfast table a little and I brushed my hair one more time and we put on our raincoats. Mine is old and too short in the sleeves, and I was sorry I had to wear it on the first day at Jefferson School. We fixed the latch on the front door so it would lock behind us, and went out.

Richard said, "Here we go, up the road, to a birthday party," which are the words to a song we learned in nursery school. We always say that when we're going someplace we worry about, like the dentist.

It was funny to walk down the driveway on the first day of school and not have anyone to look back at and wave to.

Source: *The Real Me*, by Betty Miles (New York: Alfred A. Knopf, 1974).

SCORING AID

Word Recognition

%–Miscues

99–2
95–7
90–15
85–22

Comprehension

%–Errors

100–0
90–1
80–2
70–3
60–4
50–5
40–6
30–7
20–8
10–9
0–10

143 Words
(for Word Recognition)

143 Words
(for Rate)

WPM
8580

COMPREHENSION QUESTIONS

____ main idea — 1. What is the main idea of this story? (Two children get ready for the first day of school.)

____ inference — 2. What relation is Richard to the person telling the story? (brother)

____ inference — 3. What was the weather like on the day of the story? (rainy, or at least cloudy)

____ cause and effect/detail — 4. What caused the speaker to be sorry that she had to wear her raincoat? (It was old and too short in the sleeves.)

____ sequence — 5. What was the last thing the children did before they went outside? (They fixed the latch on the front door so it would lock behind them.)

____ vocabulary — 6. What is a latch? (the catch that holds a door closed)

____ inference — 7. Was Richard worried about going to school? (yes) What did the story say that caused you to answer in that way? (Richard sang a song that they always sang when they were going someplace they worried about.)

____ detail — 8. Where had Richard learned the song he sang? (in nursery school)

____ vocabulary — 9. What does the word "funny" mean when it is used in the last sentence of the story to describe how the children felt as they walked down the driveway? (strange)

____ inference — 10. Was there anyone left in the house when the children left? (no) What fact in the story caused you to answer that way? (There was no one to look back at and wave to.)

INTRODUCTORY STATEMENT: Daedalus had made wings for himself and his son, and they had learned to fly. Read this story to find out what happened.

Daedalus kept a watchful eye on the boy, even as a mother bird does when she has brought a fledgling out of its nest in the treetops and launched it in the air. It was early morning; few people were about. But here and there a plowman in the field or a fisherman tending his nets caught sight of them.

"They must be gods!" the simple toilers cried, and they bent their bodies in reverent worship.

Father and son flew far out over the sea. Daedalus was no longer worried about Icarus, who managed his wings as easily as a bird. Already the islands of Delos and Paros were behind them. Calymne, rich in honey, was on their hand. But now Icarus began to yield to the full delight of his newfound powers; he wanted to soar and swoop. How thrilling it was to rise to a height, close his wings, and speed down, like a thunderbolt, then turn and rise again!

Time after time Icarus tried it, each time daring greater heights. Then, forgetting his father's warning, he soared higher still, far up into the cloudless sky.

Source: "Daedalus," adapted from *Golden Treasury of Myths and Legends* by Anne Terry White.
[*Note*: Do not count as miscues mispronunciation of the names Daedalus, Icarus, Delos, Paros, and Calymne. You may pronounce these words for the student if needed.]

SCORING AID

Word Recognition
%–Miscues
99–2
95–9
90–18
85–27

Comprehension
%–Errors
100–0
90–1
80–2
70–3
60–4
50–5
40–6
30–7
20–8
10–9
0–10

180 Words
(for Word Recognition)

188 Words
(for Rate)

WPM
11280

COMPREHENSION QUESTIONS

____ main idea — 1. What is the main idea of this story? (Icarus flies high; Icarus and Daedalus fly like birds.)

____ inference — 2. Was Daedalus worried about Icarus at first? (yes) What fact in the story caused you to answer in that way? (He kept a watchful eye on Icarus. Later it said he was no longer worried.)

____ vocabulary — 3. What is a fledgling? (a young bird just ready to fly)

____ vocabulary — 4. What does the word "launched" mean as it is used in this story? (shoved off into the air)

____ detail — 5. What time of day was it at the beginning of the story? (early morning)

____ detail — 6. What did the workmen think Daedalus and Icarus were? (gods)

____ inference — 7. Was Icarus good at flying? (yes) What did the story say that caused you to answer that way? (He managed his wings as easily as a bird, and birds are good at flying.)

____ cause and effect/ detail — 8. What caused Icarus to want to soar and swoop? (his delight with his newfound powers)

____ sequence — 9. Name, in order, four things Icarus did time after time. (He would rise to a height, close his wings, speed down, turn and rise again.)

____ inference — 10. What did Daedalus warn his son about? (flying too high)

INTRODUCTORY STATEMENT: During the Civil War, Jethro Creighton, who was too young to enlist, worked his family's farm. Read this story to find out about an experience he had.

By the first of March the weather was warm, and the higher fields were dry enough for plowing. Jethro carried a rifle with him when he went down to John's place to work. It was always possible that he might bring down some kind of wild game for the table or that he would have need to defend himself against a desperate deserter.

The field he plowed that day in early March was bordered on the east by dense woods, and Jethro became conscious that each time he approached the woods side of the field, the sharp, harsh call of a wild turkey would sound out with a strange kind of insistence—almost as if some stupid bird demanded that he stop and listen. Once when he halted his team and walked a little distance toward the woods, the calls came furiously, one after the other; then when he returned to his team and moved toward the west, they stopped until he had made the round of the field.

After several repetitions of this pattern, Jethro tethered his team and, taking up his rifle, walked into the woods.

Source: From *Across Five Aprils*, by Irene Hunt. © 1991 by Modern Curriculum Press, Simon & Schuster Education Group. Used by permission.

[*Note*: Do not count as a miscue mispronunciation of the name Jethro. You may pronounce this name for the student if necessary.]

SCORING AID

Word Recognition
%–Miscues
99–2
95–10
90–19
85–28

Comprehension
%–Errors
100–0
90–1
80–2
70–3
60–4
50–5
40–6
30–7
20–8
10–9
0–10

185 Words
(for Word Recognition)

188 Words
(for Rate)

WPM
11280

COMPREHENSION QUESTIONS

____ main idea	1. What is the main idea of this story? (While plowing, Jethro hears a strange wild turkey call.)
____ detail	2. What was the weather like by the first of March? (warm)
____ cause and effect/ inference	3. Why did Jethro carry a rifle with him when he went down to John's place to work? (because he might need it to shoot wild game or defend himself against a deserter) [Accept either part for full credit.]
____ vocabulary	4. What does the phrase "wild game for the table" mean? (wild animals that can be used for food)
____ detail	5. What bordered the field that Jethro was plowing on the east? (dense woods; woods)
____ detail	6. What happened each time Jethro approached the woods side of the field? (A wild turkey call would sound out.)
____ detail	7. What was the sound of a wild turkey call like? (sharp and harsh)
____ sequence	8. What happened just after he halted his team and walked a little distance toward the woods? (The calls came furiously, one after the other.)
____ vocabulary	9. What does the word "tethered" mean? (tied to something)
____ detail	10. What did Jethro take with him into the woods? (his rifle)

INTRODUCTORY STATEMENT: Maurice and Maralyn Bailey were sailing in their yacht when a whale crashed into it and made a hole that caused it to sink. They were left adrift with a dinghy, a life raft, and some things they managed to save from the sinking yacht. Read the following story to find out what Maurice said about their 104th day adrift.

SCORING AID	
Word Recognition	
%–Miscues	
99–2	
95–9	
90–18	
85–28	
Comprehension	
%–Errors	
100–0	
90–1	
80–2	
70–3	
60–4	
50–5	
40–6	
30–7	
20–8	
10–9	
0–10	
184 Words (for Word Recognition)	
184 Words (for Rate)	
WPM	
11040	

The thunderstorms came and went with increasing frequency. Then the wind increased and low, dark clouds scudded quickly across the sky foretelling the coming of another storm. Apprehensively we watched the waves heighten between periods of torrential driving rain. More and more our discomfort grew with the violently increasing motion; rain was now an ever present facet of our daily routine. It was difficult for us to imagine what it had been like to be warm and dry. My salt water sores were becoming daily more unbearable. The pain from these sapped my spirit and I found little contentment in living. I was in a state of abject misery. Rest had been a luxury that we had both forgotten. Now all our efforts went towards survival. There was no prospect of fishing in those conditions and we expended our energy ridding the raft of water. Even when it was not raining, waves would send water crashing over us and we would start all over again.

Each hour went by slowly and with tedious monotony. I wondered just how we could survive the next hour.

Source: From *Staying Alive!*, by Maurice and Maralyn Bailey.

COMPREHENSION QUESTIONS

____ main idea — 1. What is the main idea of this story? (Surviving while adrift was difficult.)

____ detail — 2. What weather problems did Maurice and Maralyn face? (frequent thunderstorms)

____ sequence — 3. What came *before* each thunderstorm? (increasing wind; dark clouds moving quickly across the sky)

____ vocabulary — 4. What does the word "apprehensively" mean? (fearfully; uneasily)

____ cause and effect/ detail — 5. What caused them more and more discomfort? (the violently increasing motion, the rain, the salt water sores) [Accept any of these answers.]

____ inference — 6. Were Maurice and Maralyn cold? (yes) What did the story say that made you believe that? (It said it was difficult for them to imagine what it had been like to be warm and dry; it said that they were wet and the wind was frequently blowing, and that will make you cold.)

____ detail or inference — 7. Other than being cold, how did Maurice feel? (discontented and miserable [detail] or tired [inference])

____ inference — 8. How much rest were Maralyn and Maurice getting? (none)

____ cause and effect/ detail or inference — 9. What caused the raft to fill up with water? (waves that crashed over them [detail] or rain [inference]) [Accept either answer.]

____ vocabulary — 10. What does the word "monotony" mean? (sameness; invariability)

INTRODUCTORY STATEMENT: After fourteen years of separation, Joe Dagget has returned to marry Louisa Ellis, to whom he had been engaged during the long separation. Read the story to find out how Louisa felt about Joe's return.

Louisa's first emotion when Joe Dagget came home (he had not apprised her of his coming) was consternation, although she would not admit it to herself, and he never dreamed of it. Fifteen years ago she had been in love with him—at least she considered herself to be. Just at that time, gently acquiescing with and falling into the natural drift of girlhood, she had seen marriage ahead as a reasonable feature and a probable desirability of life. She had listened with calm docility to her mother's views upon the subject. Her mother was remarkable for her cool sense and sweet, even temperament. She talked wisely to her daughter when Joe Dagget presented himself, and Louisa accepted him with no hesitation. He was the first love she had ever had.

She had been faithful to him all these years. She had never dreamed of the possibility of marrying anyone else. Her life, especially for the last seven years, had been full of a pleasant peace; she had never felt discontented nor impatient over her love's absence; still, she had always looked forward to his return and their marriage as the inevitable conclusion of things.

Source: From "A New England Nun," by Mary E. Wilkins Freeman.

SCORING AID

Word Recognition

%–Miscues

99	2
95	10
90	19
85	29

Comprehension

%–Errors

100	0
90	1
80	2
70	3
60	4
50	5
40	6
30	7
20	8
10	9
0	10

195 Words (for Word Recognition)

195 Words (for Rate)

WPM
)11700

COMPREHENSION QUESTIONS

____ main idea 1. In your own words, tell me one sentence that expresses the main thought in this story. (Although Louisa has looked forward to Joe's return for years, she is not very enthusiastic about it when he does return.)

____ vocabulary 2. What does the word "apprised" mean? (notified; informed)

____ inference 3. Was Louisa still in love with Joe when he came back? (no) What did the story say that made you believe that? (It said, "Fifteen years ago she had been in love with him." It also said she had not been discontented during his absence.)

____ detail 4. How had Louisa viewed marriage fifteen years ago? (as reasonable and probably desirable)

____ sequence 5. What had Louisa done after Joe presented himself as a suitor, but before she accepted him? (listened to her mother's opinions; talked with her mother)

____ cause and effect/inference 6. What was one thing other than her view of marriage in general that caused Louisa not to hesitate when Joe asked her to marry him? (her mother's advice; considering herself to be in love with him)

____ inference 7. How many boyfriends had Louisa had in her life? (only one; only Joe)

____ detail 8. What had Louisa's life been full of for the last seven years? (a pleasant peace)

____ vocabulary 9. What does the word "inevitable" mean? (sure to happen; unavoidable; inescapable; unalterable)

____ detail 10. What did Louisa see as the inevitable conclusion of things? (Joe's return and their marriage; their marriage)

INTRODUCTORY STATEMENT: This is the story of two men. Read to find out about them.

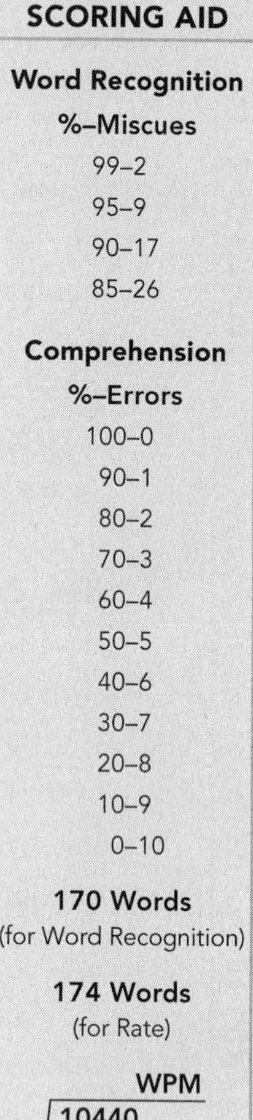

SCORING AID

Word Recognition
%–Miscues
99–2
95–9
90–17
85–26

Comprehension
%–Errors
100–0
90–1
80–2
70–3
60–4
50–5
40–6
30–7
20–8
10–9
0–10

170 Words
(for Word Recognition)

174 Words
(for Rate)

WPM
10440

Of all the eager young men working on the Verrazano-Narrows Bridge under Hard Nose Murphy in the fall of 1963, few seemed better suited to the work or happier on the bridge job than the two men working together atop the cable 385 feet over the water behind the Brooklyn Tower.

One was very small, the other very large. The small man, standing five feet seven inches and weighing only 138 pounds—but very sinewy and tough—was named Edward Iannielli. He was called "The Rabbit" by the other men because he jumped the beams and ran across wires, and everybody said of the twenty-seven-year-old Iannielli that he would never live to be thirty.

The big boy was named Gerard McKee. He was a handsome, wholesome boy, about two hundred pounds and six feet three and one-half inches. He had been a Coney Island lifeguard, had charm with women and a gentle disposition, and all the men on the bridge immediately took to him, although he was not as friendly and forward as Iannielli.

Source: *The Bridge*, by Gay Talese (New York: Harper and Row, 1964).

[*Note*: Do not count as miscues mispronunciation of the names Verrazano and Iannielli. You may pronounce these words for the student if needed.]

COMPREHENSION QUESTIONS

____ main idea — 1. What is the main idea of this story?
(Two young bridge workers are suited to the job.)

____ inference — 2. Who was in charge of the men's work at the bridge? (Murphy)

____ inference — 3. Is it likely that Murphy was a demanding boss? (yes)
What in the story made you think this? (His nickname was Hard Nose.)

____ detail — 4. When was the bridge job being done? (1963; fall of 1963)

____ inference — 5. Did Edward and Gerard enjoy their bridge job? (yes)
What in the story caused you to say that?
(It said few seemed to be happier.)

____ vocabulary — 6. What does the word "sinewy" mean in the phrase "very sinewy and tough"? (strong, muscular)

____ cause and effect/detail — 7. What caused the men to call Edward "The Rabbit"?
(He jumped beams and ran across wires.)

____ detail — 8. How old was Edward? (twenty-seven years old)

____ sequence — 9. What job did Gerard have before coming to work on the bridge?
(Coney Island lifeguard)

____ detail — 10. Which of the two men was more friendly? (Edward Iannielli)

★ TEACHER 12 ★ FORM D ★ 12 PASSAGE ★

INTRODUCTORY STATEMENT: Read this story to learn about two men as they embark upon an adventure.

Beneath their feet the diesel engine thudded slowly, sending a thrust of power trembling through the deck. Across Tauranga Harbor, against the wharf at Mount Maunganui, a Japanese timber ship lifted her long black hull fretfully on the tide, dragging at the hawser with a dark, clumsy impatience. Farrer looked away, out to the harbor mouth, mentally checking off Matakana Island, impatient to be past it, as though the approaching bird sanctuary barred their passage to the open sea and the things he knew awaited him there. The sun, still rising, spread hot, multifingered hands across the waters.

Conversation between the two men was desultory, as it is between total strangers, but the bond of mutual interest was there. Reminiscent, unembellished reflection forged a slow tie, and each saw the other through the light of his own experience and was willing to draw upon his stored knowledge of the sea's creatures.

And then, when they were long past Mayor Island, and the horizon had taken and absorbed it, leaving them alone with the sea's vastness, they saw the kahawai frantically surfacing in deafening crescendo, panic-stricken.

Source: "Black Marlin," by Cecilia Dabrowska, *Blackwood's Magazine*, August 1962. Copyright 1962 Cecilia Dabrowska. Reprinted by permission of William Blackwood & Sons, Ltd.

[*Note*: Do not count as miscues mispronunciation of the names Tauranga, Maunganui, and Matakana. You may pronounce these words for the student if needed.]

SCORING AID

Word Recognition
%–Miscues

99–2
95–10
90–19
85–28

Comprehension
%–Errors

100–0
90–1
80–2
70–3
60–4
50–5
40–6
30–7
20–8
10–9
0–10

182 Words
(for Word Recognition)

185 Words
(for Rate)

WPM
11100

COMPREHENSION QUESTIONS

____ main idea — 1. What is the main idea of this story? (Two men begin a trip on the sea; two men leave the harbor on a ship.)

____ detail — 2. How was the boat powered? (with a diesel engine)

____ detail — 3. How did Farrer feel at the beginning of the story? (impatient to reach the open sea)

____ inference — 4. What time of day was it? (morning) What fact in the story caused you to answer in this way? (The sun was still rising.)

____ vocabulary — 5. What does the word "desultory" mean in the statement, "Conversation between the two men was desultory"? (random; aimless; going from one topic to another)

____ cause and effect/ inference — 6. What caused the conversation to be desultory? (The men were strangers.)

____ inference — 7. What was the mutual interest of the men? (the sea's creatures)

____ vocabulary — 8. What does the word "unembellished" mean? (not enhanced by fanciful or fictitious details; unadorned)

____ sequence — 9. What was the last thing that happened in the story? (They saw the kahawai frantically surfacing; they saw the fish frantically surfacing.)

____ inference — 10. What are kahawai? (fish)

SUMMARY OF QUANTITATIVE ANALYSIS

Student's Name ______________________ **Grade** ______ **Date** ______ **Administrator** ______________________

Forms Used: Word Lists, Form _____ Oral Passages, Form _____ Silent Passages, Form _____ Listening Comprehension, Form _____

Performance Levels Based on Full Inventory (Oral & Silent): Independent _____ Instructional _____ Frustration _____ Listening Comprehension _____

Performance Levels Based on Oral Passages: Independent _____ Instructional _____ Frustration _____ Listening Comprehension _____

Performance Levels Based on Silent Passages: Independent _____ Instructional _____ Frustration _____ Listening Comprehension _____

Optional Comparison Levels: Independent _____ Instructional _____ Frustration _____ **Rate of Reading:** High _____ Average _____ Low _____

Performance Levels Based on Graded Word Lists: Placement _____ Independent _____ Instructional _____ Frustration _____

Types of Miscues in Context

	Mispronunciation	Substitution	Insertion	Omission	Reversal	Repetition	Refusal to Pronounce	Row Totals
Total								
Meaning changed								
Self-corrected								

Comprehension Skill Analysis Chart

Skill	Number of Questions	Number of Errors	Percent of Errors
Main idea			
Detail			
Sequence			
Cause and effect			
Inference			
Vocabulary			

Summary Table of Percentages

Level	Word Recognition	Oral Comprehension	Silent Comprehension	Average Comprehension	Listening Comprehension
PP					
P					
1					
2					
3					
4					
5					
6					
7					
8					
9					
10					
11					
12					

SUMMARY OF QUALITATIVE ANALYSIS

Summary of Strengths and Weaknesses in Word Recognition

(Include all of the important data that have been collected on word recognition skills.)

Summary of Strengths and Weaknesses in Comprehension

(Include all of the important data that have been collected about comprehension.)

Checklist of Reading Behaviors

(Place a [+] by areas that are strong and a [–] by areas that are weak.)

1. Reads in phrases _____
2. Reads with expression _____
3. Attends to punctuation _____
4. Pronounces words correctly _____
5. Sounds out unfamiliar words _____
6. Uses structure clues, when available, to recognize unfamiliar words _____
7. Uses context clues _____
8. Makes strategic attempts to recognize unfamiliar words (applies word recognition skills flexibly) _____
9. Keeps place in material being read _____
10. Shows few signs of tension when reading _____
11. Holds book at appropriate distance from face when reading _____
12. Self-corrects errors without prompting _____

WORKSHEET FOR WORD RECOGNITION MISCUE TALLY CHART

Miscue		PP	P	1	2	3	4	5	6	7	8	9	10	11	12	Totals
Mispronunciation	**A**															**A**
	MC															**MC**
	SC															**SC**
Substitution	**A**															**A**
	MC															**MC**
	SC															**SC**
Insertion	**A**															**A**
	MC															**MC**
	SC															**SC**
Omission	**A**															**A**
	MC															**MC**
	SC															**SC**
Reversal	**A**															**A**
	MC															**MC**
	SC															**SC**
Repetition	**A**															**A**
Refusal to pronounce	**A**															**A**
Totals	**A**															**A**
	MC															**MC**
	SC															**SC**

A = All miscues of that type (excluding ones that were self-corrected)
MC = Miscues that resulted in a meaning change
SC = Self-corrected miscues

Miscue Analysis of Phonic and Structural Analysis Skills

(Tally total miscues on appropriate lines.)

Miscue	For Words in Isolation	For Words in Context
Single consonants	________	________
Consonant blends	________	________
Single vowels	________	________
Vowel digraphs	________	________
Consonant digraphs	________	________
Diphthongs	________	________
Prefixes	________	________
Suffixes	________	________
Special combinations	________	________
Word beginnings	________	________
Word middles	________	________
Word endings	________	________
Compound words	________	________
Inflectional endings	________	________
Syllabication	________	________
Accent	________	________

(*Note*: In order to fill out the analysis for words in context, it is helpful to make a list of expected reader responses and unexpected responses for easy comparison as to graphic similarity, syntactic acceptability, and semantic acceptability. See page 218 for a good way to record this information.)

WORKSHEET FOR QUALITATIVE ANALYSIS OF UNCORRECTED MISCUES IN CONTEXT

(Include mispronunciations, substitutions, insertions, omissions, and reversals.)

Passage	Type of Miscue	Expected Response	Unexpected Response	Graphic Similarity	Syntactic Acceptability	Semantic Acceptability

APPENDIX A

Choosing Books to Develop and Support Children's Reading Proficiency

After using the IRI to discover the reading levels of your students, you will probably want to provide books at the appropriate levels for students to read for recreation or outside reading (books on their independent levels) or for your classroom instruction (books on their instructional levels). You can use such books for recreational reading or additional reading practice to build fluency (independent level books) or for skill and strategy development in reading groups (instructional level books). Locating books that are appropriate is a time-consuming task, however. The following lists of books have been compiled to assist you in this task.

Considerations in Using the Lists

Readability measures have indicated that the following books are appropriate for these respective levels. Remember that readability measures provide only *estimates* of difficulty because many factors that affect the difficulty of a book for a particular student are not included in formulas. Readers' backgrounds of experience and interests both greatly affect the level of book that they will be able to read. Readers with a large amount of experience with a topic will be able to read material on that topic at a much higher level than they could read material for which they had little background. Likewise, most readers can read material in which they are interested at higher levels than they can read material in which they have little or no interest. The maturity levels of the students also affect the material that they can read with comprehension. Some themes are not within the maturity levels of students who have the mechanical skills to read the texts.

Therefore, although the books on these lists can provide appropriate additional reading practice for students who are independent at these levels and can provide appropriate material for instruction for those who are at these instructional levels, some of them may not be within the range of experiences of the students involved; some of the stories/topics may not be of interest to these students; and some may not fit the maturity levels of the students. Only teacher judgment can result in the best matches of students with books.

The books listed on pages 220–225 are available in a number of editions, sometimes from different publishers. Any edition that is not listed as abridged or adapted should work for the grade levels indicated.

Books Appropriate for Each Reading Level in the IRI

Preprimer

Awdry, Rev. W. *Catch Me, Catch Me!: A Thomas the Tank Engine Story.*

Bridwell, Norman. *Clifford the Big Red Dog.*

Brown, Margaret Wise. *Goodnight Moon.*

Donnelly, Liza. *Dinosaur Garden.*

Harrison, David. *Wake Up, Sun!*

Kennedy, J., and A. Eaton. *Two Points.*

Malka, Lucy. *Fun with Hats.*

Mayer, Mercer. *All by Myself.*

Phillips, Joan. *Lucky Bear.*

Salem, Lynn, and Josie Stewart. *Here's Skipper.*

Shaw, Nancy. *Sheep in a Jeep.*

Slater, Teddy. *The Bunny Hop.*

Smith, Sue. *Honk!*

Urmston, Kathleen, and Karen Evans. *The Clown.*

Urmston, Kathleen, and Karen Evans. *Colors in the City.*

Urmston, Kathleen, and Karen Evans. *Marching Band.*

Wildsmith, Brian. *Cat on the Mat.*

Ziefert, Harriet. *A Dozen Dogs: A Read-and-Count Story.*

Ziefert, Harriet, and Emilie Boon. *Mommy, Where Are You?*

Primer

Aylesworth, Jim. *Old Black Fly.*

Bordelon, Carolyn. *Octopus Goes to School.*

Cocca-Leffler, Maryann. *Ice-Cold Birthday.*

Crews, Donald. *Shortcut.*

Diaz, Nellie. *Cool Off.*

Edwards, Roberta. *Five Silly Fishermen.*

Fleming, Denise. *In the Tall, Tall Grass.*

Frankford, Marilyn. *Going to Grandpa's.*

Geddes, Diana. *It's Football Time.*

Gelman, Rita Golden. *Why Can't I Fly?*

Gibson, Kathleen. *Where Does Teacher Sleep?*

Guarino, Deborah. *Is Your Mama a Llama?*

Hoff, Syd. *Who Will Be My Friends?*

Jonas, Ann. *Now We Can Go.*

Kalan, Robert. *Rain.*

Lake, Mary Dixon. *I Love Bugs.*

Lake, Mary Dixon. *My Circus Family.*

Lovell, Scarlett and Diane. *Is This a Monster?*

Martin, Bill. *Brown Bear, Brown Bear.*

Mayer, Mercer. *Just Me and My Puppy.*

Mayer, Mercer. *Me Too!*

Montgomery, Charlotte. *Look Again.*

Mueller, Virginia. *Playhouse for Monster.*

Pasternac, Susana. *In the City.*

Peek, Merle. *Round and Round.*

Shaw, Nancy. *Sheep Take a Hike.*

Steptoe, John. *Baby Says.*

Tafuri, Nancy. *Spots, Feathers and Curly Tails.*

Urmston, Kathleen, and Karen Evans. *Looking for Halloween.*

Urmston, Kathleen, and Karen Evans. *Sammy at the Farm.*

Vandine, JoAnn. *I Eat Leaves.*

Vandine, JoAnn. *Run! Run!*

Wildsmith, Brian. *All Fall Down.*

Wildsmith, Brian. *My Dream.*

Wildsmith, Brian. *Toot, Toot.*

Wildsmith, Brian. *What a Tale!*

Williams, Sue. *I Went Walking.*

First Reader

Asch, Frank. *Just Like Daddy.*

Barton, Byron. *Dinosaurs, Dinosaurs.*

Bogart, Jo Ellen. *Daniel's Dog.*

Bolton, Faye. *Melting.*

Brandenburg, Franz. *Cock-A-Doodle-Do.*

Brenner, Barbara. *Moon Boy.*

Brownrigg, Sheri. *All Tutus Should Be Pink.*

Campbell, Rod. *Dear Zoo.*

DeRegniers, Beatrice Schenk. *Going for a Walk.*

Doyle, Charlotte. *Freddie's Spaghetti.*

Everitt, Betsy. *Mean Soup.*

Galdone, Paul. *Cat Goes Fiddle-i-fee.*

Gerstein, Mordicai. *Roll Over.*

Henkes, Kevin. *SHHH.*

Hest, Amy. *In the Rain with Baby Duck.*

Hoff, Syd. *Sammy the Seal.*

Hood, Susan. *Too-Tall Paul, Too-Small Paul.*

Hurd, Edith Thacher. *Johnny Lion's Rubber Boots.*

Hutchins, Pat. *Rosie's Walk.*

Isadora, Rachel. *At the Crossroads.*

Joyce, William. *Friendly Snowman.*

Kraus, Robert. *Herman the Helper Lends a Hand.*

Krauss, Ruth. *Is This You?*

Lloyd, David. *Grandma and the Pirate.*

Low, Joseph. *Mice Twice.*

Maris, Ron. *Is Anyone Home?*

Mayer, Gina and Mercer. *Just Me and My Cousin.*

Mitchell, Greg. *My Grandpa.*

Parish, Peggy. *Scruffy.*

Reese, Bob. *Huzzard Buzzard.*

Rockwell, Harlow. *My Kitchen.*

Stadler, John. *Hooray for Snail.*

Stewart, Josie, and Lynn Salem. *No Luck.*

Tibo, Gilles. *Simon and the Wind.*

Udry, Janice May. *The Moon Jumpers.*

Ward, Cindy. *Cookie's Week.*

Watanabe, Shigeo. *I'm King of the Castle.*

Watanabe, Shigeo. *Where's My Daddy?*

West, Colin. *Have You Seen the Crocodile?*

West, Colin. *Pardon? Said the Giraffe.*

Wheeler, Cindy. *Marmalade's Nap.*

Wheeler, Cindy. *Marmalade's Snowy Day.*

Wheeler, Cindy. *Rose.*

Ziefert, Harriet. *Harry Takes a Bath.*

Ziefert, Harriet. *Here Comes the Bus.*

Ziefert, Harriet. *Thank You, Nicky!*

Ziefert, Harriet. *Wheels on the Bus.*

Grade 2

Alexander, Martha. *Blackboard Bear.*

Asch, Frank. *Bear's Bargain.*

Asch, Frank. *Bear Shadow.*

Benchley, Nathaniel. *Red Fox and His Canoe.*

Berenstain, Stan and Jan. *He Bear, She Bear.*

Bonsall, Crosby. *And I Mean It, Stanley.*

Brown, Margaret Wise. *Little Fireman.*

Carle, Eric. *The Very Hungry Catepillar.*

Cohen, Miriam. *Don't Eat Too Much Turkey!*

Cole, Joanna. *Norma Jean, Jumping Bean.*

Cummings, Pat. *Jimmy Lee Did It.*

Degan, Bruce. *Jamberry.*

dePaola, Tomie. *Charlie Needs a Cloak.*

Dr. Seuss. *Green Eggs and Ham.*

Dr. Seuss. *Great Day for Up.*

Dr. Seuss. *Hop on Pop.*

Dr. Seuss. *I Can Read with My Eyes Shut.*

Dr. Seuss. *The Cat in the Hat.*

Emberly, Ed. *Drummer Hoff.*

Flack, Marjorie. *Ask Mr. Bear.*

Galdone, Paul. *The Little Red Hen.*

Giff, Patricia Reilly. *Purple Climbing Days.*

Giff, Patricia Reilly. *Say Cheese.*

Gross, Ruth Belov. *The Bremen-Town Musicians.*

Hoff, Syd. *Barney's Horse.*

Hoff, Syd. *Danny and the Dinosaur.*

Hoff, Syd. *The Horse in Harry's Room.*

Hutchins, Pat. *Clocks and More Clocks.*

Hutchins, Pat. *The Doorbell Rang.*

Keats, Ezra Jack. *Peter's Chair.*

Keats, Ezra Jack. *The Snowy Day.*

Lionni, Leo. *Little Blue and Little Yellow.*

Lobel, Arnold. *Mouse Soup.*

Lobel, Arnold. *Mouse Tales.*

Mayer, Mercer. *I Was So Mad.*

Mayer, Mercer. *There's a Nightmare in My Closet.*

McCully, Emily Arnold. *The Grandma Mix-Up.*

McPhail, David M. *The Bear's Toothache.*

Parish, Peggy. *Play Ball, Amelia Bedelia.*

Peppe, Rodney. *The House that Jack Built.*

Perkins, Al. *Left Hand, Fingers, Thumb.*

Rey, Margaret, and H. A. Rey. *Curious George Goes to an Ice Cream Shop.*

Rylant, Cynthia. *Henry and Mudge and the Forever Sea.*

Rylant, Cynthia. *Henry and Mudge in Puddle Trouble.*

Rylant, Cynthia. *Henry and Mudge in the Green Time.*

Rylant, Cynthia. *Henry and Mudge: The First Book.*

Selsam, Millicent. *How Kittens Grow.*

Sendak, Maurice. *Let's Be Enemies.*

Sendak, Maurice. *Where the Wild Things Are.*

Stadler, John. *Adventures of Snail at School.*

Thaler, Mike. *A Hippopotamus Ate the Teacher.*

Waber, Bernard. *Ira Sleeps Over.*

Waddell, Martin. *Farmer Duck.*

Zion, Gene. *Harry and the Lady Next Door.*

Grade 3

Aliki. *Dinosaur Bones.*

Bemelmans, Ludwig. *Madeline.*

Blume, Judy. *Otherwise Known as Sheila the Great.*

Blume, Judy. *Tales of a Fourth Grade Nothing.*

Brett, Jan. *Berlioz the Bear.*

Brett, Jan. *The Mitten.*

Cameron, Ann. *It Takes a Village.*

Cameron, Ann. *More Stories Julian Tells.*

Cameron, Ann. *Stories Julian Tells.*

Clymer, Susan. *Key to the Treasure.*

Dahl, Roald. *Llama Pajamas.*

Danziger, Paula. *Amber Brown Goes Forth.*

Danziger, Paula. *Amber Brown Is Not a Crayon.*

Danziger, Paula. *Amber Brown Sees Red.*

Danziger, Paula. *Amber Brown Wants Extra Credit.*

Danziger, Paula. *You Can't Eat Your Chicken Pox, Amber Brown.*

dePaola, Tomie. *The Cloud Book.*

Donally, Judy. *The Titanic.*

Gag, Wanda. *Millions of Cats.*

Gibbons, Gail. *Frogs.*

Giff, Patricia Reilly. *Shark in School.*

Greene, Carol. *Martin Luther King, Jr.*

Hall, Lynn. *The Mystery of Pony Hollow.*

Hurwitz, Johanna. *School's Out.*

Lionni, Leo. *Frederick.*

MacLachlan, Patricia. *Sarah, Plain and Tall.*

MacLachlan, Patricia. *Seven Kisses in a Row.*

Mathis, Sharon Bell. *Sidewalk Story.*

Parish, Peggy. *Julian's Glorious Summer.*

Polacco, Patricia. *Pink and Say.*

Roop, Peter and Connie. *Ahyoka and the Talking Leaves.*

Say, Allen. *Grandfather's Journey.*

Scieszka, Jon. *The Frog Prince, Continued.*

Sobol, Donald J. *Encyclopedia Brown Shows the Way.*

Van Allsburg, Chris. *The Polar Express.*

Viorst, Judith. *Alexander and the Terrible, Horrible, No Good, Very Bad Day.*

Viorst, Judith. *Alexander, Who Is Not (Do You Hear Me? I Mean It!) Going to Move.*

Viorst, Judith. *Alexander, Who Used to Be Rich Last Sunday.*

Whelen, Gloria. *Next Spring an Oriole.*

Grade 4

Alberts, Nancy. *Second Grade Star.*

Buck, Pearl S. *The Big Wave.*

Byars, Betsy. *Cybil War.*

Christopher, Matt. *Pressure Play.*

Christopher, Matt. *Red-Hot Hightops.*

Cleary, Beverly. *Dear Mr. Henshaw.*

Clifford, Eth. *Help! I'm a Prisoner in the Library.*

Coatsworth, Elizabeth. *The Cat Who Went to Heaven.*

Coerr, Eleanor. *Sadako and the Thousand Paper Cranes.*

Conrad, Pam. *Pedro's Journal.*

Conrad, Pam. *Prairie Songs.*

Dahl, Roald. *James and the Giant Peach.*

Fleischman, Sid. *Ghost on Saturday Night.*

Giff, Patricia Reilly. *Fourth Grade Celebrity.*

Henry, Marguerite. *Brighty of the Grand Canyon.*

Hesse, Karen. *Just Juice.*

Hollander, Phyllis and Zander. *Amazing But True Sports Stories.*

Howe, James. *Bunnicula.*

Hudson, Wade. *Five Brave Explorers.*

Hudson, Wade. *Five Notable Inventors.*

Koller, Jackie French. *A Dragon in the Family.*

King-Smith, Dick. *Babe the Gallant Pig.*

Kinsey-Warnock, Leslie. *The Canada Geese Quilt.*

Lowry, Lois. *All About Sam.*

Lowry, Lois. *Anastasia Krupnik.*

Macdonald, Marianne. *Dragon for Sale.*

MacLachlan, Patricia. *Arthur, for the Very First Time.*

McCloskey, Robert. *Homer Price.*

McGovern, Ann. *If You Lived in Colonial Times.*

McGovern, Ann. *If You Lived with the Sioux Indians.*

McKay, Hilary. *The Amber Cat.*

Naylor, Phyllis Reynolds. *Shiloh.*

Park, Barbara. *Skinnybones.*

Paterson, Katherine. *Flip-Flop Girl.*

Peck, Robert Newton. *Soup.*

Ransom, Candice F. *Fire in the Sky.*

Sachar, Louis. *There's A Boy in the Girl's Bathroom.*

Sachar, Louis. *Wayside School Is Falling Down.*

Smith, Robert Kimmel. *Chocolate Fever.*

Speare, Elizabeth George. *The Sign of the Beaver.*

Stein, Megan. *Laura Ingalls Wilder, Pioneer Girl.*

Strasser, Todd. *Help! I'm Trapped in My Teacher's Body.*

Taylor, Mildred D. *The Friendship.*

Taylor, Mildred D. *The Gold Cadillac.*

White, E. B. *Charlotte's Web.*

Yolen, Jane. *The Girl Who Loved the Wind.*

Grade 5

Alexander, Lloyd. *The Book of Three.*

Avi. *Nothing But the Truth.*

Bloor, Edward. *Tangerine.*

Blos, Joan. *A Gathering of Days.*

Cleary, Beverly. *Ralph S. Mouse.*

Cleary, Beverly. *Ramona the Pest.*

Cleary, Beverly. *Runaway Ralph.*

Collier, James and Christopher. *Jump Ship to Freedom.*

Cooper, Susan. *The Boggart.*

Cushman, Karen. *Catherine, Called Birdy.*

Danziger, Paula. *The Cat Ate My Gymsuit.*

Danziger, Paula. *P.S. Longer Letter Later.*

de Angeli, Marguerite. *The Door in the Wall.*

Farley, Walter. *The Black Stallion.*

George, Jean Craighead. *Julie.*

George, Jean Craighead. *Julie of the Wolves.*

George, Jean Craighead. *My Side of the Mountain.*

Hobbs, Will. *Bearstone.*

Kassem, Lou. *Listen for Rachel.*

Konigsburg, E. L. *The View from Saturday.*

Krumgold, Joseph. *Onion John.*

Lasky, Kathryn. *Beyond the Burning Time.*

Levine, Gail Carson. *Ella Enchanted.*

Lewis, C. S. *The Lion, the Witch, and the Wardrobe.*

Lowry, Lois. *Number the Stars.*

Myers, Walter Dean. *A Place Called Heartbreak: A Story of Vietnam.*

Naylor, Phyllis Reynolds. *Beetles, Lightly Toasted.*

Norton, Mary. *The Borrowers.*

O'Brien, Robert. *Mrs. Frisby and the Rats of NIMH.*

Paterson, Katherine. *Bridge to Terabithia.*

Paterson, Katherine. *Lyddie.*

Paterson, Katherine. *The Sign of the Chrysanthemum.*

Paulsen, Gary. *Tiltawhirl John.*

Paulsen, Gary. *Tucket's Ride.*

Paulsen, Gary. *The Winter Room.*

Snyder, Zilpha Keatley. *The Egypt Game.*

Soto, Gary. *Baseball in April and Other Stories.*

Spinelli, Jerry. *Report to the Principal's Office.*

Sterling, Dorothy. *The Story of Harriet Tubman: Freedom.*

Uchida, Yoshiko. *Journey to Topaz.*

Wilder, Laura Ingalls. *By the Shores of Silver Lake.*

Wilder, Laura Ingalls. *Little House in the Big Woods.*

Wilder, Laura Ingalls. *Little Town on the Prairie.*

Wisler, G. Clifton. *Jericho's Journey.*

Grade 6

Cameron, Eleanor. *The Court of the Stone Children.*

Cooper, Susan. *The Dark Is Rising.*

Cushman, Karen. *The Midwife's Apprentice.*

Duncan, Lois. *Locked in Time.*

Dyson, John. *Westward with Columbus.*

Edmonds, Walter D. *Drums Along the Mohawk.*

Farmer, Nancy. *A Girl Named Disaster.*

Field, Rachel. *Calico Bush.*

Fritz, Jean. *Harriet Beecher Stowe and the Beecher Preachers.*

Hamilton, Virginia. *The House of Dies Drear.*

Hamilton, Virginia. *M.C. Higgins the Great.*

Hautzig, Esther. *The Endless Steppe: Growing Up in Siberia.*

Hesse, Karen. *Out of the Dust.*

Lauber, Patricia. *Lost Star: The Story of Amelia Earhart.*

O'Dell, Scott. *Sarah Bishop.*

Parks, Rosa. *Rosa Parks: My Story.*

Paulsen, Gary. *The Voyage of the Frog.*

Paulsen, Gary. *Woodsong.*

Rawlings, Marjorie Kinnan. *The Yearling.*

Rawls, Wilson. *Where the Red Fern Grows.*

Rinaldi, Ann. *The Blue Door.*

Sauer, Julia L. *Fog Magic.*

Snyder, Zilpha Keatley. *Libby on Wednesday.*

Soto, Gary. *Novio Boy.*

Sperry, Armstrong. *Call It Courage.*

Taylor, Mildred. *Let the Circle Be Unbroken.*

Taylor, Mildred. *The Road to Memphis.*

Yolen, Jane. *The Devil's Arithmetic.*

Young, Ronder Thomas. *Moving Mama to Town.*

Grade 7

Adamson, Joy. *Born Free: A Lioness of Two Worlds.*

Barrie, James M. *Peter Pan.*

Cleaver, Vera and Bill. *Where the Lilies Bloom.*

Collier, James and Christopher. *My Brother Sam Is Dead.*

Hargrove, Jim. *Thomas Jefferson: Third President of the United States.*

Kent, Zachary. *John F. Kennedy: Thirty-Fifth President of the United States.*

Lillegard, Dee. *Richard Nixon: Thirty-Seventh President of the United States.*

Lowry, Lois. *The Giver.*

Magorian, Michelle. *Good Night, Mr. Tom.*

Montgomery, Lucy Maud. *Anne of Green Gables.*

Myers, Walter Dean. *Scorpions.*

North, Sterling. *Rascal.*

Parkman, Francis. *The Oregon Trail: The Conspiracy of Pontiac.*

Say, Allen. *Ink-Keepers Apprentice.*

Sewell, Anna. *Black Beauty.*

Steinbeck, John. *The Pearl.*

Voigt, Cynthia. *Jackaroo.*

Wells, H. G. *The Invisible Man.*

Wilder, Thornton. *The Bridge of San Luis Rey.*

Grade 8

Dodge, Mary Mapes. *Hans Brinker or the Silver Skates.*

Frank, Anne. *The Diary of Anne Frank.*

Giblin, James Cross. *Charles A. Lindbergh: A Human Hero.*

Grahame, Kenneth. *Wind in the Willows.*

Gunther, John. *Death Be Not Proud: A Memoir.*

Guy, Rosa. *The Friends.*

Heyerdahl, Thor. *Kon-Tiki.*

Hinton, S. E. *The Outsiders.*

Keyes, Daniel. *Flowers for Algernon.*

Lee, Harper. *To Kill a Mockingbird.*

Lipsythe, Robert. *The Contender.*

London, Jack. *The Call of the Wild.*

London, Jack. *The Sea Wolf.*

Mazer, Norma Fox. *After the Rain.*

Pullman, Philip. *The Golden Compass.*

Soto, Gary. *Living Up the Street.*

Soto, Gary. *A Summer Life.*

Stevenson, Robert Lewis. *Treasure Island.*

Tolkien, J. R. R. *The Hobbit.*

Twain, Mark. *The Adventures of Huckleberry Finn.*

Twain, Mark. *Adventures of Tom Sawyer.*

Wiggin, Kate D. *Rebecca of Sunnybrook Farm.*

Grade 9

Austen, Jane. *Emma.*

Baldwin, James. *Go Tell It on the Mountain.*

Brown, Dee. *Bury My Heart at Wounded Knee.*

Burgan, Michael. *Madeleine Albright.*

Clarke, Arthur C. *2001: A Space Odyssey.*

Cohen, David. *Manhattan Project.*

Cooper, James Fenimore. *Deerslayer.*

Dana, Richard Henry. *Two Years Before the Mast.*

Dickens, Charles. *David Copperfield.*

Dickens, Charles. *Great Expectations.*

Dickens, Charles. *A Tale of Two Cities.*

Eliot, George. *Silas Marner.*

Gay, Kathleen and Martin. *Spanish-American War.*

Herb, Angela. *Beyond the Mississippi.*

King, David. *Lexington and Concord.*

Nordhoff, Charles. *Mutiny on the Bounty.*

Potok, Chaim. *The Chosen.*

Pyle, Howard. *Men of Iron.*

Verne, Jules. *Journey to the Center of the Earth.*

Washington, Booker T. *Up from Slavery.*

Williams, Tennessee. *The Glass Menagerie.*

Wister, Owen. *The Virginian.*

Zeinert, Karen. *Those Courageous Women of the Civil War.*

Grade 10

Bronte, Charlotte. *Jane Eyre.*

Bronte, Emily. *Wuthering Heights.*

Conrad, Joseph. *Heart of Darkness.*

Conrad, Joseph. *Secret Sharer.*

Cooper, James Fenimore. *The Last of the Mohicans.*

Dickens, Charles. *Oliver Twist.*

Gay, Kathleen and Martin. *Persian Gulf.*

Gay, Kathleen and Martin. *Vietnam War.*

Hammett, Dashiell. *The Maltese Falcon.*

Hardy, Thomas. *Far from the Madding Crowd.*

Hardy, Thomas. *Return of the Native.*

Lewis, C. S. *Screwtape Letters.*

Lewis, Sinclair. *Babbitt.*

Marshall, Catherine. *Christy.*

Poe, Edgar Allan. *The Gold Bug.*

Thomas, Peggy. *Medicines from Nature.*

Thoreau, Henry David. *Walden.*

Tolstoy, Leo. *Death of Ivan Ilych.*

Twain, Mark. *Life on the Mississippi.*

Uris, Leon. *Exodus.*

Uris, Leon. *QB VII.*

Zeinert, Karen. *Those Remarkable Women of the American Revolution.*

Grade 11

Blackmore, R. D. *Lorna Doone.*

Conrad, Joseph. *Lord Jim.*

Dostoyevsky, Fyodor. *Crime and Punishment.*

Hardy, Thomas. *Tess of the D'Urbervilles.*

Hawthorne, Nathaniel. *The House of Seven Gables.*

Homer. *The Iliad.*

Lewis, Sinclair. *Main Street.*

Poe, Edgar Allan. *The Purloined Letter.*

Sobel, Dava. *Longitude: The True Story of a Lone Genius Who Solved the Greatest Scientific Problem of His Time.*

Steinbeck, John. *Grapes of Wrath.*

Toffler, Alvin. *Future Shock.*

Tolstoy, Leo. *Anna Karenina.*

Verne, Jules. *Clipper of the Clouds.*

Wright, Richard. *Native Son.*

Grade 12

Austen, Jane. *Pride and Prejudice.*

Dreiser, Theodore. *An American Tragedy.*

Hawthorne, Nathaniel. *The Scarlet Letter.*

Melville, Herman. *Moby Dick.*

Miller, Arthur. *Death of a Salesman.*

Swift, Jonathan. *Gulliver's Travels.*

Thackeray, William Makepeace. *Vanity Fair.*

Time-Life Editors. *Africa's Glorious Legacy.*

Time-Life Editors. *Ancient India: Land of Mystery.*

Time-Life Editors. *Celts: Europe's People of Iron.*

Time-Life Editors. *Creative Fire.*

Time-Life Editors. *Early Europe: Mysteries in Stone.*

Time-Life Editors. *Magnificent Maya.*

Time-Life Editors. *Perseverance.*

Time-Life Editors. *Search for El Dorado.*

APPENDIX B

How the Inventory Was Constructed

Constructing the Word Lists

The items for the word lists at each grade level were randomly selected from the vocabulary lists for the respective levels of two basal reading series. After the tests were compiled, each one was administered to students at three levels—the one for which the list was designed, the level immediately below, and the level directly above. (The obvious exceptions, the preprimer and twelfth-grade lists, were each administered to students at two levels.) The percentage of students who successfully pronounced each word was then calculated for each of the tested levels. A word was assigned to a given level if 80 percent or more of the students from that level, less than 80 percent from the level below, and more than 80 percent from the level above successfully pronounced the word. Words that failed to meet the criteria were replaced by the same process. The graded word lists for levels preprimer through grade 3 were then compared with similar established lists, and a high degree of correspondence was found.

Constructing the Passages

Passages were initially chosen from each level, preprimer through grade 12, of the basal reading series used to construct the word lists and a reading and literature series. In the subsequent editions, some selections were also chosen from other reading series and a variety of trade books for the appropriate levels. In addition, some original passages were developed when passages that met all of the chosen criteria for inclusion were not available. The passages were checked for readability level using the Spache Readability Formula for preprimer through grade 3 and the Fry Readability Graph for grades 4 through 12. No selection that failed to fit the level exactly, as determined by the formula, was used.

A mix of fiction and nonfiction selections was included because students are exposed to both in their school and recreational reading activities, and only excerpts that made sense out of the context of the entire story were chosen. Any necessary background information was included in the introductory statement that precedes each passage.

The comprehension questions that accompany the readings are of six types: main idea, detail, sequence, cause and effect, inference, and vocabulary. Eight such questions are provided for each of the preprimer through grade 2 passages, and ten questions are included for each of the grade 3 through grade 12 selections. The guidelines for writing informal reading inventory questions set forth by Valmont[1] were followed in constructing the questions.

Johnson, Kress, and Pikulski[2] have also stressed that passage-independent questions should be avoided. This admonition has been taken into consideration in question development. Only some of the vocabulary questions may stand as passage independent, but since vocabulary understanding is central to comprehension, asking some such questions seemed to be justified. Questions about vocabulary terms for which there are context clues may be passage independent for students who already have the terms in their vocabularies but passage dependent for students who need to use the context to determine the meanings.

Classification of questions is sometimes difficult. Often the way a question is answered, rather than the way the question is asked, determines whether a detail has been provided or an inference has been made. In cases in which a particular question could legitimately elicit either type of response, both answers have been indicated and the question types for each specific answer given.

All questions that are not *directly* answered by the passage are inference questions. Some inferences are simpler to make than others, but if any part of the answer is not explicitly stated in the passage, the question is an inference question. Deciding on the referent for a pronoun, for example, is an inferential task, since no passage would state that "he" refers to "John." When connectives expressing cause and effect are not provided directly in the text, a question that requires a decision about cause and effect is inferential. For example, in a passage that states, "Trixie lost her dime. She was sad," the question "Why was Trixie sad?" is an inferential one, even though it is an easy inference.

A vocabulary question that has one obvious answer (i.e., the word does not have multiple meanings) will generally be asked in the form "What is the meaning of . . . ?" If a word has multiple meanings, the examiner will usually present it in a phrase from the story in order to determine whether the student knows the specific meaning of the word needed for the story.

The questions were scrutinized by several classes of graduate students in reading education who had experience in constructing informal reading inventories. They were revised in accordance with some of the suggestions received. The graduate students then administered the entire inventory to pupils in the grade ranges covered by the passages. This field testing revealed that the difficulty level of the passages did increase appropriately in each of the four forms. Analysis of the responses to the questions showed that only a few seemed to cause problems due to ambiguity, alternate responses, or other factors. These questions were revised or replaced. The levels found for the students who were tested agreed closely with their teachers' judgments of the levels at which they were performing.

In constructing the second edition of this informal test, the author replaced nineteen passages from the first edition. This was done in order to include passages that reflected current concerns and adequately represented minority groups and to raise the overall interest level of passages in the book. The new material was field-tested on students and performed successfully. Analysis of responses to the questions showed that only a few questions seemed to cause problems; these were revised or replaced. Some questions pertaining to passages retained from the first edition were also revised or replaced, based on feedback from users.

During construction of the third edition of the test, the author replaced nineteen passages from the second edition and revised questions in some other passages from that edition, based on feedback from users. The new passages were chosen for their high interest factors and timely subjects.

The entire revised inventory was field-tested on students in grades 1 through 12 by interspersing the new passages with passages from the previous edition and administering them as described in the introductory portion of this book. The passages did increase in difficulty as the grade level increased, just as they should have. A few questions were revised during the field testing because they were ambiguous as originally worded. The students were asked to rate each passage according to interest after reading it. A majority of the students reading each of the new passages

[1]William J. Valmont, "Creating Questions for Informal Reading Inventories," *Reading Teacher* 25 (March 1972): 509–512.

[2]Johnson, Marjorie Seddon, Kress, Roy A., and Pikulski, John J. *Informal Reading Inventories,* 2nd ed. (Newark, Del.: International Reading Association, 1987).

found them to be above average or average in interest level.

The fourth, fifth, sixth, and seventh editions have expanded and clarified directions for administration and interpretation of the inventory. The changes were made in response to reader queries and current information in the field.

In the seventh edition, five passages were replaced—one for the preprimer level, one for the primer level, one for grade 2, and two for grade 3. These passages were replaced in response to user feedback about passages that they would like to see replaced. Multiple passages were developed for each grade level and field tested on more than 120 students in grades 1 through 6. Field testing was done by two university professors and four graduate students who had been taught to administer the assessment. The subjects were drawn from schools in three school systems, one in a university town, one in a mid-sized town near a federal installation, and one in a rural county. As a result of the field testing of both the new passages and existing passages, some passages were moved from one form to another in order to obtain a smoother progression in difficulty for the individual forms. Levels obtained by the four forms were consistent in their indications of independent, instructional, frustration, and capacity levels. During the field testing, some problems with several questions became evident, and these questions were replaced or revised. The revised passages were found to increase appropriately in difficulty as the grade level increased, as they should.

The passages represent the materials that are actually used for school assignments and outside reading by students, and the skills that are tested are ones that are the focus of school reading programs, based upon research in the field. Therefore, the test has face validity. Alternate forms testing revealed that the levels indicated by different forms administered to the same student were consistent. The determination of levels by different experienced administrators examining the collected data was also consistent.

Development of Sections One and Two and Appendix A

Sections One and Two present background information about different aspects of testing word recognition and comprehension and give specific step-by-step directions on how to administer, score, and interpret the inventory. Over the seven editions, the sections have been continuously expanded to provide more specific information, more case study examples, and more specific and user-friendly worksheets and summary forms to help in data analysis. These sections cover administration, scoring, and interpretation of the inventory thoroughly. They explain how to make both quantitative and qualitative analyses and offer flexible ways of administering the inventory to meet specific needs. Questions that are frequently asked by users are presented with answers, to expedite the testing process for inexperienced users.

In the sixth edition, Appendix A was added to the inventory to provide a list of leveled trade books for preprimer through grade 12 that can be used for reading on the levels indicated by the inventory results. This seventh edition has a much expanded list, at the request of several users, who found the books listed to be valuable in planning instruction following administration of the inventory.